THE TRUMPET

THE
TRUMPET

Edward Tarr

Translated from the German by
S.E. Plank and Edward Tarr

Amadeus Press Portland, Oregon
Reinhard G. Pauly, Ph.D., General Editor

Jacket illustration
A natural trumpet in D (contemporary E flat) of the Charamela real,
dated 1761
Lisbon, Museu Nacional dos Coches
(Photo: LAFO, Lisbon)

Published simultaneously with this volume

The Horn
Kurt Janetzky & Bernhard Brüchle

The Oboe and the Bassoon
Gunther Joppig

The Flute
Raymond Meylan

This edition copyright © B.T. Batsford Ltd 1988

First published in 1988

All rights reserved. No part of this publication may be reproduced, in any form or by any means, without permission from the publisher

Translated from the German edition © 1977 Hallwag AG, Bern © assigned 1984 by B. Schott's Söhne, Mainz, Germany

Printed in Great Britain

First published in North America in 1988 by
Amadeus Press
9999 S.W. Wilshire
Portland, Oregon 97225, USA

ISBN 0-931340-13-6

Library of Congress Cataloging-in-Publication Data

Tarr, Edward H.
    The trumpet.

    Translation of: Die Trompete.
    Bibliography: p.
    Includes index.
    1. Trumpet—History. I. Title.
ML960.T3713   1988   788'.12   88-19280
ISBN 0-931340-13-6

Contents

List of Photographs	page 6
Introduction	7
1 The Early History of the Trumpet until the Fall of Rome (AD 476)	19
2 Some Asiatic Forms of the Trumpet	30
3 The Trumpet from the Fall of Rome until the Crusades (c 1100)	32
4 The Trumpet in the Late Middle Ages (c 1100–1400)	35
5 The Trumpet in the Renaissance (1400–1600)	50
6 The Golden Age of the Natural Trumpet (1600–1750)	85
7 The Trumpet in an Era of Decline (1750–1815)	138
8 The Modern Epoch of the Trumpet: From 1815 to Today	156
Afterword	200
Translator's Afterword	203
Bibliography	209
Notes	213
Index	214

List of Photographs

Australian aborigine playing the didjeridu	page 20
Roman soldiers capturing the sacred implements at the Temple of Jerusalem (AD 70)	23
Salpinx from the second half of the fifth century BC	24
Trumpets of the Last Judgement (c AD 1000)	34
'Cantoria' by Luca della Robbia (1431–8)	43
X-ray photograph of a trumpet mouthpiece by Jacob Steiger (1578)	51
Three angels with slide trumpets by Hans Memling (c 1490)	55
Alta ensemble at a celebration of the Burgundian court by an unknown master (c 1430)	57
Portrait of Cesare Bendinelli from a votive tablet donated by him in 1580	71
Bendinelli's trumpet made by Anton Schnitzer I (1585)	83
Thomas Harper, junior with the slide trumpet (1816–98)	152
Various trumpets from c 1700–1976	154–155
French double case with orchestral trumpet	162
Maurice André with a piccolo B-flat trumpet	178
Adolf Scherbaum with a C trumpet	181
Maynard Ferguson in action	199

Colour Photographs (between pages 96 and 97)

Tuba, hydraulus and cornua at a gladiatorial contest (second century AD)
Short and long Arabian trumpets
Angel trumpeter of the Last Judgement (1072–87)
'Niccolò Mauruzi in the Battle of S. Romano' by Paolo Uccello
'Coronation of Mary' by Beato Angelico (c 1425–40)
Two trumpets by Jacob Steiger (1578)
Trumpet by Anton Schnitzer I (1581)

Introduction

Definition of the Trumpet

No musical instrument has changed so much in the course of time as the trumpet. The Roman tuba was about 120cm long and had a conical tube with a diameter of about 10mm at the small end, expanding to about 26mm at the large end. The natural trumpet of the Baroque era was about 224cm long, and its mainly cylindrical tubing had a diameter of about 12mm. Although the inside diameter of the tubing of a modern B-flat trumpet is only slightly narrower (about 11.5mm), its length of tubing, however, is only about half that of the Baroque trumpet, that is, 130cm. The piccolo trumpet, which is sometimes – and incorrectly – called a 'Bach trumpet', and to which Adolf Scherbaum, Maurice André, and many other soloists owe a considerable measure of their success, has little in common with the Baroque instrument; it is only 65cm long, and its tubing has, with some instruments, a diameter of less than 11mm.

The illustration on page 8 demonstrates the striking differences between these four instruments, all of which, nevertheless, are referred to as 'trumpets'. It is necessary to differentiate between the visual picture of these trumpets and their actual tube length.

If we now try to define the trumpet using these four instruments as a point of departure, we will have to identify their common characteristics. For a long time, musicologists differentiated trumpets from horns on the basis of their bore. According to this old definition, the trumpet's bore is supposed to be about two thirds cylindrical and one third conical, but that of the horn one third cylindrical and two thirds conical. This definition does not apply any more. The bore of both the B-flat and the piccolo B-flat trumpet are up to 80 per cent conical; the only cylindrical portions are in the areas of the tuning slide, the valve slides, and in the windways through the valves. (The various parts of the

Introduction

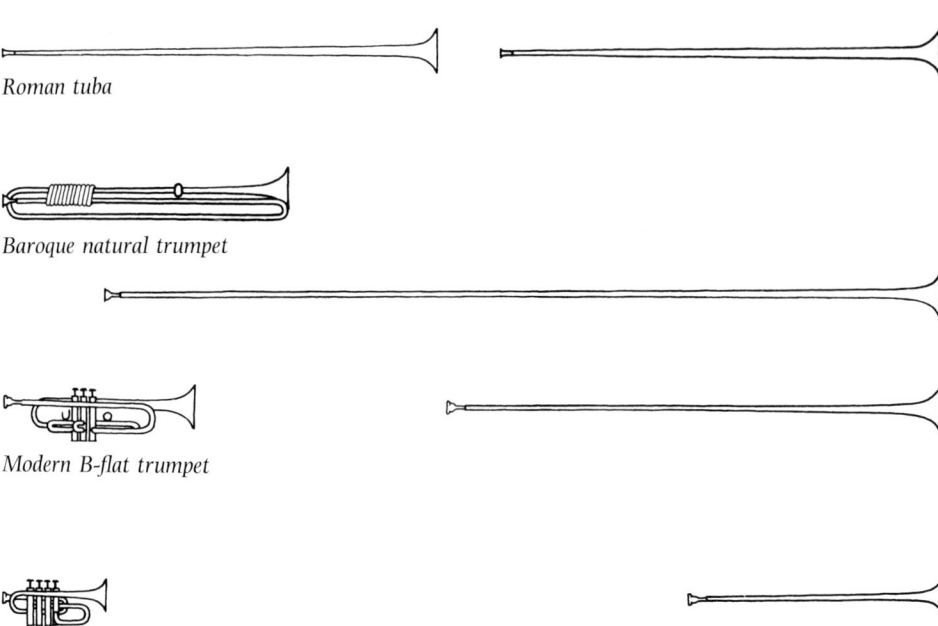

Roman tuba

Baroque natural trumpet

Modern B-flat trumpet

Modern piccolo B-flat trumpet

Four kinds of trumpets as they actually appear

The same four instruments stretched out in straight form (both modern instruments without the valves), in order to demonstrate the differences in their lengths and diameters of tubing

trumpet will be explained later.) Besides the relatively narrow bore, the common characteristics of the Roman tuba, the natural trumpet of the Baroque era, and of modern B-flat and piccolo B-flat trumpets are as follows: the mouthpiece, the bell with a more or less prominent flare, and the fact that the trumpet – with only a few exceptions – always had a form which was straight and not coiled. I would therefore like to adapt the definitions of Wilhelm Bernoulli and Herbert Heyde (*see Bibliography*) and define the trumpet as follows:

> The trumpet is a wind instrument which is made to sound by the vibrations of the player's lips; besides its more or less well-developed mouthpiece, it consists of a relatively narrow-bore conical or cylindrical tube which is not coiled, ending in a flared bell.

Introduction

The Trumpet's Characteristic Sound, its Function as a Signalling Instrument, and its Ceremonial Associations

The trumpet is set apart from all other musical instruments by the splendour of its tone. Even in the earliest of times it served as a signalling instrument, because its sound could be heard at a great distance. It soon acquired military associations, and later, religious ones. In the Old Testament the trumpet was reserved for the priests. In Numbers x:1–2 we read: 'the Lord said to Moses, "make two silver trumpets; of hammered work you shall make them . . ."'.

The trumpet was regarded as a sacred instrument. The church fathers associated the tone of the trumpet with the voices of the angels or with the voice of God. During the late Middle Ages, trumpeters entered the service of potentates and soon became an attribute of their glory. In 1768 Hiller wrote: 'A solemn event in church or state can hardly be celebrated without the sound of trumpets and kettledrums'.

In 1795, while courtly society in Europe was crumbling all around him, Johann Ernst Altenburg (1734–1801) published his famous *Essay on an Introduction to the Heroic and Musical Trumpeters' and Kettledrummers' Art*, a work in which he attempted to renew his instrument's elevated position, handed down since biblical times. His attempt was in vain, since trumpeters had already been nearly completely deprived of their courtly basis of existence.

If the trumpet's association with royalty disappeared in Romantic times, at least the splendour remained. A dynamic climax in the huge orchestra of a Richard Wagner or Anton Bruckner would be unthinkable without the impact of the brass, with, at their head, the trumpet. Rightly or wrongly listeners

Introduction

today seem to be attracted more by a strong, radiant trumpet tone than by artistic subtlety. This situation brings us to another characteristic of trumpet tone: it can be loud and radiant, as well as soft and tender. This double nature of the trumpet's tone goes back to the beginnings of the Baroque era.

Before we survey the historical development of the trumpet, its makers, its players, and its literature, let us first turn to a description of the instrument and the notes which can be played on it.

Description of the Natural Trumpet

The natural trumpet, which was in use during the entire Baroque period and even into the middle of the nineteenth century, had just as simple a form as the modern state trumpet or fanfare trumpet which derived from it. Its main components were two lengths of tubing ('yards') and the bell, as well as two bends in the tubing ('bows') connecting these straight parts. Five ferrules strengthened both the mouthpiece end of the first length of tubing and those places in which the straight and curved sections of tubing were joined together. The bell ended in a flare, the widest part of which was strengthened by a so-called garland, since the metal at that point became very thin during the process of hammering necessary to create the flare. On the garland the instrument maker often stamped or engraved his name and city, sometimes also his master's mark and the year.

In the middle of the bell section, or two thirds of the length towards the bell flare, a ball was to be found. It had a purely ornamental function and can also be seen on some illustrations of medieval trumpets, as well as on many surviving Oriental ones. In many books it has been stated that the ball covered the place at which the bell ended and the normal tubing began. This is not

Introduction

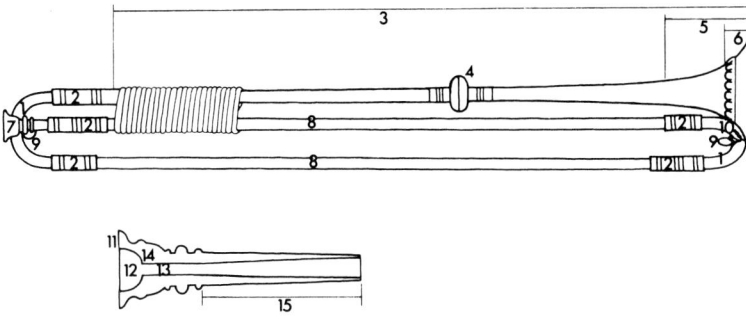

1. Bend 2. Ferrule 3. Bell section 4. Ball, pommel, knop or knob 5. Bell flare 6. Garland 7. Mouthpiece 8. First and second lengths of tubing (also called yards) 9. Loop 10. Wire attachment 11. Rim 12. Cup 13. Bore 14. This sharp edge between the cup and the bore is characteristic of Baroque mouthpieces 15. Shank

true. The bell section extended from the flared end all the way up to the next ferrule and had the same length as the other two cylindrical tubes. It is easy to verify this from surviving original instruments, since the ball is not soldered to the bell, but rather can be slid along the bell from its original position.

The individual parts of old instruments were usually not soldered, but rather inserted into each other, with more or less force, and then made airtight with rosin or beeswax. The bend in the tubing near the bell flare was attached to the bell flare by a small wire (or often a thin strip of leather) which passed through a tiny hole in the edge of the bell flare. The other end of the first length of tubing was separated from the bell section by a wooden block; the block and these two lengths of tubing were encircled and stabilized by a woollen cord.

Finally, two small metal loops were soldered to the inside of the two bends in the tubing. Through them was threaded the so-called 'banderole' – a lanyard on which the trumpet was hung over the player's shoulder. The second length of tubing was used to attach banners carrying the coat of arms of the sovereign, the bishop, or the city employing the trumpeter.

The parts of the natural trumpet are indicated in the accompanying illustration.

The Harmonic Series

By means of minute adjustments of lip tension, a trumpeter can play on the natural trumpet a series of tones fixed by nature, the

Introduction

so-called harmonic series (or series of partials). The lowest note in this series (or the fundamental), which is produced with the smallest amount of lip tension, is on a Baroque natural trumpet in C, the C two ledger lines below the bass clef.

The next note to speak on a natural trumpet is the *c* one octave higher.

With these two Cs we have the first octave of the harmonic series.

Within the second octave of the harmonic series, between *c* and *c'* (middle C on the piano), the fifth responds i.e. *g*.

This *g* is almost exactly in the middle between the second and fourth partials, *c* and *c'*. Now we can understand the principle of construction of the harmonic series; every new octave in an upward direction contains the same tones which were present in the octave below, as well as further tones between them. Let us now attempt to apply this principle to the third octave of the harmonic series. First we transpose the tones of the second octave to the third octave (*c'*, *g'*, *c''*),

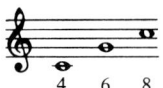

and then we add the new ones (*e'* and *b*-flat').

The fifth partial, the major third (*e'*), is almost exactly in the middle between middle *c'* and *g'*. The middle between *g'* and *c''* however is neither *b*-flat' nor *a'*, but lies in between. This note, *b*-flat', rendered here as a black note, is accompanied by an arrow pointing downwards, showing that it is too low in pitch.

By means of the first three octaves of the harmonic series it is possible to realise how the intervals between the playable notes become progressively smaller as they ascend. *C* to *c*, for example, forms an octave; *c* to *g* a fifth; *g* to *c'* a fourth; *c'* to *e'* a major third; *e'* to *g'* a minor third, etc.

The tones of the fourth octave of the harmonic series lie so closely together that they form a kind of scale. If we first imagine the tones of the third octave to be one octave higher, we arrive at *c''*, *e''*, *g''*, a too-low *b*-flat'', and high *c'''*. If we now add the intermediate notes of this octave, we arrive at the following scale: *c''*, *d''*, *e''*, *f''* (too sharp), *g''*, *a''* (too flat), *b*-flat'' (too flat), *b''* and *c'''*.

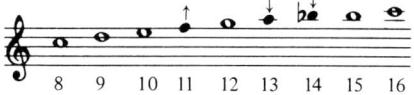

Since here too the intervals between the available notes become progressively smaller, the distance between *c''* and *d''* amounts to a large or major whole step; that between *d''* and *e''* is a small or minor whole step. The third formed by *c''* and *e''* is slightly too small for the so-called 'well-tempered system' in use on keyboard instruments today, but it was wonderfully suitable for the 'unequal temperament' of the Baroque period.

Introduction

We already know from the third octave that the fourteenth partial, *b*-flat″, will be too low in pitch. The eleventh and thirteenth partials, as well, lie outside the system of equal temperament. The eleventh partial is between *f*″ and *f*-sharp″, while the thirteenth partial is closer to *g*-sharp″ than to *a*″ (for this reason these notes are also indicated in black and with arrows). In the Baroque period, when trumpeters had to play melodies in this fourth octave of the harmonic series, they corrected the impure partials by a change in lip tension. Modern-day trumpeters employ the same technique, called 'lipping', in order to correct occasional deviations in pitch – deviations, however, which are much smaller than those encountered by the Baroque trumpet. We can therefore say that the trumpeters of the Baroque era needed more lip strength in order to play their instrument in tune. Michael Praetorius described the situation in 1619 in the following manner: 'The trumpet . . . is a magnificent instrument when it is played by a good master who can tame and rule it well and artistically'. The harmonic series can be extended to infinity. The accompanying illustration shows merely the tones of the first half of the fifth octave.

The twenty-fourth partial was reached in at least two trumpet

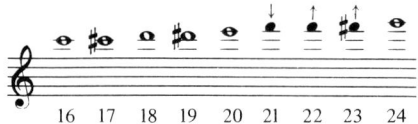

concertos written by Michael Haydn (1736–1806) and Georg von Reutter, junior (1708–72). They probably wrote these pieces around the year 1760 for the Austrian virtuoso J.B. Resenberger – 'a fine trumpeter who has made himself very famous . . . particularly in the high register' (L. Mozart). J.S. Bach, who may well have written the most outstanding trumpet parts of the

Introduction

eighteenth century, although they were not the most difficult, often demanded the sixteenth and eighteenth partials. Only once – in the final chorale of cantata 31 (*Der Himmel lacht, die Erde jubilieret*) – did Bach demand the twentieth partial, an *e'''*.

Trumpets are named after their fundamental tone. A natural trumpet in C plays the harmonic series in C as indicated above. A somewhat shorter natural trumpet in D plays the same series, but one tone higher, etc.

The Valved Trumpet and its Harmonic Series

After the invention of the valve around 1815, with which it became possible to play chromatically, the valved trumpet became more and more generally accepted in classical music, while the Baroque natural trumpet became demoted to a pure signalling instrument, today's state or fanfare trumpet. The valves produce progressive lengthenings of the air column and thus the automatic downward transposition of the harmonic series, a half tone at a time. The second valve makes the series sound a half tone lower, the first valve makes it sound a whole tone lower, and the third valve makes it sound one and a half tones lower. All further combinations of fingerings up to 1-2-3 (three whole tones lower) are possible. Descending from middle *c'*, the fingerings are as shown in the accompanying illustration.

The first valved trumpets used in orchestras were generally pitched in F, a fourth higher than the natural trumpet in C. Thus

Introduction

the harmonic series indicated above was shifted a fourth higher for the notes which were fingered 'open'.

Through the use of the valves, of course, each one of these notes can be lowered by as much as three whole steps; in the high register several fingerings are often possible on a given note.

Wagner, Bruckner, Mahler and Richard Strauss wrote the majority of their trumpet parts for the valved trumpet in F. In the second half of the nineteenth century, the B-flat trumpet became more and more generally accepted, last but not least under the influence of the cornet in B-flat. Trumpets pitched in C became used as well. These instruments were only half as long as the corresponding natural trumpets of the Baroque era. To avoid transposing the harmonic series for these short instruments further and further upwards, its notation was simply shifted by one octave. In this way the high *c'''* for the valved trumpet in C was no longer the sixteenth partial, but the eighth. The harmonic series for a modern valved trumpet in C is notated as follows:

On the B-flat trumpet, this series sounds one step lower.

Description of the Valved Trumpet

Two kinds of valved trumpets are in general use today. They differ from one another in the type of valve employed in their valve

Introduction

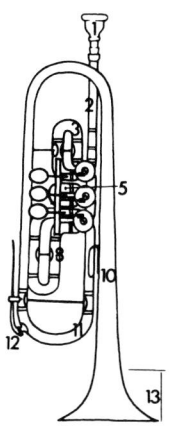
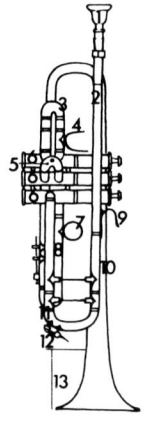

1. Mouthpiece
2. Mouthpipe
3. First valve slide (whole step)
4. Thumb hook for intonation correction
5. Second valve slide (half step)
6. Valve casings
7. Ring for intonation correction
8. Third valve slide (one and a half steps)
9. Finger hook
10. Bell section
11. Tuning slide
12. Water key
13. Bell flare

B-flat Trumpet with Rotary Valves   B-flat Trumpet with Piston Valves

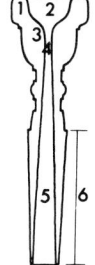

Mouthpiece for the Valved Trumpet
1. Rim
2. Cup
3. This soft shoulder between cup and bore is characteristic of the modern mouthpiece
4. Throat
5. Backbore
6. Shank

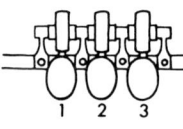

Enclosed clock spring return mechanism

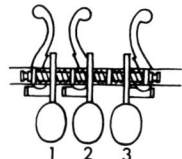

Helical spring return mechanism

mechanism. One kind is known as the rotary valve and was invented in 1835 by Joseph Riedl; the other kind is the piston valve, developed in 1839 by François Périnet (fl. 1829–55). Trumpets with piston valves are in common use everywhere today, except in some areas of Germany, in Austria, and in several countries of Eastern Europe, where trumpets with rotary valves are preferred. Not long ago, when trumpets with piston valves were little used in German-speaking countries, they were called there 'jazz trumpets' – not a very accurate name, since this type of instrument was considerably older than jazz.

Other parts of the trumpet accompanying the valves are the valve slides, the tuning slide, the water key (invented about

Introduction

1830), and sometimes a finger hook for the little finger of the right hand. The two principal kinds of return mechanisms for the rotary valve employ enclosed clock springs and helical springs, respectively.

   The illustrations on the previous page show both kinds of trumpets as well as two different rotary-valve return mechanisms.

ONE

The Early History of the Trumpet until the Fall of Rome (AD 476)

The Origin of the Trumpet

'The first trumpet was the long or short, straight or slightly bent tuba out of wood or cane; it was held in a lengthwise direction and thus blown at one end.' This sentence – as well as most of the evidence concerning the early history of the trumpet – was taken from the work of Curt Sachs (1881–1959), whose pioneering research work is, largely, still valid today, and also forms a point of departure for further research.

The earliest trumpets had no mouthpiece and no bell flare. The player did not even blow them. Rather, these were megaphones, the purpose of which was to distort the player's voice. In acoustical terms, their function was the same as that of a mask in visual terms: the distorted human voice sought to dispel evil spirits. Such megaphone trumpets were sounded at religious and magical rites: circumcisions, burials and sunset ceremonies. They were played only by men and were thus identified with the male sex, as opposed to certain drum forms which were supposed to be feminine. Trumpets such as these can still be found in the primitive cultures of New Guinea and northwest Brazil, as well as in the form of the Australian didjeridu.

Related instruments are the African transverse trumpet (which, however, is not a true trumpet in the strict sense, because it is made from an antelope horn, an elephant tusk, or even – in imitation of these – out of wood) and the shell trumpet of Oceania, an implement for signalling and for dispelling evil spirits associated with death, sacrifice and war. Two types can be distinguished:

1 The side-blown triton, fusus and strombus
2 The end-blown cassis.

It would be incorrect to speak of conch-shell trumpets.

Australian aborigine playing the didjeridu
Australia, Northern Territories
(Photo: Stuart Dempster, Seattle, Washington)

The Egyptians

The Egyptian trumpet was an instrument of war and religious ceremony and was called 'snb' in hieroglyphics. It was played by soldiers about 1415 BC. The inventor of the trumpet was said to be the god Osiris, and the trumpet was used in the mystery plays held in his honour. As with other earlier trumpets, we look in vain for a 'musical' use. Plutarch compared the sound of the Egyptian trumpet with the braying of an ass.

Through the truly sensational discovery of the grave of Tutankhamun (king of the eighth dynasty, about 1350 BC) in 1922, posterity came into possession of two Egyptian trumpets. One of them is made of silver, is 58.2cm long, and has a conical

The Early History of the Trumpet until the Fall of Rome (AD 476)

Marching Theban troops with a trumpeter at their head

bore from 1.7 to 2.6cm in diameter (with a bell 8.2cm at the large end). The other one, of bronze, is 50.5cm long and has similar dimensions. Both have a wide bell but no detachable mouthpiece. The silver one was unfortunately shattered when it was blown experimentally in 1939. A third such instrument is preserved in the Louvre in Paris.

The Assyrians

This warlike people (1160–625 BC), at the height of their power about 670, knew the trumpet. Illustrations of trumpet-playing soldiers survive.

The Israelites

We referred previously to God's command to Moses to 'make two silver trumpets . . . of hammered work'. The trumpets of the Israelites were reserved exclusively for the priests; Aaron and his descendants were the players of the sacred trumpets. In Numbers x we learn more about the use of these instruments: they served to sound alarms, to announce gatherings and to accompany offerings. Their use is described in verses 9 and 10 as follows:

> And when you go to war in your land against the adversary who oppresses you, then you shall sound an alarm with the trumpets, that you may be remembered before the Lord your God, and you should be saved from your enemies. On the day of your gladness also, and at your appointed feasts, and at the beginnings of your months, you shall blow the trumpets over

your burnt offerings and over the sacrifices of your peace offerings; they shall serve you for remembrance before your God: I am the Lord your God.

The trumpet, called *chatzotzrah*, was played in two different ways. The Hebrew expression *těķi'a* was rendered with the expression 'to blow' in the King James version of the Bible, and *těrû'āh* as 'to blow (or to sound) an alarm'. According to Altenburg, the latter was 'a broken and modulated sound caused by the interchanging of various tones and by blaring', whereas the former was 'a constant, unbroken sound'.[1] 'Blowing' was carried out either by one or two priests; 'sounding an alarm' was always done by two. Altenburg, quoting Fesselius' biblical concordance, summarized the usage of the trumpet of the Israelites in two areas:

1 *For the gathering of the entire assembly*, when *both* were blown; or for the gathering of the princes and generals, when only *one* was blown.
2 *At the breaking of the camps* (a) that lie on the east parts, when the priests sounded an alarm for the first time, and (b) of those that lie on the south side, when it happened for the second time. (pp. 16–17)

On the occasion of the dedication of Solomon's temple, 120 priests played their trumpets; 'and it was the duty of the trumpeters and singers to make themselves heard in unison in praise and thanksgiving to the Lord' (II Chronicles v:13).

According to a description of Flavius Josephus (c AD 37–100), the trumpet of the Israelites was one ell long or 45.72cm, only slightly shorter than the Egyptian trumpet. These trumpets are represented in the triumphal arch erected by Titus in Rome in the year AD 70, after he had conquered Jerusalem and carried away the sacred implements.

The Early History of the Trumpet until the Fall of Rome (AD 476)

Roman soldiers capturing the sacred implements of the Temple at Jerusalem from the Titus Arch, Rome, AD 70
(Photo: Deutches Archäologisches Institut, Rome)

For the Israelites then, the trumpet was an instrument given and hallowed by God, but an instrument which could also be put to military use. The impressive splendour of its tone is apparent in the description of the consecration of the Temple. As has already been mentioned, Altenburg called attention to the importance of the trumpet for the Israelites while he was pleading the cause of the restoration of his instrument's dignity. Particularly noteworthy is the fact that for the first time in history, the sound of the trumpet is said to have a double nature. Altenburg later compared 'blowing' and 'sounding an alarm' with *principale* and *clarino* playing, respectively.

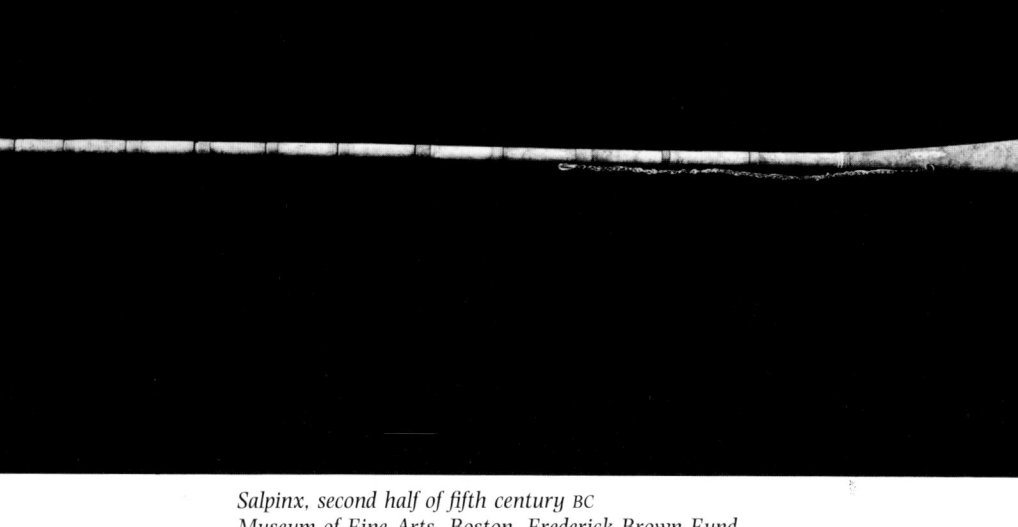

Salpinx, second half of fifth century BC
Museum of Fine Arts, Boston, Frederick Brown Fund

The Greeks

Although we are relatively well informed about Greek music theory, we know practically nothing about the use of the Greek trumpet, the *salpinx*. It seems to have been a purely military instrument. However, trumpet playing was also a discipline of the newer Olympic games, and the story has been handed down about a certain Achias, who won three times, and to whom a column of honour was erected in celebration of his excellence.

Fortunately, a salpinx has survived; it dates from the second half of the fifth century BC and is preserved in the Museum of Fine Arts in Boston. Since this instrument measures 157cm, it is longer than the chatzotzrah of the Israelites. It consists of 13 cylindrical parts made of ivory, which are held together by means of broad bronze rings. The delicate bell is made of cast bronze, as is the mouthpiece, which is a mere widening of the tubing. Aeschylus described the sound of the salpinx as 'screaming'.

The Etruscans

The Etruscans were a decidedly music-loving people. Their flutes lured wild animals into the snare, and also accompanied the rhythm of monotonous labours such as kneading. For them, the trumpet was a military instrument. In the *Eumenides* Aeschylus praised the sound of the Etruscan tuba, the *Tyrrhenica tuba*. Three Roman brass instruments, *tuba, lituus* and *cornu*, originated with the Etruscans, who played them in processions and in battle. According to Virgil (the *Aeneid*, VIII, 526), their soothsayers believed that they announced the will of the gods or even the end of an epoch.

The Romans

The Romans had several brass instruments, of which two can be considered trumpets. The confusion reigning in both old and modern works as to their nomenclature and use has been recently resolved by Meucci (1985) (*see Bibliography*). All of the brass instruments taken over by the Romans from the Etruscans were made of bronze and had removable mouthpieces.

The tuba was longer than the chatzotzrah, but shorter than the salpinx. A specimen preserved in the Etruscan Museum in Rome is 117cm long. The tuba was conical throughout its entire length; the diameter of the bronze tubing of the surviving instrument just mentioned measures at the mouthpiece end 1cm and at the other end, just before the slightly flaring bell, 2.79cm.

The *buc(c)ina* was an instrument in the shape of a hook or a 'J', and no doubt originated from a stalk of cane (or some other similar material) which was provided with a bell made out of an animal horn.

The cornu, a long, curved instrument made out of bronze in the form of a 'G', was a third Roman brass instrument, but not a trumpet in the sense of our discussion.

A fourth Roman brass instrument, the lituus, is confused in the old sources with the bucina. It was also hook-shaped and seems variously to have been made of two kinds of material: (1) up to

The Early History of the Trumpet until the Fall of Rome (AD 476)

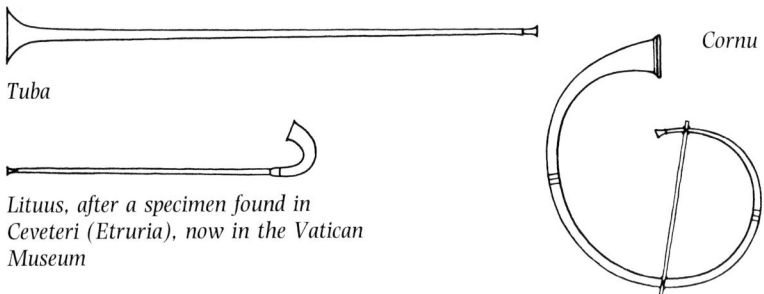

Tuba

Cornu

Lituus, after a specimen found in Ceveteri (Etruria), now in the Vatican Museum

c AD 100 out of bronze, and as such related to the Celtic *karnyx* (*see below*), and (2) in the Imperial Age, out of an animal horn with silver decorations, like the bucina. It seems, during this later period at least, to have been used in a religious and civil context rather than a military one. Surviving specimens are 78, 79.5 and 140cm long.

The Roman trumpets were first and foremost military instruments. The tuba is said to have been the instrument of the infantry, the bucina that of the cavalry. Their signals were reported on by Flavius Vegetius, who, in the history of the Roman trumpet, occupies the same position that Altenburg did later with respect to the Baroque trumpet. Vegetius wrote his treatise, *Epitoma rei militaris*, after the defeat of the Roman army at the hands of the Goths near Adrianopolis (AD 378). The decline of the once perfectly functioning Roman military machinery was already too advanced for a return to the ancient virtues of discipline and courage postulated by Vegetius. As far as the signals are concerned, Vegetius wrote:

> The music of the legion consists of tubae, cornua, and buccinae. The tuba signals charges and retreats. The cornua are only used to indicate the movements of the colours ... The classicum, a special call of the buccinae or of the cornua, is reserved for the commanding officer ...

The sounds of the Roman instruments were anything but beautiful. Authors of antiquity described the tuba's tone as horrible, terrible, raucous, and rough (*horribilis, terribilis, raucus, rudis*). The sound of the shorter lituus was logically described as *acutus*, i.e. 'high', but these instruments also produced a great din – in Latin *stridor* and *strepens*. It must have been a strenuous exertion to play these instruments. Sometimes the tuba players girded their cheeks with the so-called *capistrum* of the aulos

The Early History of the Trumpet until the Fall of Rome (AD 476)

players, in order to prevent them from being puffed out unduly.

The Roman brass instruments were also used in the arena. We know that the tuba and the cornu sounded together with the Roman hydraulus, a water-powered organ, during gladiator fights. (*See colour page i.*)

From the time of the Servian constitution (middle of the fifth century BC), the Roman military musicians formed two centuriates (groups of one hundred members) and belonged to the fifth class of the voting populace. Since the time of Septimus Severus (193–211) they were allowed to form groups called colleges. The statutes of such a legion in Lambaesis in North Africa are still preserved; they comprised 35 cornu players in all with an *optio* at the head of each group.

The Roman tuba was also an instrument of religious ceremony, sounding at public services. In addition, 'the festival of the trumpeters (*tubilustrium*) was celebrated solemnly every year, when in the month of April (on the last day of the *quinquatriorum*) the trumpets used at the sacrifices were played publically, usually at the sacrifice of a lamb. On the 23rd of May the trumpeters celebrated this festival themselves.' (J.E. Altenburg, p. 21.)

The Teutonic Tribes

From the time of the Bronze Age of the Teutonic tribes (1500–400 BC), curious brass instruments called *lurs* survive, which were apparently used for religious purposes. About three dozen of these instruments have been discovered in the moors of Norway, Sweden, Denmark, North Germany, and Ireland. The largest collection of lurs is found in the National Museum of Copenhagen. The primitive form of the lur must have been that of a long animal horn, provided later with metal reinforcements. In the Bronze Age the lur proper was developed from this. The Teutonic

The Early History of the Trumpet until the Fall of Rome (AD 476)

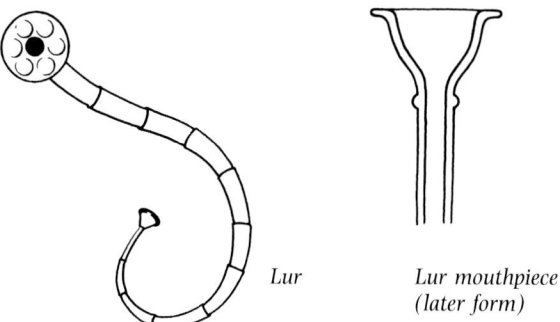

Lur

Lur mouthpiece
(later form)

workmanship shows perfect mastery in the art of casting (*see summary below*). Lurs, which were always discovered in pairs, have the shape of an 'S', whereby the second curve lies in a different plane from that of the first. Their tubing is conical throughout and does not end in a flared bell, but rather in a flat disc provided with various ornamental circular indentations. A study of their mouthpieces reveals that they underwent developmental changes. The earliest ones were mere expansions of the narrow end of the tube, whereas the later ones possess a cup-shaped form not unlike that of a modern trombone or baritone mouthpiece. One should not, however, allow oneself to be misled by this form to believe that lurs were thus played in a manner familiar to us. The writers of antiquity without exception speak in derogatory terms about the tone of instruments such as these. Lurs were probably not even played in harmony together. On the contrary, all music of primitive peoples known to us suggests the opposite conclusion, that is, that lurs were either played together in unison or else separately.

The Celts

The Celts too had a trumpet-like military instrument, the *karnyx*. Like the Roman lituus, it developed from the union of a cane stalk and a cowhorn, forming a hook-shaped instrument made entirely of bronze. The most recent karnykes had a fanciful bell in the shape of a dragon's head and were depicted in bas-relief on Hadrian's Arch in Rome, AD 113. The karnyx seems to have influenced the shape of the lituus for a time, since the latter took over the dragon's head; the most recent and most typical litui, however, display a simpler form.

The Early History of the Trumpet until the Fall of Rome (AD 476)

Summary

Except for the chatzotzrah of the Israelites, which was made out of hammered silver, and the Egyptian 'snb', most metal trumpets of the earliest time seem to have been made of bronze by the so-called 'lost-wax' process. With this method, the desired form of the tubing – whether straight as with the tuba, or bent, as with the lur – was modelled in wax around an indestructible core and surrounded by a clay mantle. When the liquid bronze was poured in, the wax melted. Tubing made in this way was generally rather thick-walled. It was not until the time of the Saracens that brass instruments seem to have been made from hammered sheet.

It is significant to note that the various kinds of trumpets, from prehistoric beginnings up to the Romans, had either a military or a religious function. Among the civilized people of old it was certainly the Israelites who gave their trumpeters the highest rank; the trumpet was allowed to be played only by priests.

The trumpet of prehistoric times and of antiquity served only as a signalling instrument, and certainly not to produce music in the modern sense. The sound of these instruments was described as terrible, that is, producing terror, and was compared to the braying of an ass.

TWO
Some Asiatic Forms of the Trumpet

The Indians

The South Indian trumpet, called *tirucinnam* in Tamil, was similar to the Assyrian and Egyptian trumpet. It was about 75cm long, had a wide cylindrical bore, and a narrow, conical bell, but no mouthpiece. The reason for the lack of mouthpiece is clear; the tirucinnam player always blew two of these instruments simultaneously.

Another kind of Indian trumpet, the end-blown shell trumpet called *šankha* in Sanscrit, is mentioned here only because of its exclusively religious use. On the last day of the earth, when everything goes up in flames, the god Siva will play the shell trumpet – as will the seven angels of the biblical Last Judgement.

The modern North Indian trumpet seems to be derived from central Asiatic and Far Eastern trumpets or at least to be related to them. Like the Chinese trumpet, it is narrow and conical and consists of four telescoping sections, the ends of which are each provided with a kind of knob.

The Chinese and Tibetans

Besides the end-blown shell trumpet (*hai lo* in Chinese, *hora* in Japanese), which is played by sailors and Buddhist priests, there was also in China a very long cylindrical metal trumpet (*hao t'ung* in Chinese, *dokaku* in Japanese), the bell end of which rests on the ground while the instrument is being played. Instead of a bell, it possesses a long, broad cylinder made out of wood, iron, or brass; the telescoping tubing can be made to disappear into this cylinder. The hao t'ung was played at burials.

The ordinary Chinese metal trumpet, *la pa* (*rapa* in Japanese), came from Mongolia, where it was called *rapal*. It had a narrow conical bore and consisted of two or three telescoping sections

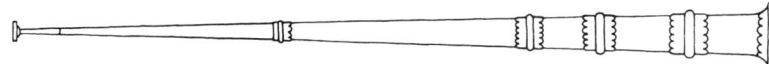

Dung (Tibet), after a specimen in the author's collection

which, as with the later North Indian trumpet mentioned above, were separated from one another by knobs. Its bell had a considerable flare.

The Tibetan trumpet, called *dung*, can be as long as nearly five metres. It is made of copper, has a conical bore, and also consists of several telescoping sections with knobs. When it is blown during lama rites, it usually rests on the ground. Like many Asiatic trumpet instruments related to it, the dung has a broad, very flat mouthpiece. Only low, roaring tones are played on it.

Summary

Thus the Asian trumpets had the same common characteristics as the prehistoric and ancient ones. They apparently were and are played at religious ceremonies and perhaps also in times of war; a 'musical' use in the Western sense can be excluded. Particularly noteworthy is the presence of several knobs on the instruments. On the Asiatic trumpets these knobs served to mark the ends of the telescoping sections of tubing. Rudimentary knobs can also be observed on the primitive German lurs which also consist of several sections, although they do not telescope into each other. This component can be seen on the Baroque natural trumpet, although on these latter instruments the ball – as it is called – has a merely ornamental function. It is possible that the knob or ball was brought to the West from the Orient by the Saracens during the Crusades.

THREE

The Trumpet from the Fall of Rome until the Crusades (*c* 1100)

With the conquering of Rome by the West Goths under Alarich (410) and by the Vandals under Geiserich (455), the way was prepared for the decay of the Western Roman Empire. Decadent Roman culture came to an abrupt end in AD 476 when the Germanic general Odoaker deposed the last Western Roman emperor Romulus Augustulus, who was only 14 years old. While older historians agreed that with the end of the West Roman empire many cultural assets of the Romans also disappeared, among them the trumpet, recent writers – particularly Baines (1976) and Žak (1979) – point out a slender tradition of brass instruments in the West up to the time of the Third Crusade, when a new type of long cylindrical trumpet, the busine, was introduced by way of the Arabs. During this intervening period, the Teutonic tribes were acquainted with military instruments made out of buffalo or aurochs horns and were also apparently familiar with metal instruments. Some of the following forms of trumpets lived on in works of art and the writings of the Church Fathers.

The words 'salpinx' (in the Greek version of the Holy Bible) and 'tuba' (in the later Latin version) designated indiscriminately both the wind instruments of the Israelites – shofar (a ram's horn) and chatzotzrah – as well as later instruments, which can generally be recognized in works of art as animal horns. It is an interesting anomaly in the German language that Martin Luther, in his German translation of the Bible from 1552, used the word 'Posaune' – the modern word for trombone – as a translation for 'shofar', while the King James version of the Bible, for example, employs the word 'trumpet'. Thus, while we speak of trumpeting angels, the Germans still today refer to 'Posaunenengel', which would seem to be trombone-playing angels. Even in the German translation of Handel's *Messiah*, Germans know the famous air, 'The Trumpet Shall Sound', as 'Es erschallt die Posaun'. Žak has shown, however, that 'Posaune' for Luther did not mean the trombone but rather a trumpet in the then old-fashioned straight form as can be seen in contemporary biblical illustrations, since, as we will see below, 'S'-shaped trumpets were in use by then and the term was not exclusively used to designate the trombone.

The Church Fathers identified the salpinx or tuba with the voice of the angels; they were apparently influenced by the Book of Revelation (written about AD 95–96), where, in Chapter 1:10 the voice of God is compared with a salpinx. The music theorist Cassiodorus (c AD 485–580) was influenced by the Church Fathers when, in his interpretation of Psalm 46:6, he described the awesome sound of these instruments as follows: 'The voice of the tuba represents the words of the angels, which resounded with a great uproar of the trembling air.'

Among the representations of the tuba in works of art, those of the Apocalypse are distinctive. The immediate effectiveness of the tuba in the Last Judgement can be seen in an illustration from a book once belonging to the Emperor Heinrich II (beginning of the eleventh century). Four angels, in four corners of the book, are sounding four animal horns. The resurrected ones, just emerging from their graves, perceive the 'great uproar' as if transfixed (*see p. 34*).

Ancient forms of the trumpet, next to the otherwise usual animal horn, seem to live on in two other works of art. First, the long straight, conical instruments from a Last Judgement of an Irish Gospel of the eighth century in St Gall are strongly reminiscent of the Greek salpinx; like the latter, the former consist of several parts, although the salpinx was cylindrical and not conical. Second, a medium-long conical instrument similar to a Roman tuba appears in the Trier Apocalypse (first half of the ninth century).

The Trumpet from the Fall of Rome until the Crusades (c 1100)

Trumpets (animal horns) of the Last Judgement from the Pericope Book of Heinrich II, early eleventh century
Munich, Staatsbibliothek
(Photo: Bildarchiv Foto Marburg)

FOUR

The Trumpet in the Late Middle Ages (*c* 1100–1400)

Introduction
In the late Middle Ages, literature and art flourished greatly, creating a profusion of new forms of trumpet and therefore new names as well. This variety was due largely to contact with the Arabs, known at that time as 'Saracens'. This was the time of the founding of great courts and cities, the future employers of trumpeters, as well as the emergence of two kinds of instrumental ensemble using trumpets: the pure trumpet ensemble, sometimes including kettledrums, and the so-called alta ensemble consisting of shawms and trumpets. It was also during this period that musicians, including trumpeters, first banded together into brotherhoods or confederations. However by far the most important use of the trumpet was in war; and it was easy for the itinerant musicians of the time to find temporary employment in the service of one of the numerous armies going off to the Crusades.

Western Contact with the Saracens during the Crusades
The Saracens subjugated Spain in the years 711 to 713, and centuries passed before the Saracens, after laborious struggles, could be forced to retreat. Only in 1492 did Spain become entirely freed. Between 1071 and 1073 the Saracens also conquered Palestine and as the Greek Emperor Alexios I called for help from the Pope, all of Europe became possessed by a veritable fever to liberate the Holy Land: the Crusades had begun.

The first Crusade lasted from 1096 to 1099, the second occurred between 1147 and 1149 under Konrad III and Louis VII, the third occurred from 1189 to 1192 under Friederich Barbarossa, Richard the Lionheart and Phillip II, and the sixth lasted from 1248 to 1252 and was led by Louis IX, who was later pronounced a saint. Numerous other, smaller Crusades followed.

In the eleventh century, the Islamic world was superior to the West in many areas, such as astronomy, trade, and the conduct of war and as a result the Western world profited enormously from its contact with the Orient. For example, it took over the Arabian system of numbers and increased its trading capacities immeasurably. It was also from the Saracens that many musical instruments were taken over, often together with their Arabic names.

Saracen Trumpets

The Saracens possessed many noisy instruments such as *anafīr* (trumpets), *būqāt* (trumpets or horns), *zumūr* (shawms), *naqqāra* (kettledrums), *tubūl* (drums) and *kāsāt* (cymbals). Like the Christian wind instruments, these too were used 'to frighten the enemy', as John of Spain wrote around 1138. All of the chroniclers of the Crusades agree that the Saracen military musicians produced a true din in battle; in particular, the noise of their kettledrums was said to have created such confusion that the Christians found it necessary to blind the eyes and stop the ears of their horses (Pseudo-Turpin, eleventh century).

Short and long Arabian trumpets can be seen on two miniatures of the manuscript *F-Pbn fonds arabe 5847* (fols 19 and 94ᵛ) (*colour pp. ii and iii*). The scenes depicted are quite realistic. The long trumpets are accompanied by a pair of large kettledrums, and the trumpeters playing shorter instruments are accompanied by colleagues beating smaller kettledrums. The trumpets, which are blown in pairs, have ornamented garlands reinforcing the flared bell ends. The long instruments have a greater degree of bell flare than do the short ones, and they also possess one or more knobs. It is easy to imagine these mobile groups of musicians spurring

The Trumpet in the Late Middle Ages (c 1100–1400)

their troops on to battle from the top of a low hill.

The Arabian word *buq*, which is probably derived from the Latin word bucina, has two meanings. Around the year 800, it designated a horn- or trumpet-like instrument – as did the word tuba in Latin writings. Then, from the tenth century, it meant a short kind of animal horn used by the militia. In the eleventh century it began to be constructed out of metal.

The other Arabian kind of trumpet, the *nafīr*, is first heard of in the eleventh century, first under the name of *buq-al-nafīr*. We can assume that the nafir was usually longer than the buq because of a source (probably from the twelfth century) which speaks of a large buq resembling the buq-al-nafir. This word was taken over in later Iberian literature as *añafil*. There were shorter and longer ones, and the longer ones have survived even until today in North Africa under the original name of nafir.

Still another Saracen instrument, the form of which has not yet been determined, is the *cor Sarrazinnois*, described by Joinville in his chronicle of the Sixth Crusade.

The Use of the Saracen Trumpets in War

All high Saracen officers had their own military band, the size of which depended on the officer's rank. The band of Sultan Baibars (d. 1277), for example, consisted of 68 members: 20 trumpets (anfār), four shawms (zumūr), four drums (*duhul*) and 40 kettledrums (kūsāt). The *amir* of a division had the same-sized band, but without the kettledrummers. An *atabeg* had 16 players, the amir of a smaller fighting force had eight players, and others had only one buq. The band's tent was next to that of the Sultan. A kettledrum signal called the riders and footsoldiers to battle. During the fighting, these warlike instruments played unceasingly; as long as they could be heard, the soldiers knew that the

The Trumpet in the Late Middle Ages (c 1100–1400)

battle was running according to plan. As early as the ninth century, musical instruments and banners were among the most coveted spoils of war.

Western Trumpets at the Time of the Crusades

The most important kind of trumpet in the Western world came to be the busine. The busine is generally agreed to be a long, usually cylindrical trumpet of metal. The word was derived from the French term *buisine* around the year 1250; both terms go back to the Latin word bucina. The sources of the twelfth and thirteenth centuries, however, are contradictory. For example, in the *Song of Roland*, written around the year 1100, busines are mentioned which are hung around the neck. These must therefore have been rather short instruments, probably like the oliphant, which was made of ivory; other sources mentioned animal horn as the material. Even if the word 'busine' designated the long metal trumpet then, there are so many other definitions that this term must be used with the greatest care. In the fifteenth century, with the invention of the double slide, the trombone was born, and from the original term busine, by way of the word *pusune*, the German word for trombone, Posaune, originated, as we have seen above.

It is thought that the long metal trumpet – whether it was called busine or nafir – was brought to the Western world by the Saracens. The earliest example of such an instrument was thought to be the four trumpets in the representation of the Last Judgement on the west wall of the basilica of S. Angelo in Formis, near Capua, painted in the years 1072–87 (*see colour page iv*). Although these instruments do indeed demonstrate the new, long form and are to be termed trumpets rather than horns, Capua lies outside the Saracen sphere of influence; the early

The Trumpet in the Late Middle Ages (c 1100–1400)

dating also excludes the influence of the first Crusades which did not start until 1096. Baines (1976) has also pointed out that there are no contemporary Arabian representations of trumpets which can be drawn on for comparison. The Formis frescoes therefore seem to present us with a riddle. However, Žak (1979) has demonstrated a clear Byzantine influence: in the training of the artists and in the style of their frescoes, in the former occupation of the territories surrounding Capua, and finally, in the use of trumpets themselves in the Byzantine empire, both in war and at court.

The Use of Trumpets in the West: the Trumpa

Details of the fighting and of the use of musical instruments in the Third Crusade have been handed down by both sides. Entering Messina in the year 1190, Richard the Lionheart was greeted by 'resounding tubae and clear, bright litui'; there on the third day, he encouraged his army to follow him 'to the sound of the buccina'.

As Richard was pausing in Sicily before setting out for Palestine, a new kind of instrument – the *trumpa* – was demonstrated to him. Roger of Wendover (d. 1236) wrote about 'tubae called trumpae'. This instrument was mentioned for the first time around the year 1180 in the writings of William of Palermo. It is possible that the trumpa, too, was of Arabian origin, because the Normans had driven the Saracens out of Sicily only nine years before, taking over many of their customs. The word 'trumpa' was to become particularly important in the future, for the modern terms for the trumpet in the most important European languages developed from diminutive forms of this term: in German, *trumpa, trumb, Trum(m)et, Trompete*; in French, *trompe, trompette*; and in English, trump, trumpet. At

The Trumpet in the Late Middle Ages (c 1100–1400)

first, in the fourteenth century, the diminutive form designated the short straight trumpet; afterwards, in the fifteenth century, and thanks to a new technique in instrument making, it came to mean the modern, folded trumpet.

The noise-making function of the Saracen military music was soon taken over by the Christians. Courtly epic poems often described battle music. (*See colour page v.*)

The sound of the trumpet called the troops to battle: 'mìn busùner hiez ich dò / blàsen unde machen schal' (*Frauendienst, c* 1255, verse 590, 6). The warlike music was not allowed to cease at the height of the battle:

> Biaus fu li jors et li solaus luist clers,
> Et la bataille fist molt à redouter.
> En cc lieus i véissiés capler,
> Cors et buisines et olifans soner,
> Molt hautement ensegnes escrier,
> Païne gent et glatir et huper . . .
> (The day was beautiful and the sun shone clear,
> and the battle was fearsome.
> In two hundred places you could see them fighting,
> and you heard horns, trumpets, and oliphants sounding
> and making very loud signals,
> and you heard the pagans shouting and screaming . . .)

(From Aliscans, *Chanson de Geste*, lines 5617–22)

The expression 'machen schal', or 'to make noise during the battle', is quite probably related to the later Baroque term, 'Lärmblasen'. In the Middle Ages, this music-making by trumpeters was called 'classicum'. The *classicum* was described by John of Janua as follows: 'Properly speaking, classicum is the unison made by all the instruments sounding together, whether they be

The Trumpet in the Late Middle Ages (c 1100–1400)

the tubae and cornua in war, or the bells'. The 'unison of all the instruments sounding together' seems to have been organized in some way. But at other times, however, 'the tubae were sounded at random to frighten the enemy' (Aymeric de Peyrac, fifteenth century). The performance of the classicum will be discussed below.

The magical sound resulting from all these instruments being played together comes out clearly in these descriptions, especially when 'trumpets and bells ring out together', as stated in *Lohengrin*, verse 5037. The word 'sonnerie', still in use today in French, means both a military signal and a ringing of bells. Military signals seem to have developed only gradually. At the time of the courtly epic poems, there was just a 'ringing out' of trumpets. By contrast, fixed tunes seemed to have existed on marches; these were called 'Reisenoten': 'Mîn busûnaere die bliesen dò / mit kunst ein reisenot vil hò' (*Frauendienst*, verse 996, 6–7).

The Claro or Clarion

In English glossaries and chronicles of the twelfth and thirteenth centuries, we come across certain trumpet-like instruments with names such as claro, clario, clarone and clarasius. Claro and clario were derived from the Latin word 'clarus', meaning bright or clear, whereas the origin of the ending 'asius' is uncertain. Around 1350–70, the modern word 'clairon' already existed in French. A typical use of these words, found in a passage of unique poetic strength, appears in *The Knighte's Tale* by Chaucer (*c* 1340–1400):

> Pypes, trompes, nakers, clariounes,
> that in the bataille blowen blody sounes.

The Trumpet in the Late Middle Ages (c 1100–1400)

In the bloody business of war, 'trompes' and 'clariounes' must have been different instruments. (In England and France, the word 'trompe' often designated a hunting horn.)

The Range of the Late Medieval Trumpet

Thanks to the music theorist Johannes de Grocheo, we are well informed about the range of trumpets around the year 1300. In his treatise *De arte musicae*, he wrote that the trumpet had command of the three perfect consonances – that is, the octave, fifth, and fourth. These are the intervals formed by the first four partials of the harmonic series. In other words, trumpeters of the late Middle Ages played in the low register of their instrument.

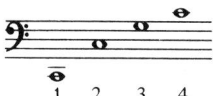

This fact is corroborated by the loose way of blowing that we see in many works of art. For example, in the left upper field of the famous choir loft, or *cantoria*, built between 1431 and 1438 by Luca della Robbia (now preserved in the Museum of the Cathedral of Florence), three trumpeters are playing. They are illustrating a verse of the 150th Psalm, *Laudate eum in sono tubae*. The mouthpieces seem to be constructed simply by having that end of the tubing widened slightly, a fact which suggests a large inside diameter. The trumpeters are playing with loose lip muscles and puffed-out cheeks. Both of these factors – mouthpiece bore and method of playing – suggest a low, somewhat rough sound.

The Trumpet in the Late Middle Ages (c 1100–1400)

Luca della Robbia, Cantoria, *1431–38 Trumpeters in the upper left field*

Florence, Museo dell' Opera del Duomo (Photo: Fratelli Alinari, Florence)

The Social Status of Medieval Trumpeters

In the Middle Ages, musicians, actors, and the like were not regarded as having any rights at all, because they generally had no permanent place of residence, appearing here and there at festivals and fairs. The church even denied them the sacraments. In this respect, the trumpeters' lot was no different from that of other musicians. On the other hand, if any musician succeeded in gaining employment with a court or a city, he was then considered to have rights.

The Court Trumpeters

Despite incomplete documentation, we can say with certainty that trumpeters were among the first musicians hired by courts. The reason for this is doubtlessly because of their important function in war. Fighting wars seems to have been one of the favourite pastimes of rulers of that day, and trumpeters were indispensable for giving signals. They served purely ceremonial functions as well, for which they wore costly uniforms, and had a banner with the coat of arms of their employer decorating their instruments; in addition they were often given a horse.

On no account, however, can we assume that the trumpeters themselves had a high social position. They were regarded merely as servants. Among the duties of court trumpeters were playing at table and announcing the public appearances of their ruler. These functions were already delineated in one of the earliest surviving court ordinances, the *Leges Palatinae*, decreed by Jaime II, King of Mallorca, in 1337. He was referring to the five musicians employed by him: two trumpeters and a drummer or kettledrummer, as well as two other musicians playing a number of different instruments. The first duty above all else was to make their king of good cheer and to dispel his anger and sadness. The trumpeters and kettledrummers had the special task of playing whenever the king showed himself in public – one of the most important functions of court trumpeters everywhere up to the nineteenth century. Another important duty, and similarly one which was also important later on, was playing at table, except for certain times of fasting or mourning. In the court records, trumpeters and timpanists belonged specifically to the *mimis et joculatores*.

Like the battle in wartime, the tournament in times of peace was one of the main occupations of both the rulers and their trumpeters. A tournament usually lasted an entire day. In the early morning after mass, trumpets were sounded to announce the beginning of the event. Sometimes, but not always accompanied by other instruments such as 'pipes', they played at certain moments before the competition, such as at the challenge, as well as during the tournament itself. In so doing the trumpeters did not necessarily remain at a safe distance from the field of activity. The day usually ended with a banquet and with dancing. Trumpeters played at other festive occasions at court, such as coronations, weddings, baptisms and the like.

The Trumpet in the Late Middle Ages (c 1100–1400)

The City Trumpeters

The wealthy trading cities in Italy, Germany and Flanders were first to feel the wish to emulate the splendour of the courts, taking trumpeters into their service. In Italy, we know of municipal trumpeters starting with the twelfth century and in Germany from the thirteenth. These musicians first performed watchmen's functions and were an important symbol of the judiciary, but gradually they came to participate in festivities of all kinds.

The example of Bologna, a city which was to become important for the trumpet in the seventeenth century, well illustrates the duties of municipal trumpeters. Already in the thirteenth century (1281) there were two *tubatores* who made official proclamations. They received splendid uniforms from the city; their trumpets were made of silver and were decorated with various kinds of pennants. By 1328, eight city trumpeters positioned themselves in groups of two in the watchtowers of the four principal city gates: the Porta Piera, Porta Procula, Porta Stiera, and Porta Ravegnana. In Italian, the trumpeters were called *trombetti della Signoria*, and in Latin, the official language of city business, they were still named *tubatores*. Their duties consisted not only of playing signals to announce legal proclamations and the like, but also of furnishing the decorative framework for the installation festivities of university rectors as well as for processions on the occasion of doctoral celebrations. During the fifteenth century they formed the nucleus of a group of Bolognese musicians called the Concerto Palatino della Signoria, an institution related to that of the German city-pipers or *Stadtpfeifereien*.

We have documentary evidence of six such trumpeters in Florence in 1292 and five in Lucca in 1310. In Flanders, trumpeters are known to have served as tower watchmen in the fourteenth and fifteenth centuries, for example, in Bruges,

Antwerp, Leiden and Ghent. It is typical to find them mentioned in archival documents as performing together with other instruments; shawm and busine, mentioned in 1342 in Mons; *trompers* and minstrels, in 1368 in Bruges; and the playing for a procession in 1377 in Mecheln by three *tromperen*, three pipers, a shawm player, and a kettledrummer.

North of the Alps, city watchmen's functions seemed to have first been filled not by a trumpeter, but rather by a musician playing on an animal horn – except for a few early instances, such as in Görlitz (1376) and Basel (before 1384). In general the trumpet does not seem to have taken over these duties from the horn until gradually during the course of the fourteenth and fifteenth centuries.

The Musicians' Brotherhoods

In order to protect their own interests, musicians of the fourteenth century, living in a particular region, began to form brotherhoods. Following the example of feudal society, these brotherhoods had a *Spielgraf* or *Spielkönig* at their head. Trumpeters also belonged to these brotherhoods and occasionally even headed them. The earliest brotherhood of musicians, the so-called Nicolai-Zechbrüder, was founded in Vienna in 1288 and was disbanded only in 1782. In 1310, five trumpeters in Lucca formed such a brotherhood. The Confrérie de Saint-Julien was founded in Paris in 1321 and was dissolved in 1773. In 1330, representatives of 31 musicians' brotherhoods met in Tournai. English minstrel kings are mentioned as early as 1381.

The Trumpet in the Late Middle Ages (c 1100–1400)

The Music of Medieval Trumpeters

According to Žak, four kinds of ensembles using trumpets existed during the late Middle Ages:

1 trumpets with percussion instruments (first for warfare, then for ceremony), from *c* 1150 to *c* 1300, at which point the percussion instruments faded away, this combination practically ceasing to exist *c* 1350, only to be revived in a completely new, forward-looking manner a hundred years later with the rise of the large kettledrums;
2 trumpets with woodwind and percussion instruments (generally for ceremonial use), from *c* 1180 to *c* 1330;
3 trumpets with woodwind instruments (also for ceremonial use), from *c* 1300, first for processions, then after *c* 1400 for dancing as well;
4 trumpets alone, by far the largest group, from 1150 to 1350.

By 1400 two kinds of ensemble could be clearly differentiated. One kind, arising from the first or fourth group above, was the trumpet ensemble, often after 1450 with kettledrummers, a group which later developed into the courtly trumpet corps. At first they performed signalling functions at war, but later assumed ceremonial duties as well. The other group (group 3 above) was the so-called 'alta' ensemble, consisting of loud instruments (*instruments hauts*), such as shawms (woodwind instruments with a double reed) and trumpets, as opposed to the soft instruments (*instruments bas*), such as vieles, psalteries, and lutes.

The trumpet ensemble played the classicum, both in battle and at court. Taking Johannes de Grocheo's information on the range of the trumpet, we can presume that all of the trumpeters played

The Trumpet in the Late Middle Ages (c 1100–1400)

low notes. Several observations confirm this supposition: (1) the loose way of blowing, mentioned above; (2) contemporary accounts mentioning great loudness, recalling primitive usage; (3) the fact that the trumpet in the alta ensemble always played the low part and that the trombone – a low-pitched instrument emerging in the fifteenth century (*see below*) – was descended from the (slide) trumpet. If all the trumpets had the same pitch or if all of the trumpets playing together, long and short, were tuned together, the result was a consonance, or a kind of constantly reiterated chord. (Still today we recognize this kind of sustained, unchanging accompaniment, called a drone, with bagpipes.) The effect of such a sustained, constantly reiterated chord must indeed have been magical. Notably, the first surviving 'sonatas' of late sixteenth-century trumpet ensembles also display the same features: a constant repetition of a single chord, which in the lower voices has the effect of a drone.

We can thus understand why all the authors of the late Middle Ages called attention to the great loudness of trumpets playing in an ensemble. Their sound was not blasting, but rather roaring and vibrant. In *Parzival* Wolfram von Eschenbach says that 'die hellen pusînen / mit krache vor im gâben dôs', that is, the clear trumpets, called busines, produced a thundering roar. In another epic poem, the *Jüngerer Titurel*, the busines were said to have roared as if the dry branches of a large forest were splintering:

> *Und mit dem ruffe der busîn krachen*
> *Als ob mit donres duzzen*
> *breche ein grozzer walt*
> *mit durren spachen*[.]

At the same time that the trumpet ensemble was developing, the alta ensemble also came to light. Like the trumpet ensemble, the alta ensemble fulfilled ceremonial functions, but it also performed at all kinds of festivities, in particular accompanying dancing. How did such a group sound, consisting mainly of two shawms and one trumpet? The musicologist Herbert Heyde has reconstructed the music of alta ensembles from surviving minstrel music of the thirteenth century. According to him, the shawms played a lively melody above a drone sustained in the trumpet part. At the ends of the phrases, the trumpet might leap a fifth. In music of this kind, the trumpet could make do with the second and third partials of the harmonic series and thus remain within the boundaries of the possibilities explained in 1300 by Johannes de Grocheo.

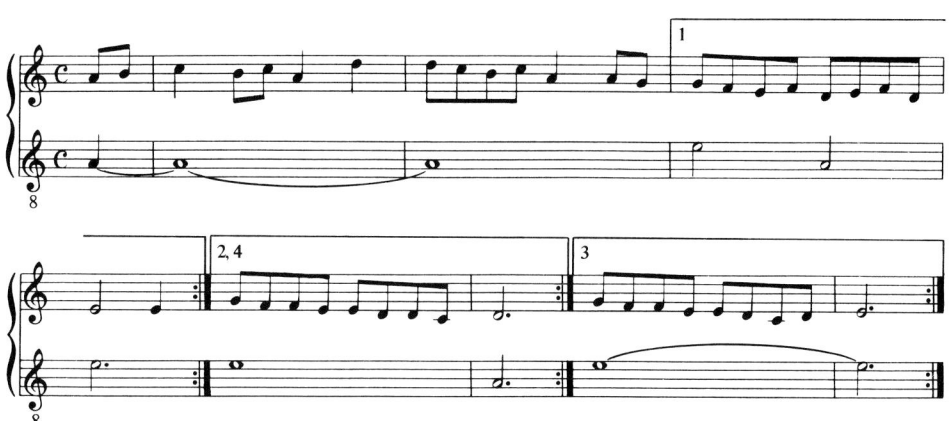

FIVE

The Trumpet in the Renaissance (1400–1600)

Mouthpieces between 1400 and 1600

The earliest mouthpieces originated by slightly expanding the blowing end of an instrument to a kind of softer lip support, as we have already seen with the trumpets on the choir loft made by Luca della Robbia. By 1600, parallel to the development of trumpet playing, more and more complicated forms of mouthpieces had developed. Whereas the older ones were constructed of many parts made from sheet metal, the later ones were cast. The process of casting as used in the construction of mouthpieces was probably developed sometime between 1400 and 1500. The illustration shows the possible development of mouthpiece-making, from the mere expansion of the tube and the construction out of sheet metal to casting. As late as 1578, Jacob Steiger, city trumpeter in Basel, constructed a mouthpiece (which still exists) with great artifice out of seven individual parts, as seen in an X-ray photo and an exploded drawing.

Instrument-Making until c 1400

As we have already seen, most metal trumpets of antiquity consisted of cast bronze. Only the silver trumpets of the ancient Israelites, the Egyptian trumpets, and certain exceptional instruments were chased, that is, made out of sheet metal. The Saracens, too, are supposed to have known this second method, which corresponds to the modern way of construction. During the Crusades then, the West imported not only Saracen instrument forms and names, but also their method of construction.

The reader will certainly have noticed by now that all of the trumpets shown from the late Middle Ages, whether short or long, are straight. At that time it was relatively simple to make a trumpet. The true profession of a brass instrument maker did not yet exist, for the most important skill necessary for the construc-

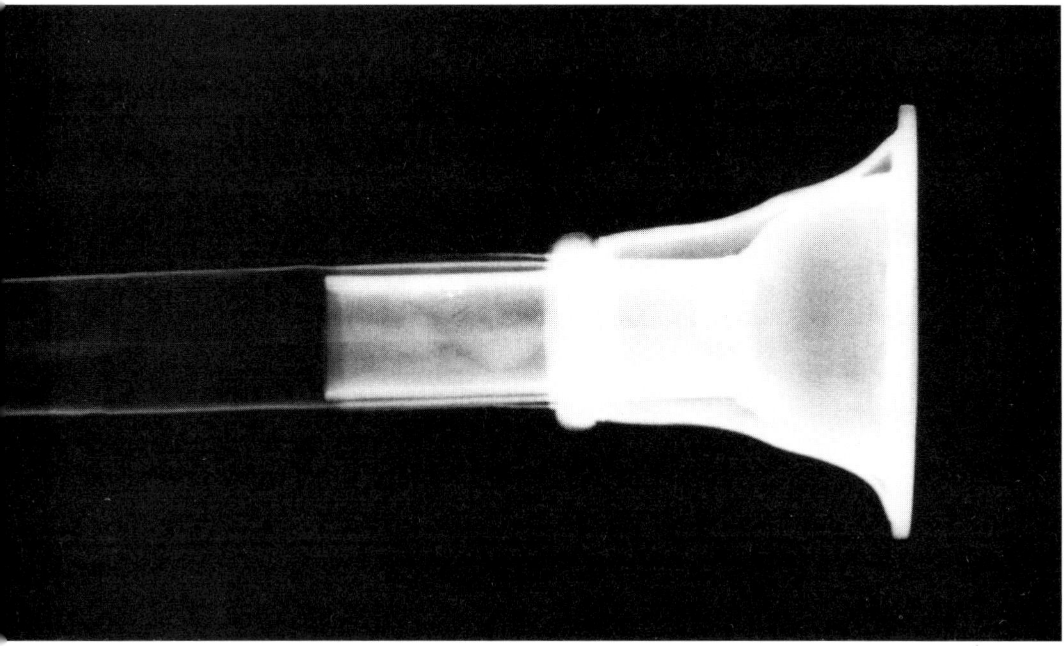

The Trumpet in the Renaissance (1400–1600)

X-ray photograph of the seven individual parts of a trumpet mouthpiece by Jacob Steiger, Basel, 1578
Basel, Historisches Museum
(Photo: Röntgeninstitut H.J. Nidecker, Basel)

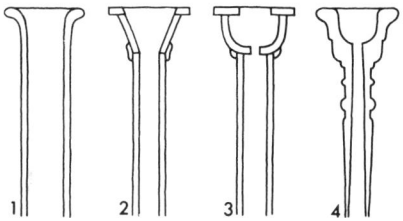

The possible development of mouthpiece construction, from the cushioned expansion of the tube (1) and the manufacture out of sheet metal (2, 3) to the modern cast mouthpiece (4)

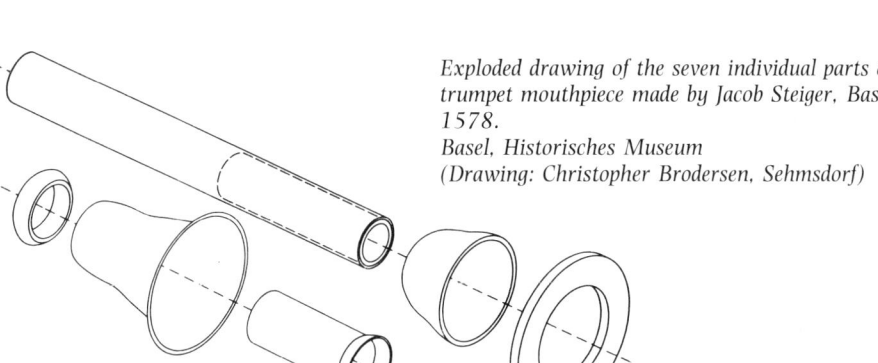

Exploded drawing of the seven individual parts of a trumpet mouthpiece made by Jacob Steiger, Basel, 1578.
Basel, Historisches Museum
(Drawing: Christopher Brodersen, Sehmsdorf)

The Trumpet in the Renaissance (1400–1600)

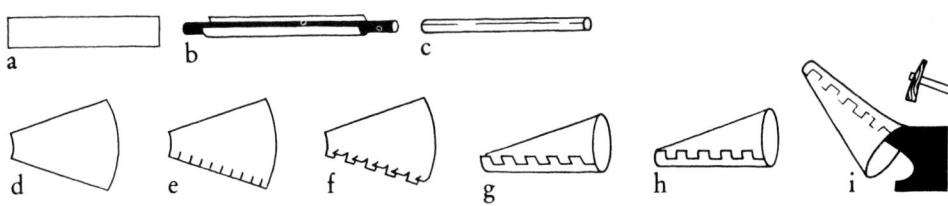

tion of a brass instrument of that time was the mere making of tubing. It is certainly no accident that the profession of brass instrument making developed in Nuremberg around 1500 from that of the coppersmith, and in Paris from that of the *chaudronnier* or kettle maker.

The illustration above shows the processes necessary for making tubing and bells. To make a cylindrical tube, one takes a flat, thin rectangular piece of metal – usually brass or another alloy, sometimes silver – of the desired length (a), and bends it around a round bar (b). After more or less sustained scraping of the parallel sides, they are fitted together and soldered to a seam (c). Long trumpets consisted of several such tubes fitted into one another.

The bell was made in a similar way from a piece of sheet metal, but with the difference that this sheet was not in the shape of a rectangle but rather a kind of trapezoid with two rounded sides (d). Teeth were cut out of one of the long sides (e), each second one being bent over slightly (f); the other long side was bent around so as to fit into these teeth (g), the whole being soldered together to form the bell in its rough shape (h). Afterwards the seam, which of course was thicker, was hammered down to the normal sheet-metal thickness. The desired bell flare was obtained by hammering on an anvil (i).

It was necessary to make the bell section using teeth, because a simple seam such as that used in tubes could split during the hammering process of making the flare. One can see from surviving bells between the sixteenth and nineteenth centuries that the toothed construction was used only in the place where the sheet metal was stretched the most, that is, in the area of the bell flare. Towards the middle of the bell section the number of teeth usually decreases, and the remainder of the bell section towards the ferrule was generally made with a straight seam, just like a simple piece of tubing.

The Trumpet in the Renaissance (1400–1600)

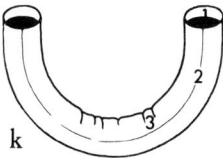

1. Lead filling
2. Seam
3. Folds (to be tapped out)

The Innovation in Brass Instrument Making around 1400

Shortly before 1400, instrument makers discovered a new technique: the bending of tubing. Before then, the Teutons, Etruscans and Romans had generally cast their curved lurs and cornua in the finished form by means of the lost-wax process. Late medieval instrument makers took advantage of the knowledge that different metals have different melting points. Copper, for example, which has always formed the principal ingredient of brass, has a melting point of 1083°C; a normal brass alloy (70 per cent copper, 30 per cent zinc) melts at about 900°C, whilst lead is already melted at 327°C. If a straight piece of tubing, such as (c) in the preceding illustration, is filled with liquid lead and allowed to stand until the lead cools and becomes firm, the piece of tubing can be bent. In so doing, one has to be careful that the metal on the outside of the bend does not tear and that the metal on the inside does not form too many folds. Skilful taps with the hammer during the bending process will miminize the forming of folds. A precautionary measure is to lay the sensitive seam neither on the inside nor on the outside of the bend, but rather only somewhat towards the inside (k). As soon as the bend has been made, the lead is melted once again and drawn off, so that the bend can now be joined to other pieces of tubing.

Two New Kinds of Trumpet around 1400

This innovation in brass-instrument making revolutionized the outward appearance of trumpets. Because their tubing could now be bent, trumpets could be made in an 'S'-shape or also in the folded shape still known today, whereby the length of a given instrument – which in some cases attained two metres – could be reduced to about one third of that of the actual tube. Thus, the

The Trumpet in the Renaissance (1400–1600)

folded trumpet was developed from the uncomfortably long busine, and could easily be transported on military campaigns or to ceremonial events, without danger of damage which had always been present with particularly long instruments. The earliest depiction of a trumpet in 'S'-shape is from 1377 and comes from a miniature of the *Chronicles of France* in the British Library. Luca della Robbia's choir loft also contains one of the earliest known examples of a trumpet in folded shape; this instrument is to be found behind the other two long, straight trumpets already discussed (*see illustration p. 43*). The majority of trumpets were made in a folded shape from about 1500 onwards. This was to become the common form of the Baroque trumpet, and it can still be seen today in the state or fanfare trumpet.

At almost the same time as the discovery of the process of bent tubing, a new kind of trumpet was developed: the slide trumpet. The slide was at first not a 'U'-shaped slide, as found on the modern trombone, but consisted instead of an extension of the mouthpiece within the trumpet's entire first length of tubing. It was not the slide, but rather the entire instrument which was slid back and forth. A detail from doors on an organ case, painted around 1490 by Hans Memling, shows three trumpeters in a group of angel musicians. The one in the middle plays a straight trumpet, and others are blowing folded slide trumpets which are slightly extended. Both kinds of trumpets, since they appeared to be shorter than the long straight trumpet, were called by the diminutive form not 'trump' but 'trumpet'; in German *Trompete*, in French *trompette*. Still earlier diminutive forms probably applied to shorter straight trumpets, such as the *trombetta* of Dante (1265–1321), in the *Inferno* XXI, 47, and the above-mentioned Bolognese city trumpeters called *Trombetti*. English usage seems to have formed an exception. Here Horman wrote in 1529: 'a Trompette is straight, but a Clarion is wounde in and out

The Trumpet in the Renaissance (1400–1600)

Hans Memling, Three Angels with slide trumpets from the organ case doors at Najera, c 1490 Antwerp, Koninklijk Museum voor Schone Kunsten

with a hope' [hoop]. Whereas the folded trumpet was called *Trompete* or *trompette* on the continent, it was thus called clarion in England.

The Trompette de Guerre and the Trompette des Ménestrels at the Burgundian Court

From about 1400, a clear separation in the usage of the two kinds of trumpets can be observed. The folded trumpet was used as a natural trumpet at court and in battle. The slide trumpet was taken into the alta ensemble, thereby providing new musical impulses, since the now chromatic trumpet was no longer confined to the playing of a mere drone.

The Trumpet in the Renaissance (1400–1600)

The separation of the two kinds of trumpets is documented in particularly clear form at the Burgundian court, starting in 1422. Already in 1404 under Philip the Hardy, there was a player of the *trompette de guerre*. From 1420 under Philip the Good (1396–1467), four such trumpeters were in court service, as well as four minstrels and a harpist. In 1422, a new instrument is mentioned in the court records for the first time, the *trompette des ménestrels*. For 50 years, these two kinds of trumpets were listed side by side in court documents. It is striking that with few exceptions there were always four to six players of the *trompette de guerre*, but with a single exception there was only one player of the *trompette des ménestrels*, together with the ministrels with whom this trumpeter obviously performed. We are therefore sure to be right in our supposition that the *trompettes de guerre* designated an ensemble of four to six natural trumpets. The *ménestrels* referred to an alta ensemble with a slide trumpet.

The Alta Ensemble and the Origin of the Trombone

Around 1430, an unknown master painted a picture of a stately dance at the Burgundian court. One can see not only the duke, but also – on the left side – the alta ensemble, consisting of a shawm, an alto bombarde, and an 'S'-shaped trumpet which is probably a slide trumpet. Since the ceremonial of the Burgundian court was exemplary for all of Europe, such alta ensembles were soon to be found everywhere. Only slightly later the double slide was invented, and with it the trombone emerged from the slide trumpet (although both instruments can still be called *trompette* in the sources). The trombone is depicted for the first time, together with three shawms, in the well-known illustration of the so-called Adimari wedding in Florence, *c* 1450.

Unknown master, Alta ensemble at a celebration of the Burgundian court,
c 1430 Musée National du Château de Versailles (Photo: Musées Nationaux)

The Trumpet in the Renaissance (1400–1600)

In Italy, the alta ensemble reached its peak of popularity in the second half of the fifteenth century. In Spain and Portugal, this kind of band of instruments was popular into the middle of the sixteenth century. An alta ensemble consisting of *quatro trompetillas bastardas y seis menestriles* played on 17 November 1543 at the festivities for the wedding of Philip II of Spain, the future king, and in another place we read about a group there consisting of *quatro menestriles y quatro trompetas bastardas*. This instrumental group, with several shawms and a trombone, can be seen very frequently in the middle of the sixteenth century in Portuguese paintings of the Assumption of Mary. In his valuable article (*see Bibliography*), Lorenz Welker discusses the repertoire of the alta ensemble – basses danses – and reports on the work done at the Schola Cantorum Basiliensis in recent years by such a group.

Early Church Music for Slide Trumpet

Until this time, with certain exceptions in England, the trumpet had not been allowed in church, presumably because of its military associations. However, as a slide trumpet, it seems to have been willingly accepted in a series of compositions. Some of these are the *Missa trompetta* by Estienne Grossin (*c* 1420), two settings of *Et in terra* by Richard de Loqueville and Arnold de Lantins, *Ave virgo* by Johannes Franchois, *Virgo dulcis* by Heinrich von Freiburg, the *Missa tubae* by Cousins, and an anonymous *Kyrie tubae*, besides Dufay's *Et in terra* 'ad modum tubae', a piece in which natural trumpets are either to be played or else imitated by other instruments. In these works, the presumed slide trumpet is called *trompette*, appearing mainly in the contra-tenor part. These parts can be differentiated from the other parts by their frequent leaps of fourths and fifths. It is thus possible to speak of a

The Trumpet in the Renaissance (1400–1600)

'(slide) trumpet style' and also to associate the slide trumpet with similar parts in other compositions. Furthermore, trumpet style was described in this way, referring to secular instrumental music, in a German theoretical treatise of the early fifteenth century (Breslau Universitätsbibliothek, cart. IV. Qu. 16, fol. 18).

Since slide trumpets have been recently reconstructed by German and Swiss instrument makers (the firm of Ewald Meine in Geretsried, Upper Bavaria, and the firm of A. Egger & Söhn in Basel), it is possible to study the relationship of this instrument to its music. Until now, scholars had been confronted with what seemed to have been an insoluble riddle: the music for the slide trumpet seemed to have been noted, without exception, in the wrong octave of the instrument. We are taking as a starting point the fact that the slide trumpet was mostly played within the second octave of the harmonic series and that, as a result of our practical studies with the reconstructed instrument, each partial could be lowered with the slide by three half-steps. On a slide trumpet in C, we thus arrive at the following pitch reservoir:

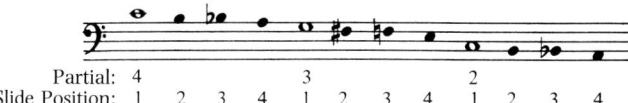

Partial: 4   3   2
Slide Position: 1   2   3   4   1   2   3   4   1   2   3   4

In this reservoir there is a gap between e and c. However, the compositions written expressly for the slide trumpet demand the note d between the second and third partials.

With the instrument as it exists and a modern playing technique, it is impossible to play this note. If the instrument were an octave lower and consequently twice as long, the player's arm would also have to be twice as long in order to reach the last slide

The Trumpet in the Renaissance (1400–1600)

positions. And such giant instruments are not to be seen in pictures of the fifteenth century. Three solutions to the problem are possible: (1) It would be possible to play the missing *d* by means of the 'lipping' technique described in the introduction to this book. Michael Praetorius described precisely this technique in 1619, applying it to the trombone for reaching still lower notes. (2) The trombone with a double slide would have been able to play the missing *d*, but then it would have had to have been invented before the presence of any other documentary evidence of its existence. (3) The music could have been played and sung in a higher transposition. Welker proposes a fourth solution: that these parts are *all* trumpet imitations, the word 'trompette' in the parts referring to 'trumpet style' mentioned above.

The Slide Trumpet on the City Towers

The slide trumpet was the preferred instrument of tower watchmen until far into the Baroque period. They chose this instrument because during the course of the fifteenth and sixteenth centuries they had been assigned a new duty in addition to that of mere signalling: tower playing (*Abblasen* in German). As we have seen, the earliest tower watchmen used animal horns. Trumpeters were not hired for this function until the late thirteenth century in Italy and the fourteenth century in Flanders; in 1376, the German city of Görlitz hired a trumpeter as a tower watchman.

Good documentation survives for the city of Basel. Here too, the office of tower watchman with a horn goes back at least to the beginning of the fourteenth century. In 1429, the watchmen on the towers of St Martin's church already had trumpets. In 1497, the city council expressed a desire to hear tower playing in two-part harmony 'every evening and every morning'. At this time

The Trumpet in the Renaissance (1400–1600)

Thurner Horn

Thurner Horn
From Musica getutscht *by Sebastian Virdung*
(Photo: Bildarchiv Preussischer Kulturbesitz, Berlin)

there were five such musicians, two each on the towers of the cathedral and of St Martin's church, as well as another one on the other side of the Rhine. In 1511, in his book *Musica getutscht*, printed in Basel, Sebastian Virdung published a woodcut of an 'S'-shaped 'Thurner Horn', which can only be a slide trumpet.

An excerpt from *The Tower Players' and Trumpeters' Oath* from Basel, written in the first half of the sixteenth century, will show what severe demands were made on the tower players of that city:

> The trumpeters . . . shall swear to ascend the tower . . . daily . . . in the evening, from that moment ringing the watch bells on the cathedral tower, immediately thereafter playing the trumpet, and then ringing the small bell for a half of a quarter of an hour; they shall never lead anyone up on to the tower, but rather shall walk up and down until six o'clock in the morning in the winter and until five o'clock in the morning in the summer; furthermore both are to play four or five entire compositions of proper length, both in the evening . . . and in the morning at daybreak. And this shall be done from both sides of the tower. . . .

The watchmen were not allowed to make things too easy for themselves with their tower playing, for four or five 'entire compositions of proper length' were demanded of them. If a tower watchman should forget to sound the beginning of day or night, he was to 'lose a week's salary without the right of appeal'. The players on the various towers were not to sound their instruments simultaneously, but rather one after the other. If someone rang 'the bell at the city gates', the tower watchman was to 'announce it properly and distinctly with the trumpet . . . before and after midnight'.

They were also required to participate in banquets: 'every

The Trumpet in the Renaissance (1400–1600)

Sunday afternoon, at the stroke of one' they were required to go 'to the city hall or to any other place where they might be required and where the city council is dining, to make music and wait on them.'

Keeping a lookout for fires and the enemy was a particularly important duty of the tower watchmen:

And when they smell a fire beginning in the city, God forbid, and the aforementioned fire has not yet broken out, then they shall call . . .'fire'; however, if flames are already leaping up, then they shall ring an alarm with the bells, . . . and . . . avoid ringing the council bells for a fire alarm, since these are to be used only in the case of an enemy alarm.

They were not allowed out of the city without permission. In wartime they were required 'to serve the city council during the day in the towers or in the field'. If they wanted to leave, they had to announce this intention to the city council a quarter of a year in advance; if they wished to quit service entirely, they had to take a parting oath.

Similar duties were required of watchmen in other cities as well. In Lübeck, the instrument of the tower watchmen seems not to have been the slide trumpet, but rather, in 1474, the *Klaritte* or Clareta. In that city, their service began with the playing of a chorale at four o'clock in the morning, when the labourers went to work. More chorales followed at the mid-day pause at ten or eleven o'clock, at the resumption of work at 12 noon, and finally at the end of the day at nine o'clock in the evening.

The Trumpet in the Renaissance (1400–1600)

Municipal Organizations of Musicians

The gradual process of musicians settling down and also forming local and regional organizations, such as brotherhoods or city-pipers' associations (*Stadtpfeifereien*), can still be observed in the fifteenth century, following its inception in the late Middle Ages.

Typical of the regional groupings were the brotherhoods founded around 1400 in the area of Mainz: the brotherhood of travelling folk, fiddlers and pipers begun in 1407 in Uznach (Switzerland), and the musicians' brotherhood founded in Zürich in 1430. In 1469, Edward IV of England decreed that his minstrels were henceforth to have rights.

Although trumpeters are not expressly mentioned as members of the above associations, no doubts regarding their participation are left by the statutes of a society founded in 1458 in Stuttgart; they state that the convocation of 'trumpeters, pipers and lute-players . . . into a brotherhood' is confirmed.

There was a significant difference between such organizations and the courtly trumpet corps (an institution which will be discussed below): the court trumpeters either played a single instrument, the trumpet, or if they had also mastered another instrument, the trumpet remained their principal one. The municipal musicians, on the other hand, were required to master half a dozen musical instruments, the trumpet among them.

The musicians' social position was bettered by their grouping together into local and regional organizations. In particular they were freed from the stigma of possessing no rights and were henceforth allowed to receive the sacraments. Their rights and duties were clearly delineated, and they were protected in their own area against musicians from other parts. The fact that the brotherhoods regulated the learning process led to an increase in respect for the profession as a whole.

The Trumpet in the Renaissance (1400–1600)

Training and Duties of Municipal Trumpeters

At the beginning of his training period, after he had produced documentation of his honourable birth, the apprentice musician was given a so-called letter of assumption, in which the duration of the training period was set down, and he was required to promise to serve his master diligently. The length of the training period varied from one place to another; it usually lasted between two and five years. During this time, the apprentice musician learned to play various instruments. In the fifteenth and sixteenth centuries, these could be the cornett, trombone, recorder and shawm, as well as the trumpet. After passing his examination, he received a letter of release from his articles of apprenticeship and was considered a journeyman. After the time of his service as a journeyman was over – a period which also varied greatly, depending upon the place – he was given the title of master. Only then was he allowed to take on pupils.

The duties of municipal musicians could include tower playing, although the office of tower musician was often kept completely separate from that of the other musicians. It was an important duty of municipal musicians to play at city council meetings and at court sessions, as well as in church.

In Bologna, the local musicians' organization, the so-called Concerto Palatino della Signora, emerged from the institution of the eight city trumpeters. This group of trumpeters was expanded for the first time in 1417 by the admission of three pipers and one kettledrummer (*naccarino*). In 1442, a lutenist and a harpist were added. The Concerto Palatino, properly speaking, was founded in 1533; at that time, the eight trumpeters were separated from the pipers, now eight in number, the harpist, and the lutenist. The instruments played by the pipers included cornett, trombone and sometimes a stringed instrument. The duties of these two groups of musicians were delineated clearly in two documents from

The Trumpet in the Renaissance (1400–1600)

1508 and 1573. They were to practise daily in a room set apart especially for them. In the morning and evening, before and after meals, they gave a regular concert from the *Ringhiera*, an open balcony on the upper floor of the Palazzo Pubblico on the main square, the Piazza Maggiore. On high religious feast days they played in church; first the trumpeters, and then the cornettists and trombonists. This duty of playing at the beginning of mass led in the second half of the seventeenth century to the custom of having a trumpet sonata or sinfonia open the celebration of the mass.

Furthermore, the 'musicians' and 'trumpeters' were required to accompany the city council in its comings and goings. At banquets they announced each new course with music. We do not know exactly what kind of music was played by Bolognese trumpeters in the sixteenth century, but we can surmise that it was similar to the sonatas played by the court trumpeters in the Holy Roman Empire, to be discussed below. The cornettists and trombonists played transcriptions of vocal music (a motet is mentioned in one document), later certainly enlarging their repertoire with instrumental canzonas, a very popular category of composition which the Venetian masters Andrea and Giovanni Gabrieli led to perfection.

It is interesting that the Gabrielis, contrary to a widespread notion, did not compose their canzonas for trumpets. Today these pieces occupy a central position in the repertoire of many brass ensembles and are played on modern valved trumpets and trombones; however, at that time, composers of canzonas used the chromatic possibilities of the cornett as a point of departure and avoided the trumpet, which, as we know, was limited to the notes of the harmonic series. (The cornett was a curved woodwind instrument covered with leather; it had seven finger-holes and was played with a small, cup-shaped mouthpiece.)

The Trumpet in the Renaissance (1400–1600)

The Concerto Palatino survived in Bologna until 1779. However, the orchestras of the large churches, especially that of the Basilica of S. Petronio, began at the end of the sixteenth century to compete with them, and this to such an extent that the municipal musicians' organization had already passed its artistic peak by around 1630.

In passing, it should be noted that the Bolognese pipers were called *zalamella* in the local dialect, a word which means the same as 'shawm' in English, *Schalmei* in German and *charamela* in Portuguese. In the sixteenth century, the *Charamela real* of the court of Lisbon consisted of shawms and a trombone; it was a true alta ensemble. In the late eighteenth century, however, that same name was given to the royal Portuguese trumpet corps, consisting of 24 trumpeters and four kettledrummers.

The Court Trumpeters

During the course of the fifteenth and sixteenth centuries, the purely ceremonial duties of trumpeters became increasingly important. More and more trumpeters went into court service. Their number (compiled by the musicologist Detlef Altenburg) was a kind of yard stick for the Renaissance sovereigns' individual needs to display their power.

A few figures will make this situation clear. The King of England ordered a set of trumpets from the Nuremberg instrument maker Jorg Stengel, called Neuschel. There were 16 trumpeters at the English court starting in the year 1514; in 1610 there were 26 of them. The beginnings of the trumpet corps at the Danish court go back to the coronation of Christian I in 1449; after 1530, 15 trumpeters and kettledrummers were employed there. There were as many as 23 at the coronation of Christian IV in 1596, when the royal guests from Germany

The Trumpet in the Renaissance (1400–1600)

brought 31 more trumpeters with them, ten of them from Dresden alone. The ceremonial of the French court, published in 1619, mentions trumpet playing at royal festivities there between 1467 and 1594.

At the imperial court of Innsbruck one year before the death of Maximilian I (1518) there were 13 trumpeters and two timpanists. It was a sad fact at this otherwise illustrious court that payments due to trumpeters, especially extra payments for trips and military campaigns, were often not made. The case of the Innsbruck tower watchman, Jacob Seidemann, was especially striking: in 1497 he wrote an official complaint that his salary had not been paid to him for 19 years! He must have led a beggar's life. At the Spanish court ten trumpeters seem to have been in service; this number is mentioned once in 1548–49 in connection with a trip made by Prince Philip, the future Philip II, to Italy, Flanders and Germany, and once again in 1552. Twenty trumpeters were in the service of the Emperor Rudolf II in 1582; in 1594 there were 27. At the court of the Dukes of Bavaria in Munich, there were 12 trumpeters in 1513. During the period of Orlando di Lasso's activity there (1568–94), their number varied between six (1589) and 15 (1569–71) with a median of ten.

The Trumpeters under Imperial Protection

In the old German empire, trumpeters seem to have stood under some kind of imperial protection in the early fifteenth century. If cities wished to take trumpeters into their service, they first had to apply to the imperial court for the necessary privilege. The earliest known case was in 1416, and had to do with the installation of Friderich Winsperg as trumpeter for the city council of Basel, where the validity of the contract was made explicitly contingent on a possible objection by 'Sygmund, the

The Trumpet in the Renaissance (1400–1600)

Roman king, ... or the queen, his wedded wife'. In the following year, during the Council of Constance (1414–18) ending the schism of the papacy, the Emperor Sigismund gave the right of employing trumpeters to that city as well. The next cities to receive this privilege were Nuremberg in 1431, as well as Augsburg and Ulm in 1434. A century later, at the Imperial Diet of the Holy Roman Empire convening in Augsburg, trumpeters were given the right to gather together in local guilds; the 37th article of the Decree of the Imperial Police in 1548 stated that

> weavers, barbers, shepherds, millers, customs officers, pipers, trumpeters, barber-surgeons, as well as their parents ... and their children, if of an honourable birth and of good conduct, shall henceforth not be excluded from corporations ... guilds, or public office, but rather be taken up and accepted into them, like other honest craftsmen.

In 1577, this edict was confirmed in a further decree of the Imperial Diet. Finally, in 1623, the Imperial Trumpeters' and Kettledrummers' Guild was founded – an organization of more than just local importance which will be discussed below.

The Music of the Court Trumpeters and the Development of the Clarino Register

At court the trumpeters occupied a special position among the groups of musicians, and can be considered as a kind of symbol of the princely courts themselves. They played at tournaments and other equestrian games, at table, at courtly festivities, and also – during the course of the sixteenth century – in church.

Since no actual music survives from the earliest times, it is necessary to reconstruct the kind of music which was performed by a courtly trumpet ensemble. First of all, we know that

The Trumpet in the Renaissance (1400–1600)

*Top: Equestrian games in the Brussels marketplace.
Etching by Peter van der Borcht (detail), c 1570
Author's Collection (Photo: Universitätsbibliothek, Basel)*

*Beneath: Lucas Cranach, the elder
Tournament of 15, 16 November 1508 in Wittenberg
Woodcut from 1509 Basel, Kupferstichkabinett*

trumpeters performed their music by improvising. Secondly, we know that around 1300 the trumpet was played only in the low register; this was probably true as well for the period between 1400 and 1450, since the trombone was developed in this time from the trumpet and was, of course, played in the low register. In the following years, trumpeters apparently learned to play in the high register as well.

The Trumpet in the Renaissance (1400–1600)

By the 1550s, the typical five-part trumpet ensemble of the Baroque period had emerged, a group in which every player performed in a different register of the natural trumpet. Once the Archduchess Maria of Bavaria wrote from Graz to her brother in Munich, Wilhelm V (reigned 1579–97), apparently asking him for the music performed by his trumpeters. In his answer, he said: 'the music that my trumpeters use, in case that is what you mean, then they don't play anything except the kind of music played at table: this is not written down, and they make it only out of their heads'.

The rules of improvisation were written down for the first time in the trumpet method of Cesare Bendinelli (c 1542–1617), *Tutta l'arte della Trombetta* (1614). Bendinelli was born in Verona, served first in Schwerin, then in Vienna, and from 1580 to his death was the leader of the court trumpet corps in Munich. Since the dated pieces in his method all come from the 1580s, he probably compiled the work in that period, using compositions of his own and those of leading German trumpeters.

According to Bendinelli there were five trumpets in an ensemble – or ten, if the trumpeters were divided into two choirs and placed in two different locations. Of the five parts, however, only one was pre-eminent, the second part from the top. Bendinelli called it the *Sonata* part; other later authors called it the *Quinta* or *Prinzipal*. The second part was imitated note for note, one step lower in the harmonic series, by the third part, called *Alto e basso*. The fourth and fifth parts (*Vulgano* and *Basso*) had only to play a single note as a foundation for the ensemble, g and c respectively. (Michael Praetorius even mentions a possible sixth part or *Fladdergrob*, playing the fundamental or C.) The highest part was called *Clarino* and moved about in the fourth octave of the harmonic series.

Thus, if a theme, such as that of line *a* in the musical example,

The Trumpet in the Renaissance (1400–1600)

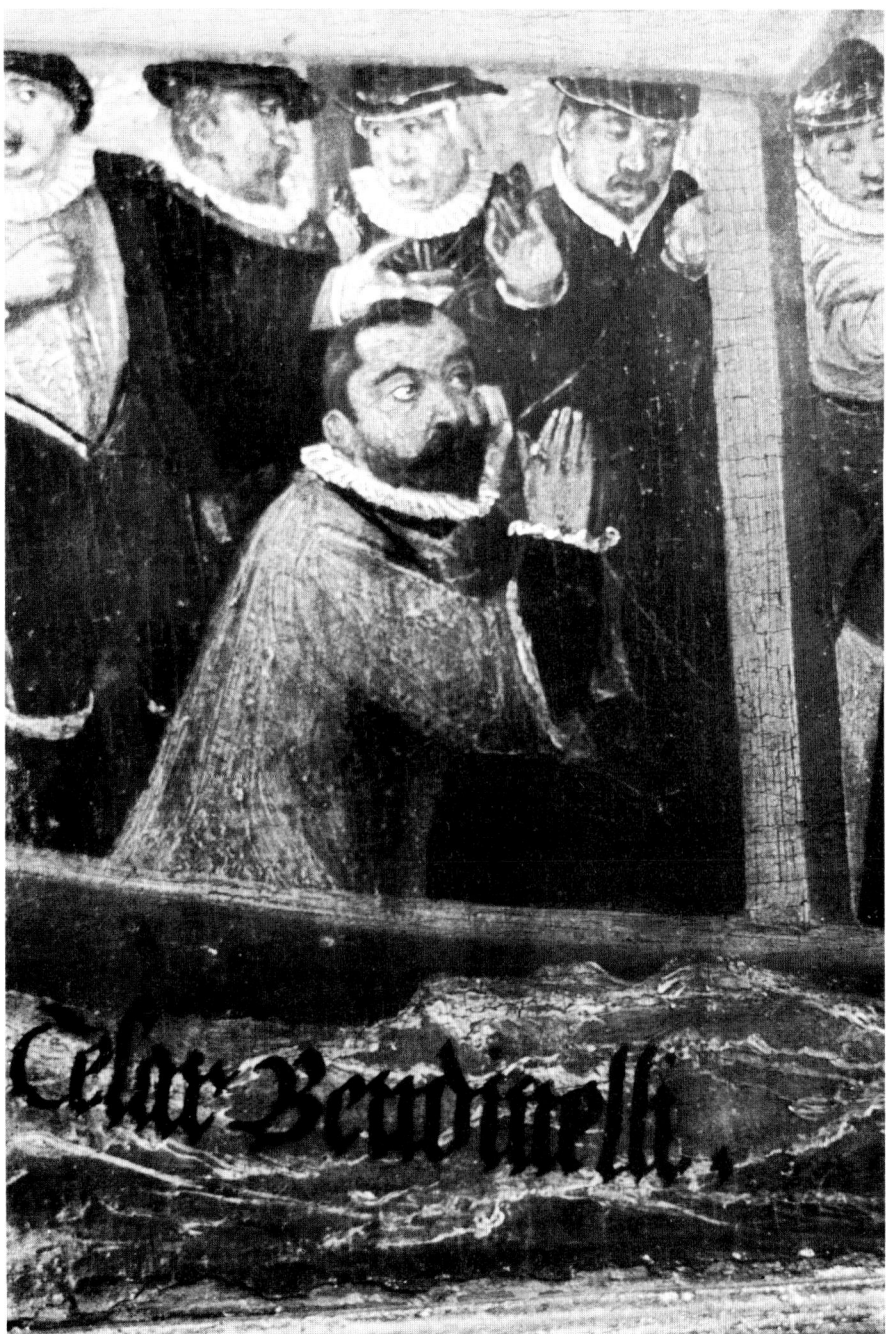

Cesare Bendinelli
from a votive tablet donated by him in 1580 to the Wallfahrtskirche Aufkirchen
Starnberg, Oberbayern
(Photo: Wörsching, Starnberg)

The Trumpet in the Renaissance (1400–1600)

(*see above*) was given in the second (sonata) part, the player of the third part improvised as in line *b*, the fourth and fifth parts remaining on low *g* and *c*, as in line *c* in the musical example. Above these parts the clarino player spun his melody, such as in line *d* in the musical example. A pair of kettledrums completed the ensemble.

Since the pieces in Bendinelli's method which are dated were written in the 1580s, as mentioned above, we can assume with certainty that trumpeters of that period played – that is, improvised – pieces of this kind for processions, tournaments, mealtimes and similar functions. The pieces themselves were called 'sonatas'; Praetorius described their form and use in 1619. The imposing effect of the medieval trumpet ensemble remained alive with such pieces. A single chord was repeated incessantly, and the rhythms of the individual parts grew faster and faster during the course of a given sonata. An example of this kind of music is the Sonata No. 336 from Bendinelli's method, which has been published in a modern edition.

Playing in the clarino register was thought to be particularly strenuous. For that reason, the sonatas contained sections in which the clarino player rested while the other trumpeters continued to play. For the wedding in 1584 of Ludwig, Count of Leuchtenberg (1567–1621), Bendinelli composed a sonata containing the first surviving clarino part in history. Bendinelli's directions for the trumpeters performing this wedding music ran as follows:

> The player of the clarino part is required to hold a large glass of wine in his hand, and every time he stops playing he has to drink a little, until the sonata is over; then the other trumpeters also drink, to imitate the text of the song.

(The melody of this particular sonata must have been a drinking

The Trumpet in the Renaissance (1400–1600)

song! Peter Downey has identified it as an anonymous chanson, 'J'ai vu le cenf', from the Danish court instrumental music collection Gl. kgl. Saml. 1873, 4°, of 1556.)

Contrary to a rather widespread opinion, the term 'clarino' did not designate an instrument, but rather the highest part in a trumpet ensemble and also the high register of the natural trumpet. The great theorist of the late eighteenth century, Johann Ernst Altenburg, compared the clarino part with the soprano part in vocal music, calling it 'a certain melody which is played mostly in the two-line octave [and which is] thus high and clear' (p. 94).

This term 'clarino' emerges relatively late in music history. In 1561 a clarin player is recorded for the first time in Annaberg (Saxony). A further document from 1596 is particularly interesting, because in it the difficulties of clarino playing are given special prominence. In this document, a letter, the Wolfenbüttel trumpeter Hans Göseke complains about the fact that he had already served at court for three years as a clarino player, 'the most difficult and distinguished duty of a trumpeter', without having been specially paid for doing so. It is interesting that *clarin* or *clarino* was a German term, even though the word form itself seems to be Italian. In Italy, the designation was generally *tromba*, sometimes *trombetta*; Girolamo Fantini, in his trumpet method of 1638, called the high register *soprano*.

Although the term 'clarin trumpeter' does not appear until 1561 and the first dated piece in the clarino register is from 1584, we know that trumpeters had then played in the high register for about 100 years. At that time, however, the highest part was not called 'clarino' but rather 'Clareta'. (As late as 1614, Bendinelli uses the term *Claretto* in reference to the high register, but explicitly as a *trombetta Antiqua*, an old-fashioned instrument.) The term 'Clareta' is found between 1460 and 1512, sometimes

The Trumpet in the Renaissance (1400–1600)

Clareta *and* Felttrumet
from Musica getutscht *by Sebastian Virdung*
(Photo: Bildarchiv Preussischer Kulturbesitz, Berlin)

to designate the high register, sometimes an instrument. Here are some examples of its use: in 1460, the Innsbruck court bought two *Glaretan Trometen* in Munich; at the same court, several *Claretter* (players of the clareta) are mentioned between 1496 and 1510. In 1474, *Klarytter* (again, players of the clareta) were hired for the first time in the Church of St Mary's of Lübeck. In 1504, the Nuremberg brass instrument maker, Jorg Stengel, advertised the fact that he made trumpets, claretas and trombones. In his book *Musica getutscht* of 1511, Virdung published a woodcut not only of the 'Thurner Horn' or slide trumpet already mentioned, but also a slender clareta and a somewhat more robust-looking *Felttrumet* or field trumpet.

Of course, the name *clareta* by itself does not necessarily mean that high playing was involved, despite Bendinelli's rather late association of the two. Convincing proof that trumpeters did in fact play in the high register during the second half of the fifteenth century comes from Amberg (Upper Palatinate). There, in 1474, Saxon dukes took their trumpeters to the wedding of Duke Philip. Playing for dancing, the trumpeters caused a stir because of their instruments, on which they played 'higher than one could imagine'.

Musical and Non-Musical Trumpters

Already around 1566–76, among the 15 trumpeters employed by the court of Vienna, we find four 'musical' (*musikalisch*) ones. This designation came to have more importance in the seventeenth and eighteenth centuries, after the trumpet had secured a place in serious music. The term refers to trumpeters with a higher degree of training which enabled them not only to play

The Trumpet in the Renaissance (1400–1600)

simple signals, but also notated music. Later on, 'musical' trumpeters were also called 'chamber' or 'concert' trumpeters. The non-musical trumpeters were employed strictly for signalling.

A third group was called 'musician and trumpeter' (*Musicus und Trompeter*) or 'instrumentalist and trumpeter'. These were trumpeters who played another instrument beside their main one. In the sixteenth century this other instrument could be the cornett or the trombone, as was the case with two great trumpeters, Alessandro Orologio (Vienna, cornett) and Bendinelli (trombone). The violin was often demanded as a second instrument during the eighteenth century.

It goes without saying that the non-musical trumpeters received the lowest pay, while the musical ones were better remunerated, and the trumpeters playing a subsidiary instrument rewarded the best of all.

The Field Trumpeters

When a trumpeter signed up for court service, he was required to swear to accompany his sovereign into the field in the case of war. With his signals he directed military operations.

From ancient times, the trumpet belonged to the cavalry, and the drums (as well as the military fife) to the infantry. In 1521, Machiavelli recommended this division in his book entitled *The Art of War*, dedicated to Lorenzo de' Medici. (In connection with the infantry, the *Heerhorn* or *Harsthorn* should be mentioned, a kind of instrument influencing the construction of the later Flügelhorn.) The military signals seem to have originated in Italy, but soon spread over the entire European continent. Clement Jannequin (*c* 1480–1560) published in 1528 a remarkable composition entitled *La Bataille*, a description of the battle of

The Trumpet in the Renaissance (1400–1600)

Marignano (1515). The second part of this work contains the first surviving trumpet signals, 'Saddle Up' and 'To the Standard', embedded in the vocal composition.

The *Kriegsbuch* by Leonhardt Fronsperger (1566) contains detailed allusions to well-known trumpet signals in the poem 'The Field Trumpeter'. It can be seen in the accompanying illustration (from the second edition, Frankfurt, 1573).

Magnus Thomsen, a German trumpeter employed at the Danish court between 1596 and his death in 1612, notated six of the most important signals for his own use; they were: (1) Entry; (2) Saddle Up; (3) To Horse; (4) Watch; (5) March; (6) To the Standard. In 1614, Bendinelli added still more: (7) To Horse – two signals, one of them in the French style and the other in the Italian style; (8) Call for Falling into Rank against the Enemy; (9) Call to the Skirmish; (10) Retreat; (11) Pitch Tents. Similar signals have been handed down by Fantini (1638) and Marin Mersenne (*Harmonie universelle*, 1636–37).

In the accompanying musical example, the beginning of the signal 'To Horse in the French Style' is given as notated by Thomsen and Bendinelli. Several features stand out. As opposed to the five-part improvised 'sonatas' of the court trumpet corps, this call consists of only one part; if several trumpeters were to play a signal such as this simultaneously, they all played the same notes. The differences between Thomsen's and Bendinelli's versions can be explained first by oral tradition and second by the fact that each trumpeter elaborated on the well-known signals in his own way. The rhythm is notated in a free manner, without bar lines; this was a characteristic of all military signals, until they were codified in France between 1803 and 1829 by David Buhl (b. 1781), who also provided them with new rhythms.

Furthermore and most important, this signal, like all others, is written in a very low register of the trumpet. It consists only of the

Der Feldt Trommeter.

Zu eim Feldtrommeter bin ich
   Erwählt/ beim Hauptmañ halt ich mich/
Vnd wart auff jhn/ die nacht/ vnd tag
   Daß er mich allzeit haben mag/
Im Zug reyt ich vorm Hauptmann her
   Mein blasen/ erschelt nah vnd ferr/
Kan vnderschiedlich blasen wol
   Also/ wannman sich satlen sol/
Zum anzug/ vnd auff sitzen fein/
   Auch so der Feindt vorhand wärd sein/
Lärmen blasen/ zugreiffen an
   Allzeit halt ich mich bey dem Fahn/
Mit blasen zu dem Essen rieff
   Auch so man etwan ein Feindtsbrieff/
Oder gefangner wirt hingsendt
   Dem Feindt oder eynige stendt/
Oder Bsatzung auff fordern wil/
   Bottschafften schicken/ in der stil/
Weiß ich zu reden/ wie/ woh/ was
   Zuschweigen/ wie sich zimet das.

Jost Ammann, Der Feldt Trommeter
from Leonhardt Fronsperger, Kriegsbuch *(Frankfurt a.M., 1566), illustration from the*
second edition (1573)
Trompetenmuseum Bad Säckingen

The Trumpet in the Renaissance (1400–1600)

Monttacawalla (Thomsen)

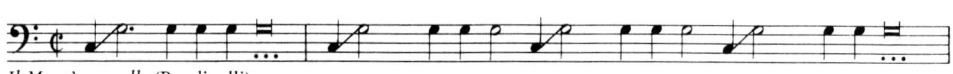

Il Mont'a cavallo (Bendinelli)

second and third partial. Other signals ascend to the fourth and fifth partials, but not higher (with the exception of some parts of Fantini's signals – preludes and postludes – which he composed himself). The military signals were probably written in the low register so they could be recognized by the soldiers, who of course had not been trained as musicians. Also since the range of the military signals in use in the sixteenth century corresponds with the range of the trumpet around 1300, we see in these signals older material which could reach back into the Middle Ages. In addition, the oft-recurring two note motif *c-g* (which was called 'Dran' and was actually pronounced in this way by players) is in itself a rather primitive form of signalling.

As related in the poem by Fronsperger, the field trumpeter had his place near the captain, in order that he could receive from him the commands for his signalling. Moreover, trumpeters were often employed in a diplomatic function. They rode over to the enemy lines, bringing dispatches. This activity was indeed fraught with danger and demanded great tact of the trumpeter. Fronsperger's poem makes it quite clear that the trumpeter sent out as an ambassador to the enemy should know 'how, where, what' he is to say, as well as knowing 'how to keep still, as is fitting'. According to the rules of war, the trumpeter was usually blindfolded until he laid his dispatches in the hands of the enemy commander and into his hands only; and he enjoyed even greater privileges than a political ambassador, since he was allowed to approach enemy lines without a passport. Nevertheless, Altenburg advised all prospective field trumpeters to comport themselves 'soberly, moderately, and carefully, since one can otherwise easily run the risk of being shot dead'. (p. 45)

It was certainly the most dangerous duty of a field trumpeter to demand the enemy to capitulate. In 1472, a trumpeter of Charles the Bold was killed by an enemy shot as he ordered the inhabitants of the besieged French city of Nesle to surrender.

The Trumpet in the Renaissance (1400–1600)

When he had finally captured the city, the Duke meted out a cruel punishment for such a scandalous breach of martial law: he collected a group of prisoners and had their hands hacked off.

The Earliest Surviving Trumpets and Early Brass Instrument Makers up to 1600

The five earliest surviving trumpets all come from the fifteenth century. Four of these are straight instruments of a medium length between 80 and 150cm. The oldest has the inscription S[I]ENA MIIIIVI (1406) and belongs to Williams College in Williamstown, Massachusetts (USA). It is pitched in A. The second oldest has the inscription MACHT SEBASTIAN HAINLEIN *M*CDLX (1460), and belongs to the Museum of Fine Arts in Boston. This one is shorter and is pitched in D, one octave higher than the normal Baroque trumpet. A third trumpet in the Gorga Collection, Rome, is about 120cm long and bears the inscription MACHT—SEBASTIANO—HAINLEIN—S[I]ENA—1461. A fourth, anonymous instrument of a similar type (stated to be from the fifteenth or sixteenth century) is in the Stearns Collection, Ann Arbor, Michigan.

Siena as the place of origin is also found on the garland of another trumpet from 1523 preserved in the Musical Instrument Museum of Berlin. The inscription reads: VBALDO/MONTINI/IN·SIEENA/15·23. Unfortunately, only the garland is original. The trumpet itself was reconstructed in the nineteenth century, presumably in imitation of the form of instruments to be found in paintings of Fra Angelico.

The Hainlein trumpets are probably authentic, even though the name of Hainlein as an instrument-making family in Nuremberg does not occur in archival documents until close to 1600. Sebastian Hainlein the Elder died in 1631; his son,

The Trumpet in the Renaissance (1400–1600)

Sebastian the Younger, was born in 1594 and died in 1655. How this name can have occurred already in the fifteenth century, and in Italy to boot, is another of the many riddles in the history of the trumpet. Another Montini instrument without date has a short fold and survives in the Leipzig collection (no. 1785). A riddle is posed by the name of Ubaldo Montini. According to Carlo Gervasoni's *Nuova Teoria di Musica* (Parma 1812), p. 46, Montini was born in Siena in 1722 and died there in 1803. The provenance of all these instruments clearly warrants a new scrutiny.

The oldest surviving trumpets in the traditional folded form (except for the more primitive shape of the Montini instrument mentioned above) are two silver- and gold-plated trumpets from the year 1578, made by Jacob Steiger (*colour page vii*). Steiger was employed by the city of Basel as a city trumpeter, a role reaching back to 1384. An x-ray of one of the two mouthpieces is shown on page 51. Both mouthpieces are so large that they can only be played in the low register, in the range of military signals. The fact that a mouthpiece can often give more clues as to the use of an instrument than the instrument itself is emphasized by the further fact that these trumpets, as soon as a smaller Baroque mouthpiece is inserted into them, can be played in the highest reaches lightly, clearly and comfortably.

The most famous European centre for the making of brass instruments from the beginning of the sixteenth century into the last third of the eighteenth was Nuremberg. During the sixteenth century, there were two families making brass instruments, the families Neuschel and Schnitzer.

The name of Hans Neuschel, the founder of one of these families of musical-instrument makers, can be found in documents from 1479; in this year he is recorded as having made slides (*Ziehstücke*) for slide trumpets or trombones. He died in

The Trumpet in the Renaissance (1400–1600)

1503 or 1504. He was originally a coppersmith (*Rotschmied*). His son, Hans the Younger, who died in 1533, was probably the most famous member of the family. The Emperor Maximilian I frequently ordered instruments from him and also preserved his image for posterity as a trombonist on a chariot in one of Hans Burgkmaier's woodcuts in the 'Triumph of Maximilian' (*c* 1518). He personally brought silver trombones to Rome, demonstrating them to Pope Leo X.

In Nuremberg, Meuschel Street [*sic*!] is named after him. Unfortunately, no trumpets made by the Neuschels survive, although the second oldest dated trombone, made in 1557 by the stepbrother of Hans the Younger, Jorg Stengel, now forms part of the Vienna Collection (ex. Clemencic, ex. Baines, ex. Galpin). Jorg Stengel, called Neuschel, also made *welsche Trompeten*, a kind of trumpet which is to be discussed below. The Neuschel family delivered their instruments to all the great European courts: Berlin, Dresden, Munich, Warsaw and London. Only Duke Albrecht of Prussia did not receive a desired shipment of instruments; a commission given by him in 1541 was never carried out, because he was too stingy to pay more than 60 guilders for a set of instruments worth 200 guilders in the estimation of their maker.

There were two branches of the other famous Nuremberg family of instrument makers, the Schnitzer family; one made woodwind instruments, the other brass. We are most fortunate to know of as many as four trumpets made by Anton Schnitzer in 1581, 1585, 1598 and 1599. (Anton I died in 1608. Anton II was born in 1564 and became a master in 1591; we do not know when he died.) Of these four trumpets, the first two, made by Anton I, are extremely interesting. The oldest is in the Collection of Old Musical Instruments in Vienna (*colour page viii*), probably the most beautiful trumpet ever made. It is silver- and gold-plated. The gold-plated parts – the ferrules, the ball and the garland – are made in such a way with lattice-work that the silver-plated tubing or bell section, respectively, can be seen underneath. Every millimetre of the silver-plated surface of the instrument is filled with costly engravings; on the bell section, allegorical female figures are to be seen holding a lute, a harp, a cornett and a trombone. This trumpet is pitched in E-flat. Once again the mouthpiece, which is attached permanently to the instrument's tubing, is so large, with a bore of 8.3mm, that only very low notes can be produced on it.

The second oldest surviving Schnitzer trumpet, made in 1585, was presented to the Accademia Filarmonica in Verona in 1614 by Cesare Bendinelli, leader of the trumpet corps at the court of Munich. It has a pretzel shape and holds the coat of arms of the Munich court in one of its lateral loops. It is pitched slightly higher than modern E; the mouthpiece is not preserved with it. The pretzel shape certainly had nothing to do with hand-stopping (a technique arising only at the end of the eighteenth century in works of the Classical period), although this opinion is sometimes voiced. In actual fact, both these instruments are quite obviously ceremonial pieces of the highest order, made for some specific occasion. In all details of their construction, they show the highest mastery of the instrument-maker's art.

Summary: the Middle Ages and the Renaissance

During the Middle Ages and the Renaissance, the trumpet was generally used as a signalling instrument in war. Itinerant trumpeters, occupying the same social position as any other kind of musician, came to be employed by courts or cities during the course of the twelfth to fourteenth centuries. At court, their duties became clearly defined at quite an early date; their tasks,

The Trumpet in the Renaissance (1400–1600)

The author with Bendinelli's trumpet, made in 1585 by Anton Schnitzer I in Nuremberg, and given to the Accademia Filarmonica of Verona in 1614 by Bendinelli
(Photo: Enrico Paganuzzi, Verona)

The Trumpet in the Renaissance (1400–1600)

spelt out in the *Leges Palatinae* of 1337, applied in principle to all court trumpeters until the beginning of the nineteenth century. Soon trumpeters became a kind of symbol of their sovereigns.

At first, their instruments were not played in a 'musical' way in the modern sense. Only around 1400, when instrument makers had discovered a method of bending tubing, did the slide trumpet find limited use in the so-called alta ensemble. Soon the trombone emerged from the slide trumpet. The court trumpeters, however, clung to their natural trumpet. By 1460 or 1470 they had probably assigned the various registers of their instrument to different players; performers of high parts in this period played in the clareta register, and from 1560 in the clarino register. The far-reaching, droning music of the court trumpeters' corps can be seen as an acoustical symbol of sovereignty.

The first surviving trumpets of this time come from the fifteenth century and are straight. The first surviving trumpets in the modern folded shape were made in 1578 by Jacob Steiger of Basel. Starting in approximately 1500, Nuremberg became the leading city for brass instrument making.

SIX

The Golden Age of the Natural Trumpet (1600–1750)

Introduction

During this period, the military function of the trumpet was just as important as before, largely because of the cruel wars waged in this epoch, known as the Thirty Years' War and the Seven Years' War. A trumpet corps belonged just as much to a court as the sovereign himself. Even though most of the pieces of music played by court trumpeters were still improvised, many of the processional fanfares, ceremonial sonatas, and the like, were written down and still survive in many archives.

One of the two most important events in the modern history of the trumpet took place during the seventeenth century: the acceptance of the trumpet into art music. (The second important event was the invention of the valve around 1815.) Since the actual time in which the trumpet was accepted into art music varied from country to country, our survey of the period 1600 to 1750 is organized geographically.

First of all, some thoughts on the playing technique of the natural trumpet of the Baroque era.

The Playing Technique of the Baroque Trumpet

In order for their instruments to become accepted into art music, Baroque trumpeters had to develop two new techniques: they had to play softly, and they had to play the impure partials of the harmonic series in tune.

During the Middle Ages it was only the sheer din of the trumpets which counted. This loud method of playing was naturally retained for signalling in later epochs, and we can imagine that the court trumpeters' corps did not particularly hold back their volume when they played for tournaments and other events in the open air. However, if a concert trumpeter wished to play a sonata or concerto together with the court orchestra, he

The Golden Age of the Natural Trumpet (1600–1750)

needed to know how to manage his instrument in a more delicate manner. There were, then, two ways of playing. J.E. Altenburg (p. 24) derived these from the 'blowing' and 'sounding an alarm' of the ancient Israelites, writing:

> with us they are called *field piece playing* (wherein principale playing is included) and *clarino playing*; consequently, the kinds of trumpet sound, *as with the ancients*, are *two-fold*.

In order to play in the high register, trumpeters had to give up the medieval embouchure and puffing-out of the cheeks. In 1614, Bendinelli forbade the puffing-out of cheeks, and for Altenburg the most important signs of a clarino embouchure were 'a strong thrust of air and a tight drawing together of the teeth and lips'. This 'proper embouchure' was – and still is – 'extraordinarily difficult to obtain'. Then, as now, there was only one secret to success: practice. 'Practice should perform the best service hereby' (Altenburg). Altenburg also wrote that 'the chamber or concert trumpeter is spared the weekly playing at table, because through the blaring he would spoil the delicate and subtle embouchure needed for clarino playing'.

As long as trumpeters were only playing in the court trumpeters' corps, it did not matter if the impure eleventh and thirteenth partials were in tune or not, since they were only passing notes within the great din. However, as soon as trumpeters were supposed to play together with other instruments, it became important to bring intonation under control. This phenomenon has not been understood properly until now, and many modern authors, sitting at their desks, have either invented the most adventurous techniques of playing or else have merely contented themselves with the trivial observation that trumpeters in earlier days simply did not play in tune. As far as playing in tune is concerned, it should be remembered that the

The Golden Age of the Natural Trumpet (1600–1750)

Baroque system of temperament was an unequal one; that is, in contrast to the present-day system of equal temperament, not every interval was of the same size. The harmonic series, with its large whole step between c'' and d'' and its beatless third between c'' and e'' (or $c'-e'$), as well as the somewhat too high f'', corresponded in many details to the system of temperament in use at that time.

Two techniques of playing, incorrectly associated by some modern authors with the Baroque period, are first, hand-stopping, by means of which the pitch of individual notes can be lowered (a technique originating only in the second half of the eighteenth century and therefore having nothing at all to do with the Baroque period), and second, correcting the pitch by means of finger-holes (a possibility discovered only after 1760, but most incorrectly described in our time – in 1960 to be precise – as the long-sought 'secret' of Baroque trumpet playing).

If we do not take the easy way out, either by accusing all Baroque trumpet players from Bendinelli and Fantini up to Gottfried Reiche and Johann Heinisch of playing out of tune, or by pre-dating techniques of a later time by 150 years, we will have to find a valid answer to the question: how were the trumpeters of the Baroque era able to play in tune? The answer: by means of the technique of 'lipping'.

Even today, no modern valved trumpet is completely in tune. Here and there, trumpeters must push a given note upwards or downwards by the strength of their lips, a process which of course presupposes a good ear, since it is necessary to grasp the tiny differences of pitch practically by instinct. Trumpeters of the Baroque era used the same technique. It was such a matter of course that theorists did not waste many words on it. Today a teacher tells his pupil: 'You'll have to lip this note a little bit upwards' or 'downwards'. In the Baroque era, it was just the same, except for the intervals that had to be lipped; they were larger, and thus more lip strength was demanded.

As far as the notes which had to be lipped into tune were concerned, it was actually only a matter of the eleventh and thirteenth partials, and sometimes of the seventh and fourteenth partials. These latter two, however, were not used very often. Altenburg wrote about this matter in a short chapter with the title 'Improving the Sounds which Are Out of Tune':

> He who is endowed with a healthy sense of pitch will soon perceive that the aforementioned four sounds – a-sharp', f'', a'', a-sharp'' – are . . . not perfectly in tune,

and he recommended the technique of lipping in order to bring them into tune:

> Therefore one must necessarily try to correct them by using a skilled embouchure and a proper amount of exertion, if one wishes rightfully to deserve to be called artistic and expert.

Concerning the low a-sharp' or b-flat', he simply wrote:

> When making use of this tone one must attempt to raise its pitch.

The eleventh partial was used both as f'' and f-sharp'':

> If, now, this tone is to produce its proper effect, one must necessarily let it fall, or lower it for F; but for F-sharp one must seek to drive it upwards to raise it. The latter situation is also to be observed with a'', in that the tone as well sounds a bit too low.

It is to be noted in this connection that it is much easier to lip notes downwards than upwards. With some practice it is even possible to play in between partials, by lipping downwards the

The Golden Age of the Natural Trumpet (1600–1750)

(from J.S. Bach, Cantata No. 137)

next upper note. Such a passage as the obbligato trumpet part in the tenor aria from Bach's Cantata No. 137 can be executed easily without any other technique than that of lipping. The b' (note no. 1) is reached by lipping the eighth partial a semitone downwards. Note no. 2 (a') is a lipped-down b'-flat, the seventh partial, which is already somewhat low in pitch. As far as note no. 3 is concerned, the eleventh partial or f'', 'one must necessarily let it fall' (J.E. Altenburg).

By means of this technique, the player can perform many passing notes written outside the harmonic series by Bach, Biber, and other composers, as shown in the two other accompanying musical examples.

Trumpet 1 in D

(from J.S. Bach, Orchestral Suite No. 4 in D)

Trumpet 2 in C

(from H.I.F. Biber, *Sonata Sancti Polycarpi a 9*, in C)

Lipping presupposes only light mouthpiece pressure on the lips. This is the method used by all professional players today, and yet much nonsense has been written about this very matter. We should not speak of the 'non-pressure system', because some mouthpiece pressure against the lips is always necessary to retain contact between the lips and the mouthpiece as well as to ensure that no air escapes from the corners of the mouth. On the other hand, no good professional player could play with heavy pressure, because this would hinder the circulation of blood in the lips, thus reducing endurance. We should therefore choose the middle road in our terminology, not speaking of 'heavy' or 'no' pressure, but rather of 'light' pressure. In this connection, moreover, it is necessary to point out that this term can have various meanings, depending upon a given player's experience, lip muscles, etc. We realise that a beginner, whose lips are still rather undeveloped for playing a brass instrument, should not use as much mouthpiece pressure as a full-grown professional trumpeter, whose highly developed lip muscles can stand a good deal of stress. Furthermore, a trumpeter will always use slightly more pressure for high notes than for low ones. Modern trumpet methods always emphasize an embouchure using light mouthpiece pressure, and of course correct breathing as well; and we can assume that the modern and the Baroque embouchure have much in common in this respect.

   In order to 'lip' a given partial downwards, the player should pucker the lips slightly, seeing to it that as much upper lip as possible is inside the mouthpiece cup. At the same time the oral cavity is somewhat enlarged by a slight displacement of the lower jaw and the tongue. At the beginning it is difficult to prevent a given partial from cracking into the next lower one; however, a player with well-developed lip muscles will succeed in mastering the technique of lipping after a short time. In producing these artificial notes, the trumpet functions like a kind of megaphone for the vibrations which are produced by the lips alone. The natural trumpet class of the Schola Cantorum Basiliensis, a division of the Musical Academy of the city of Basel devoted to research and teaching in early music, has worked on this technique since 1973.

The Golden Age of the Natural Trumpet (1600–1750)

An Introduction to Style on the Baroque Trumpet

In the Renaissance and Baroque periods, it was the most important duty of an instrumentalist to imitate the human voice. For this reason, brass instruments were preferred to the strings because with their air stream they more closely approached the singing voice.

> It is well known that the human voice is supposed to serve as the model for all instruments; thus should the clarino player try to imitate it as much as possible, and seek to bring forth the so-called *cantabile* on his instrument. (Altenburg, p. 96.)

The 'so-called *cantabile*' was attained, especially in fast melodic passages, by a particular method of tonguing. In the modern school of orchestral trumpet playing, we are used to tonguing all semi-quavers equally hard. In earlier days, however, unequal tonguing was taught. Unequal tonguing was the principal method of articulation on all wind instruments, woodwind and brass, since the late Renaissance. On longer note values up to the quaver, players tongued as today, da da da or ta ta ta. Semi-quavers, however, as well as quavers in fast tempos, were tongued as shown below:

(from Fantini, *Modo per imparare a sonare di tromba*, 1638, p. 11.)

The result was a subtle grouping of such notes in groups of two.

The Golden Age of the Natural Trumpet (1600–1750)

This grouping could also be expressed in terms of volume, as illustrated

(Altenburg, p. 96).

An old poem read:

> If you want your piping to be here to stay,
> learn well your *diridiride*.

(Martin Agricola, *Musica Instrumentalis Deudsch*, Wittenberg, 1545.)

Broken chords were tongued with short notes, as is the custom today. True slurs were performed principally on 'sighing' motifs, falling a second.

(From G. Torelli, *Suonata con instromenti e Tromba, 1690, G. 1.*)

It was not until the late Baroque and the early Classical period that players began to slur larger groups of notes.

in D

(From L. Mozart, *Concerto per il Clarino solo*, 1762.)

The Golden Age of the Natural Trumpet (1600–1750)

The early Baroque period was a time devoted to experimentation. Girolamo Fantini (1600–c 1675) imitated on the trumpet an extravagant vocal ornamentation called the *messa di voce*. It was performed on long held notes by making a crescendo to the middle of the note and then a diminuendo until the end 'so that it can hardly be heard'.

Trills could be performed on all notes in the fourth octave of the harmonic series, generally beginning with the upper note. Bach once wrote a trill on the sixth and once even on the fourth partial (Christmas Oratorio, bass aria 'Grosser Herr, o starker König', Part 1, No. 8). In Fantini's day (1638), however, the modern trill did not yet exist; instead, he called for the *trillo*, a fast kind of 'huffing' on one pitch, as well as the *groppo*, which looks like a written-out articulated trill.

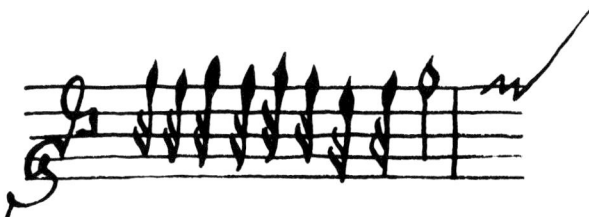

This example was taken from Bendinelli's method of 1614. Bendinelli knew the *groppo*, but not the *trillo*.

According to Altenburg, a solo trumpeter was required to 'perform purely and clearly every musical composition . . . according to the intentions of the composer'. That meant that the player should make the structure of a piece clear by his articulation – a good rule even today!

The Golden Age of the Natural Trumpet (1600–1750)

Germany and the Holy Roman Empire of the German-Speaking People

The Imperial Trumpeters' and Kettledrummers' Guild
Ever since the Imperial Police decree of 1548 mentioned on page 68, differences were constantly occurring between court trumpeters – trumpeters who had developed a high degree of self-confidence because they were answerable only to the highest secular sovereign, the emperor, and were vitally important in the conduct of war – and both city and itinerant musicians. The court trumpeters complained that the ceremonial character of their instrument was compromised when it was used in lower social circles. Furthermore, many trumpeters from these 'lower' circles entered court service, bringing the entire profession into disrepute because of their insufficient training.

In a book published in 1620 with the pompous title *Oratorischer Hall und Schall / Vom löblichen Ursprung, lieblicher Anmuth und empfindlichen Nutzen der rittermessigen Kunst der Trommeten*, Caspar Hentzschel, himself a court and field trumpeter at the electoral court of Brandenburg, warned against the great danger of a decline in the trumpeters' art through lack of sufficient training:

> Now in our time, our art is in great danger not only because of the great defects and lacks with which untrained people bring our profession . . . into disrepute, . . . but also because . . . by means of imperfect instruction and comprehension, so many bumblers and stumblers can be found in all cities and villages – . . . mixing among our colleagues like mouse-droppings among pepper – that an honest and experienced trumpeter is almost afraid to admit to his profession.

Hentzschel recommended to the sovereigns that they restore the

The Golden Age of the Natural Trumpet (1600–1750)

traditional rights which trumpeters had already possessed in Old Testament times. The Thirty Years' War had begun to rage since 1618, and an organization of trumpeters truly seemed to be in the sovereigns' interest. Finally, in 1623, all the trumpeters and kettledrummers active within the boundaries of the Holy Roman Empire of the German-Speaking People banded together to form a guild, the articles of which were confirmed by the Emperor Ferdinand II on 27 February 1623. He confirmed them anew on 24 October 1630. The 12 articles of the Imperial Privilege fulfilled two main functions: first, to keep the number of trumpet players small and the level of their art high by means of strict regulation of instruction, and second, to ensure the exclusivity of the trumpet by means of restrictions as to its use.

As far as instruction was concerned, a teacher was not allowed to instruct more than one pupil at a time unless his own son was to be included, in which case – as an exception to the rule – he was allowed to teach two pupils. Before beginning his two-year period of instruction, the pupil had to pay half of the teacher's fee or 50 thalers, paying the other 50 thalers after the two years were over. At the beginning of his period of instruction, he received a so-called 'letter of apprenticeship' and at the end the coveted 'letter of release' signed by his teacher and a certain number of other experts, as testimony to a passed examination. In the examination, the prospective trumpeter had to play the most important military signals and show some knowledge of clarino playing. As today, he first learned to play in the low register, gradually ascending higher and higher. After his release from his articles, the trumpeter had to wait seven more years before he was allowed to instruct pupils, and this was only allowed if in the meantime he had participated in at least one military campaign, a prerequisite for receiving the all-important title of Field Trumpeter.

The Golden Age of the Natural Trumpet (1600–1750)

The places in which the trumpet was allowed to be played were defined exactly in the seventh and eighth articles of the Imperial Privilege:

> Seventh, no respectable trumpeter... shall play together with jugglers, caretakers, or tower watchmen...: furthermore, no tower watchman shall use the trumpet except on his tower; and also, if a tower watchman should come into the field of a military campaign, such a person should not be tolerated among honest trumpeters... unless he has previously learned trumpet playing... in a proper manner, thus being able to show his proper Letter of Release.... Tower watchmen shall not have the power to serve, either with trumpets or with military kettledrums, at weddings, baptisms, or other respectable gatherings.

Tower musicians were thus not prohibited completely from playing the trumpet, but were allowed to use it only on their towers. On the other hand, court trumpeters were to play exclusively within the circle of nobility:

> Eighth, no respectable trumpeter shall allow himself to be employed with his instrument otherwise than by princes, counts, lords, and noble bodies of knights, or otherwise by highly qualified persons....

The patron saint of the trumpeters' guild was the archangel Gabriel; its protector was the Elector of Saxony, who had the task of settling all disputes. And disputes there were. Saxon mandates 'against unauthorized trumpet playing and military kettledrum playing' had to be issued in 1650, 1661, 1711, 1736 and 1804, they in their turn influencing revisions of the Imperial Privilege. In particular, 'comedians, jugglers, gamblers, city pipers... and especially each and every city or peasant musician' were

Tuba, hydraulus (water organ), and cornua at a gladiatorial contest
Floor mosaic from second century AD. Dar Buc Ammera, Zliten. Musée des Antiquités de Tripoli. (Photo: Pierre Belzeaux/Time-Life Books/ABC Press, Amsterdam)

This page and opposite: Short and long Arabian trumpets. F Pbn fonds arabe 5847, fols. 19 and 94ᵛ. (Photo: Tilman Seebass, Duke University)

وكاد يبزع الجمال الشر وانشد
ما الحج يبرك ثاوياً ولاداعياً ولا غنياً انل اجمالاً واجدلاً

الحج ان تقصد البيت الحرام على الحج نيل كل الحج لا يبغى به جاجا
وتجلى كامل الانصاف شئا ارد ع الهوى هادياً والحق مهاجا

Paolo Uccello, Niccolò Mauruzi in the Battle of S. Romano, with battle trumpets. London, National Gallery

Left: Angel trumpeter of the Last Judgement, 1072–87, on the west wall of the Basilica of S. Angelo in Formis

Beato Angelico, Coronation of Mary, c. 1425–40. Florence, Galleria degli Uffizi. (Photo: Scala, Antella/Florence)

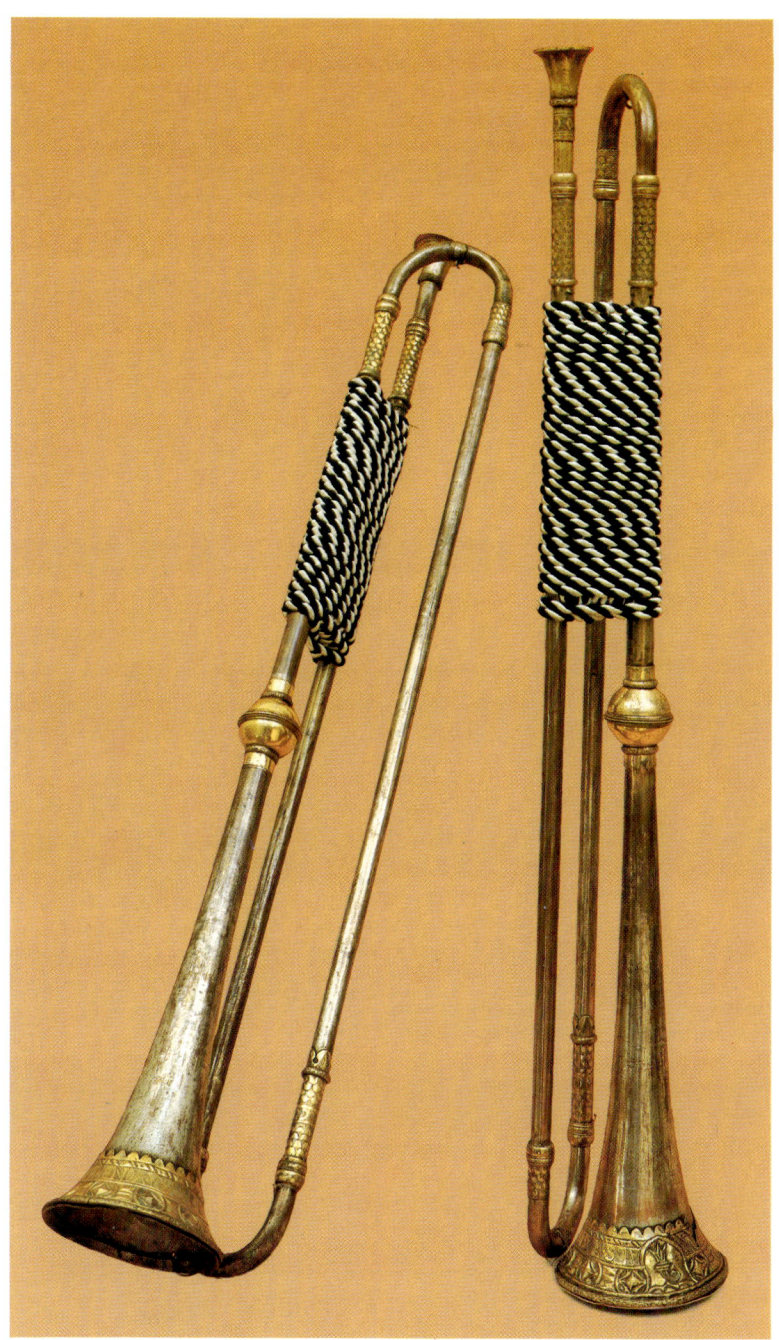

Two trumpets by Jacob Steiger, Basle, 1578. Basle, Historiches Museum. (Photo: Maurice Babey/Historisches Museum, Basle)

Trumpet by Anton Schnitzer I, Nuremberg, 1581. Vienna, Sammlung alter Musikinstrumente. (Photo: Erwin Meyer, Vienna)

The Golden Age of the Natural Trumpet (1600–1750)

expressly forbidden to play the trumpet outside their normal area of work, that is:

> outside of their comedies, juggling games, gambling stands, and towers, or at noble, civic or peasant weddings, baptisms, annual fairs, church fairs, dances of rejoicing, or similar revels.

In 1653, the Imperial Privilege was expanded from 12 articles to 23 by Friedrich III. A concession was made to the tower musicians, inasmuch as the church was henceforth recognized as one of their areas of work. Students were also allowed to use the trumpet in 'academic solemnities'. Nevertheless, quarrels continued to arise. Once in the city of Hanover, court trumpeters broke into the house of the tower watchman while he was practising, and 'smashed the latter's trumpet, as well as mishandling him thereby very badly and knocking out his teeth'. In the resulting lawsuit, the court trumpeters got off scot-free, since they had only been protecting their legitimate interests.

In confirming the Privilege in 1747, Franz I reduced the 23 articles once again to 12. The Privilege was confirmed for the last time by Josef II in 1767.

In the second half of the eighteenth century, many small and middle-sized courts went under. Each disappearance of a court meant the dismissal of five to ten trumpeters and consequently a weakening of the guild.

The Berlin court played a particular part in the decline of the trumpeters' guild. One of the first official duties of Friedrich Wilhelm I, the 'soldier king', recognized by historians as a man of great prescience, was in 1713 to dissolve the trumpeters' corps consisting of 24 trumpeters and two kettledrummers. In this process, the court trumpeters were demoted to military musicians, and worse still, were employed with the infantry! Henceforth, the two descant oboes, two tenor oboes, and two bassoons of the infantry band of each regiment were joined by a trumpeter who often marched ahead of the column, sounding his fanfares into the air. In order to secure potential talent for future military bands, Friedrich Wilhelm II, 'the Great', had a military orphanage constructed between 1772 and 1774, in which Gottfried Pepusch, the leader of the 'Long Fellows', as they were called, selected suitable candidates and trained them in the Oboists' School. The still-continuing fraternal relationship among the trumpeters of Prussian cavalry regiments was finally dissolved by Friedrich Wilhelm III on 8 November 1810.

In Saxony, the Privilege remained valid until the general abolition of guilds in 1831, the trumpeters' corps surviving even without the Privilege until 1918. In Vienna, the Union of Court Trumpeters, the successor organization to the Imperial Guild, was dissolved on 28 August 1878.

The Imperial Trumpeters' and Kettledrummers' Guild was recognized throughout the entire Roman Empire of the German-Speaking People and in the cities of the Hanseatic League of Germany. Other trumpeters however,

> who [have] not learned this trade in the above-mentioned way and who are at a court or in an army outside the Roman Empire, are simply called 'untrained', and for that very reason are not tolerated among us. (J.E. Altenburg, p. 27.)

Altenburg complained about the fact that improperly trained trumpeters had mingled among the trumpeters of the French army. In Switzerland, the Imperial Privilege was disdainfully ignored; a city trumpeter from Schaffhausen who went to Dresden to receive special training was looked upon unkindly when, after his return, and merely referring to the Imperial Privilege, he tried to secure certain advantages for himself.

The Golden Age of the Natural Trumpet (1600–1750)

Instrument Making in Nuremberg
Two years after the founding of the Imperial Trumpeters' and Kettledrummers' Guild, the brass instrument makers of Nuremberg came together, receiving a charter of their guild from the City Council. After 1640 it became the custom for each new master to enter his mark on a brass plaque, in order to register it and protect it against unauthorized imitation. The customs of the Nuremberg instrument makers were even more severe than those of the Imperial trumpeters; the periods of apprenticeship and of being a journeyman lasted six years each. Apprenticeship usually began at the age of 14. In order to be taken on as an apprentice, it was necessary to be a Nuremberg citizen.

When the Nuremberg instrument makers received their charter in 1625, there were ten masters there. Being worried 'that a number of them could not nourish or provide for themselves', the City Council decreed a *numerus clausus* on the profession; no master was henceforth allowed to take on an apprentice 'until the number of present masters shall have died out to six'. This number was reached relatively quickly, after only 11 years, and although the craft of brass instrument making flourished, there were never again so many masters in Nuremberg as in 1625.

Some familiar names can be found among the ten masters of that date, whereas others were only to become famous in the seventeenth and eighteenth centuries. The ten were Hans Doll, Conrad Droschel, Isaac and Georg Ehe, Sebastian Hainlein the Elder, Hans Kümmelmann, Elias Linssner, Hans Müller, Anton Schnitzer the Younger, and Hans Hainlein. The old names are Schnitzer and Hainlein, and the most important new name is that of the Ehe family. Besides Isaac (1586–1632) and Georg Ehe (1595–1668), three generations of instrument makers with the name Johann Leonhard Ehe are worthy of note: J.L. Ehe I (1638–

The Golden Age of the Natural Trumpet (1600–1750)

1707), II (1663–1724) and III (1700–71).

Another name missing in 1625 was Johann Wilhelm Haas. This family, too, was active over several generations. Surviving instruments were made by three generations: J.W. Haas (1649–1723), Wolf Wilhelm Haas (1681–1760) and Ernst Johann Conrad Haas (1723–92). This family was probably the most famous of all. Wolf Wilhelm and Ernst Johann Conrad honoured the family tradition by signing their instruments not with their own names, but with that of the founder. Their trumpets were sought after throughout all Europe. As late as 1795, Altenburg set trumpets made by the Haas family over those of all others:

> Be that as it may, [those] trumpets made by J.W. Haas in Nuremberg and set with angel-heads are commonly held to be the best. (p. 10)

The brass instrument makers of Nuremberg built trumpets, trombones and horns of various kinds. According to Christoph Weigel's detailed account of the various crafts of Nuremberg in 1698 (*Abbildung der gemein nützlichen Hauptstände*),

> The trumpets are of various kinds, namely *German* and so-called ordinary trumpets; *French*, one step higher than the former; and *English*, which surpass the pitch of the ordinary trumpets by an entire third. A species of *coiled* trumpets are also found, they being the *Italian* or *Welsh*, which are wound round six times; the *trumpet sticks* . . . also belong to this group.

Despite the above description, it has never been possible to discern a difference in the pitch of German, French and English trumpets. On the contrary, Marin Mersenne (*Harmonie universelle*, Paris 1636–37) and Altenburg determined independently of one another the length of tubing of the natural trumpet to be 224cm (7 *pieds* or 4 *ells*, respectively), resulting in a pitch

The Golden Age of the Natural Trumpet (1600–1750)

slightly lower than modern D. Surviving English trumpets are pitched in D or E-flat. As far as the coiled 'Italian or Welsh' trumpet is concerned, we hold the opinion that the Leipzig city-piper Gottfried Reiche is holding an instrument of this kind in his hand in the famous portrait by E.G. Haussmann (*see p. 106*), even though it is not 'wound around six times', but only four and a half. In 1620, Praetorius called such a coiled trumpet a *Jäger Trommet*. Only two instruments of this kind, made by Heinrich Pfeiffer (Leipzig) and J.W. Haas, survived up to the Second World War. Today, the first is considered to be lost.

The brass instrument makers of the city of Nuremberg constructed their instruments out of brass or silver. The heavy, richly ornamented trumpets, of which eight or 12 at a time were generally sold to the great courts and which were reserved for ceremonial occasions, were often made of silver. This does not mean they had to have a beautiful tone. Here too, we must differentiate between the music of the court trumpeters' corps and art music. Altenburg (pp. 9–10) wrote in unmistakable terms:

> However, the opinion that [the silver trumpets used on ceremonial occasions at the large courts] are superior in sound to those made of brass is unfounded. Rather the contrary is proven by experience.

To be sure, an exception was represented by silver trumpets made out of thin metal, as opposed to the heavy ceremonial instruments mentioned above. They were very rare, however.

Thanks to the work of Willi Wörthmüller (1954), we can differentiate three stages in the construction of trumpet bells in Nuremberg, according to the degree of flare. For example, the Renaissance and early Baroque bells made by the Schnitzer and Hainlein families had little flare, and the middle Baroque bells of

The Golden Age of the Natural Trumpet (1600–1750)

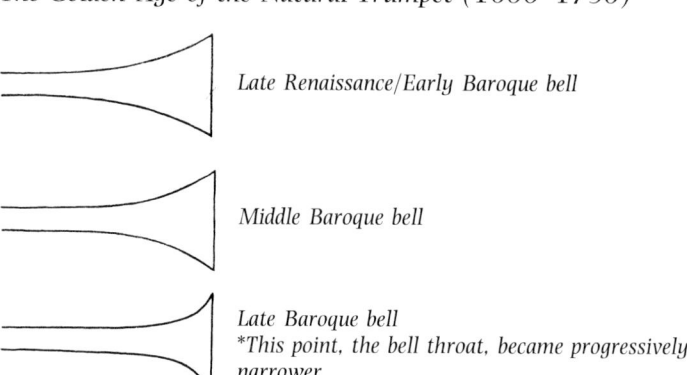

Michael Nagel, Jacob Schmidt and Friedrich Ehe more, while the late Baroque bells of Wolf Wilhelm Hass and Ernst Johann Conrad Haas had the steepest degree of flare. Together with the development of the flare, the point on the bell just before the flare which is called the bell throat became successively narrower.

The development of the Nuremberg bell went hand in hand with a transformation of Baroque sound from dark and heavy to light and clear. In addition, Nuremberg brass instrument making itself followed a parallel development to that of baroque clarino playing. Both had their origins around 1500 (clarino playing perhaps as early as 1460), experienced their peak during the seventeenth and first half of the eighteenth century, and both died out in the early nineteenth century. The last two Nuremberg brass instrument makers, Johann Jacob Frank and Johann David Frank, earned their master's title in 1822 and 1834. By this time, however, Nuremberg trumpets were already old-fashioned; a new musical style demanded new kinds of instruments.

The Acceptance of the Trumpet into Art Music in the German-Speaking World

In the German-speaking world, the trumpet was accepted into art music around 1616–20. The very first piece employing trumpets seems to be a 'Missa con le trombe a 16,' written before 1616 by the Graz court musician Reimundo Ballestra. At first, the entire trumpet ensemble was taken over lock, stock and barrel, and simply transplanted into a vocal composition; later, only two clarino parts were retained. Significantly, two settings of the Christmas carol *In dulci jubilo* belonged to the first compositions in which trumpets were called for; during the sixteenth century,

The Golden Age of the Natural Trumpet (1600–1750)

this carol was one of the pieces most frequently performed by the courtly trumpeters' corps (Thomsen, Bendinelli). When Michael Praetorius (1571–1621) published this carol in 1618 as no. 34 of his collection of church music entitled *Polyhymnia Panegyrica et Caduceatrix*, he simply took over the full six-part trumpet ensemble consisting of two Clarien, Prinzipal, Alter Bass, Volgan and Grob. Samuel Scheidt (1587–1654), in his setting of the same carol two years later, retained only the two clarien parts, which he treated equally, and which decorate the chorale melody in an extremely rich fashion by ornaments or passage-work. Until that time, the clarino register ended with the thirteenth partial of the harmonic series, or a''. The first composer to demand a high c''', the sixteenth partial, was probably Heinrich Schütz (1585–1672) in his setting of *Buccinate in neomenia tuba* (*Symphoniae Sacrae* I, No. 19, 1629).

The two-fold manner of playing the Baroque trumpet described by Altenburg can easily be seen in the structure of these pieces. Praetorius' composition has several choirs, which were doubtlessly placed at various points throughout the entire church building. The six-part trumpet choir played only at climactic points in which all the performing forces were working together, also playing an 'Intrada as a finale'. Fearing that this large group might drown the other instruments and voices, Praetorius recommended that the trumpeters be placed 'in a special place nearby the church'. Scheidt and Schütz, in the works mentioned above, presupposed the other style of playing the trumpet. In particular, *Buccinate in neomenia tuba* by Schütz requires absolute mastery of the instrument – not just a pompous sound – for the solo trumpet plays together with only two other instruments (cornett and dolcian), three men's voices (TTB), and basso continuo.

The trumpet was used in art music symbolically: it could be

The Golden Age of the Natural Trumpet (1600–1750)

called the instrument of heavenly and earthly power. It sounded on high festival days of the church in works such as Magnificats, Masses and Te Deums, as well as on ceremonial events of a secular nature for processions, tournaments, coronations, and the like. The festival masses with trumpets and kettledrums became so pompous that Pope Benedict XIV forbade them entirely in 1749 in his encyclical *Annus qui*, designed to oppose superfluous pomp in the church. It is fortunate that this prohibition came as late as it did, for otherwise posterity might not possess the so-called B-minor Mass, the Kyrie and Gloria of which J.S. Bach composed for the court of Dresden in 1733.

Centres of Trumpet Playing in the German-Speaking World
It would be too much to list all the composers and centres of Baroque trumpet music in the German-speaking world (Germany, Austria, Switzerland and parts of today's Czechoslavakia). The reader will already be familiar with many of them through recordings. Here we only wish to mention the city of Leipzig, as well as the most important courts: Weissenfels, Dresden, Kremsier and Vienna.

Leipzig
During the entire Baroque period, the city of Leipzig placed special importance on trumpet playing. The performers were the city pipers. In 1618 and 1620, before the founding of the Imperial Trumpeters' and Kettledrummers' Guild, the then cantor of St Thomas, Johann Hermann Schein (1586–1630), came in to conflict with a habitual right of the Elector of Saxony because he had included parts for trumpets and kettledrums in pieces written for weddings not involving the nobility. After the Thirty Years' War, large festival cantatas, often featuring two and even as many as four trumpets, were very popular in Leipzig. The

The Golden Age of the Natural Trumpet (1600–1750)

composers were the cantors of St Thomas: from 1657 Sebastian Knüpfer (1633–76), from 1677 Johann Schelle (1648–1701), from 1701 Johann Kuhnau (1660–1722) and from 1723 the composer regarded by many as producing the quintessence of Baroque music: Johann Sebastian Bach (1685–1750). When Bach arrived in Leipzig in 1723, he thus found a long-standing local tradition in the use of trumpets.

The city piper who performed the trumpet parts in Kuhnau's and Schelle's time was Johann Pezel (1639–94). He was also well-known as the composer of so-called tower music for two cornetts and three trombones. His own trumpet works (six sonatinas for two trumpets and basso continuo; one sonata for trumpet, bassoon and basso continuo) contained difficulties of every kind, such as lipped leading tones, and ascended to the sixteenth and even the eighteenth partials. Good trumpeters were sought after in Leipzig. When Pezel was taken into the circle of Leipzig city pipers as a *Kunstgeiger* in 1664, it was duly noted in the archival document that he was an 'approved clarino player'.

The trumpeter active at the beginning of Bach's Leipzig period was Gottfried Reiche (1667–1734). He too was known as a composer of tower music, performed by the city pipers at their so-called *Abblasen*. The City Council held Reiche's art in high esteem. Once in 1694, during a general period of mourning, when civic musical manifestations for weddings and the like were prohibited and the city pipers were thus deprived of an important source of secondary income, the City Council gave him a special financial bonus payment in order that he would not be tempted to seek employment elsewhere. The famous portrait of Reiche painted by E.G. Haussmann, a portrait which is also controversial because of the special form of instrument depicted in it, also represented a commission by the City Council (1727). Bach wrote the trumpet parts of most of his great cantatas for Reiche.

The Golden Age of the Natural Trumpet (1600–1750)

Engraving by Rosbach after E.G. Haussmann: the Leipzig city piper Gottfried Reiche with a coiled instrument (possibly called Jägertrompete *or also* italienische Trompete*), 1727; from* Musik in Geschichte und Gegenwart, *Barenreiter-Verlag, Kassel*

About half of Bach's works with trumpet were written for the C trumpet, the other half for the D. In keeping with the festive occasions, he usually wrote for three *Trombe* and *Tamburi* (kettledrums), but cantatas with a solo trumpet are also numerous. In only one cantata did he write for two trumpets, and only in two did he write for four trumpets (of these one is from the Weimar period). Only in his very first cantata from 1708 (*Gott ist mein König*, BWV 71) did Bach divide the three trumpet parts into two clarino and one principale part. In all his other works with three trumpets he was somewhat less hierarchical, a principle of composition exercising the greatest influence on the third

The Golden Age of the Natural Trumpet (1600–1750)

Trompete 1–3 in D

J.S. Bach, Christmas Oratorio, *beginning of the trumpet parts*

trumpet part. As a true principale, the third part would be restricted to the third to eighth partials; in Bach's writing, however, the third part sometimes ascends higher than even the first. The best-known example of such trumpet writing in Bach's works is probably in the opening chorus of the Christmas oratorio, a piece which originally sounded on 8 December 1733 for the birthday of the Electoress of Saxony under the title *Tönet, ihr Pauken! Erschallet, Trompeten!* (BWV 214).

Bach's first trumpet parts, like those of Pezel, often ascend to the sixteenth or eighteenth partial, sometimes requiring the lipped leading tone b', less often c-sharp''. Bach by no means avoided the impure partials f'' and a'', treating them instead just like any other note of the harmonic series.

These characteristics of Bach's handling of the trumpet are to be seen not only during his Leipzig period, but also in his earlier works. During the Weimar and Cöthen periods Bach composed important and difficult trumpet parts. Even in his earliest works, he knew how to integrate the trumpet organically into the rest of the orchestra without losing any of its dignity.

The following well-known cantatas with trumpets come from the Weimar period (1708–17): *Ich hatte viel Bekümmernis*, BWV 21 (1713); *Christen, ätzet diesen Tag*, BWV 63 (1713, one of two examples with four trumpets); *Erschallet, ihr Lieder*, BWV 172 (20 May, 1714, a cantata containing one of the most difficult of all first trumpet parts – one of the most stunning passages is a chain of 44 demisemiquavers ending on high C); *Der Himmel lacht*, BWV 31 (Easter 1715, a work containing a number of lipped c-sharps''); and *Herz und Mund und That und Leben*, BWV 147 (Advent IV, 1716). All of these cantatas were written for

The Golden Age of the Natural Trumpet (1600–1750)

trumpets in C; however, since they were composed in so-called choir pitch, they thus sounded in today's pitch of D or even E-flat. Later, in Leipzig, Bach composed an obbligato trumpet part for the final chorale of Cantata 31, a part which is doubled by violins and – the only such case in all of Bach's works – ascends to the twentieth partial, an e''' above high c'''. The trumpet parts of the cantatas written in Weimar are just as difficult as those composed in Leipzig.

During the Cöthen period (1717–23), Bach composed the six Brandenburg concertos. The second of these works is feared by trumpeters more than any other composition by Bach, in spite of our unbounded admiration for his masterful treatment of themes. The difficulties are three-fold. In the first place, it is not purely a solo work for trumpet in which the soloist might allow his tone to develop freely. On the contrary, it is a kind of concerto grosso with four solo instruments: trumpet, recorder, oboe and violin. It is necessary for the trumpeter to hold back his volume continually, in order to balance with the recorder and other instruments. In the second place, the first movement in particular is extremely strenuous, because it contains only a few rests. And finally, all of these problems are magnified because the trumpet is pitched in F, a third or fourth higher than usual. The eighteenth partial, reached three times in the first movement, is thus a sounding g'''.

This concerto, composed in 1721, occupies a special place in the trumpet repertoire. Only rarely in music history do we find trumpet works ascending to such heights. The high register of the second Brandenburg concerto was reached again, and even surpassed, in works written at the court of Vienna for Johann Heinisch (fl. 1727–50) and his successors, as well as in today's jazz and commmercial music, such as that written for Cat Anderson (1916–81) and others. (Some cornet virtuosos of the

The Golden Age of the Natural Trumpet (1600–1750)

late nineteenth and early twentieth centuries also reached g''', a''', and b-flat$'''$. In this connection it should be realized that it is easier to play high notes in improvisations than in written music.)

In recent years it has been suggested that the trumpet part in Bach's Second Brandenburg Concerto may have originally been written for a horn instead, on the basis of a later set of parts with the indication *Tromba ò vero Corno da caccia*. At the present, however, the burden of proof still rests with the advocates of the horn. From the existing source material we cannot see that the use of the horn was anything but an alternative possibility introduced later.

In Leipzig (1723–50), J.S. Bach wrote some of his most important choral works. Among which Reiche played are the following: *Die Himmel erzählen die Ehre Gottes*, BWV 76 (6 June 1723); *Schauet doch und sehet*, BWV 46 (1 August 1723, composed for a slide trumpet or *tromba da tirarsi*, a kind of trumpet surviving from the Renaissance in the hands of tower watchmen (Bach wrote several cantatas for slide trumpet, following the example of his predecessor Kuhnau); the Magnificat in E-flat major, BWV 243a (Christmas, 1723); *Jesu, nun sei grepreiset*, BWV 41 (New Year, 1724, a cantata containing what is probably the most strenuous opening chorus); the Easter Oratorio, BWV 249 (1 April 1725); *Der zufriedengestellte Äolus*, BWV 205 (3 August 1726, noteworthy because of the rare simultaneous use of three trumpets and two horns); and *Jauchzet Gott in allen Landen*, BWV 51 (17 September 1730 [?], a virtuoso contest between soprano and trumpet).

The fateful work *Preise dein Glücke, gesegnetes Sachsen*, BWV 215, deserves special mention. It was performed for the first time in the open air on 5 October 1734, the occasion of the first anniversary of the succession of August III, the Elector of Saxony,

109

The Golden Age of the Natural Trumpet (1600–1750)

to the throne of Poland. The opening chorus, for three D trumpets, was of virtuoso character, ascending to a sounding e''' already in the first bars. We will never know whether it was due to the strenuousness of the cantata or to the smoke of the many torches, but in any case, Reiche, now 67 years old, collapsed on the way home and died the following day.

Reiche's successor, Ulrich Heinrich Ruhe (d. 1787), played many important works of Bach. They include the entire Christmas Oratorio, BWV 248 (25 December 1734 to 6 January 1735); *Lobet Gott in seinen Reichen*, the so-called Ascension Oratorio, BWV 11 (19 May 1735); *Auf, schmetternde Töne der muntern Trompeten*, BWV 207a (for the name-day of August III on 3 August 1735 [?]); *Schleicht, spielende Wellen*, BWV 206 (7 October 1736 [?] – a cantata with difficult slurs); and *Gloria in excelsis Deo*, BWV 191 (Christmas, c 1741–49). It is important to mention the activity of Ruhe, since it is otherwise easy to overestimate the importance of the better known Reiche. Ruhe played for Bach for 16 years; Reiche for only 11.

On what kind of a trumpet were Bach's works originally performed? Certainly not on a Bach trumpet. This special instrument with valves only came into being at the end of the nineteenth century. (*See p. 155.*) Bach's works, like all others during the Baroque period, were played on the natural trumpet, except for those few cantatas composed for the *tromba da tirarsi*. In Weimar and Cöthen the natural trumpet certainly had the usual folded form. In Leipzig one is inclined to consider the coiled instrument known as *Jägertrompete* or 'Italian trumpet', because Reiche was depicted in his portrait holding such an instrument. It is possible that this was Reiche's favourite trumpet, on which he played everything. (It seems to have been constructed in the pitch of D with an additional crook for C.) However, it is also possible that Reiche, when sitting for the

The Golden Age of the Natural Trumpet (1600–1750)

portrait, reached for his most bizarre instrument, or that he preferred to be painted holding this coiled one in order to avoid any conflict with Saxon court trumpeters, or that the artist chose an instrument of a suitable size which could be reproduced whole. Accordingly, it is at least tenable that Reiche, and certainly Ruhe as well, played on the Baroque trumpet in the normal folded shape. However this may be, we do know that Leipzig occupied a special place among the cities. In the German-speaking countries, trumpet literature of this high degree of virtuousity is otherwise to be found only at the courts.

Weissenfels

In his dissertation of 1973, Detlef Altenburg showed how the number of trumpeters serving at the various courts declined during the Thirty Years' War (1618–48), afterwards increasing again; only towards the middle of the eighteenth century do we start to notice the dissolving of courts, as well as a reduction in the number of trumpeters serving at those courts which continued to exist. The following court trumpeters' corps were dissolved in this order: Güstrow in 1696, Berlin in 1713, Innsbruck in 1724, Eisenach and Wartburg in 1741 and Weissenfels in 1746. Only those 'musical' trumpeters who could be used in the court orchestra were retained. The age of absolutism yielded to modern times.

Weissenfels, seat of the Dukes of Saxony-Weissenfels from 1680 to 1746, occupies a position of special importance both because of its connection with Leipzig and also because of the high quality of trumpeters trained there. Gottfried Reiche came from there, as did J.S. Bach's father-in-law, the court trumpeter Johann Caspar Wülcken (d. before 1732). Johann Ernst Altenburg (1734–1801) was also trained in Weissenfels. He and his father, Johann Caspar Altenburg (1687–1761), an important

The Golden Age of the Natural Trumpet (1600–1750)

soloist, themselves experienced the severe consequences of the breaking up of their court after the death of the third duke, Johann Adolph, in 1746. After a long and illustrious career, Johann Caspar went into retirement. However, Johann Ernst was not able to find a proper position as a trumpeter. He first scraped through the Seven Years' War (1756–63) as a field trumpeter in the French army, later finding a modest position as organist in the then small town of Bitterfeld, where he died impoverished and embittered.

Dresden

Dresden always had a large trumpeters' corps. In 1548, ten trumpeters were already employed there, with the number increasing to 12 trumpeters and one kettledrummer in 1606, and 14 trumpeters and two kettledrummers in 1629, the largest number being reached in 1680, when there were 15 trumpeters and three kettledrummers. In 1736 there were 13 trumpeters and two kettledrummers, in 1771 ten trumpeters and one kettledrummer, and in 1795 eight trumpeters and one kettledrummer. The corps was not dissolved until 1918.

Both J.S. Bach and J.E. Altenburg, as good Saxon subjects, genuflected in the direction of the Elector of Saxony, whose seat was at the court in Dresden. According to the Imperial Privilege and as Archmarshal of the Holy Roman Empire of the German-Speaking Peoples, the Elector of Saxony was the arbiter of all disputes arising among Imperial Trumpeters. Not only did the Electors of Saxony issue mandates against unauthorized trumpet playing, but they also confirmed the Imperial Privilege between 1658 and 1769. Next to the trumpeters' corps at the Imperial court of Vienna, the Dresden trumpeters' corps was the most powerful in the entire empire; only the leaders of these two ensembles were allowed to call themselves 'Chief Court Trumpeter' (*Oberhoftrompeter*).

The Golden Age of the Natural Trumpet (1600–1750)

One of the duties of the Chief Court Trumpeter in Dresden was 'either to invent and to compose new sonatas, processional fanfares, and other pieces, or else to acquire such pieces from others'. A collection of 102 processional fanfares of the Dresden court trumpeters survived until the beginning of the Second World War. They were presumably written around 1760 for two clarini, one principale, and kettledrums. The high level of trumpet playing in Dresden is demonstrated not only by the remarkable singing texture of the three or four of these pieces which have survived, but also by the range of the first part, which ascended as high as the twentieth partial.

The Dresden court trumpeters were called on to play at major festivals both of a sacred and a secular nature. An important religious occasion was celebrated on the hundreth anniversary of Martin Luther's Wittenberg theses in 1617, an occasion for which Heinrich Schütz composed a Magnificat, now lost, featuring 18 trumpets and two pairs of kettledrums. A Mass Ritual from Dresden in 1665 required '1. Kyrie, 2. Gloria – with trumpets and kettledrums . . . 6. Credo – with trumpets and kettledrums (and) . . . 9. Doxology, in German with trumpets and kettledrums'. Masses and Te Deums with as many as 20 trumpets were extremely popular in Dresden until the papal edict of 1749 forbidding such extravagance. Tournaments, masked processions, and other such festivities were celebrated with similar large numbers of trumpets and kettledrums.

Musical forms underwent gradual changes. An edict of 1665 concerning playing at table read in part as follows:

> Trumpets and kettledrums usually sound the call to table at 11 o'clock on all Sundays and holidays . . . ; this function is performed at noon on weekdays by one trumpeter.

On weekdays, a single trumpeter played in the principale register,

The Golden Age of the Natural Trumpet (1600–1750)

in the words of Altenburg 'with blaring tonguings'. On Sundays and holidays the trumpeters and kettledrummers seem to have improvised music in several parts. The so-called *Tafelkonzert*, a very popular category of composition, arose from this practice. It seems that German sovereigns were not able to dine pleasantly or with appropriate pomp without the sound of kettledrums and trumpets. Altenburg described the *Tafelsonate* as a concerto in three movements for two choirs of trumpets and one or two soloists. The Concerto for Seven Clarini with Kettledrums, which displays a similar form and was printed as an appendix to his book, shows signs of not having been composed by him; it was probably written in Dresden.

Kremsier

Bohemia was an important possession of the Habsburg dynasty. For a short time, from Maximilian II (reigned 1564–76) until 1619, Prague was the capital of Bohemia, the residence of the Emperor, and thus an important centre of the trumpeter's art, even though the Bohemian trumpeters did not join the Guild in 1623. In Prague, a court trumpeter by the name of Alessandro Orologio even became music director in 1606. It was there, too, that the Thirty Years' War began with a Protestant uprising. In its brutal suppression, the old noble families were driven away, their possessions being given over to German and Austrian families.

After the war, the court in Kremsier flourished musically in an unprecedented way as the residence of the Prince-Bishop of Olmuetz (Moravia), Karl Lichtenstein-Kastellkorn (reigned 1664–95). In Kremsier, as well as in the city of Bologna – which, interestingly enough, was similarly an archbishop's city – more instrumental works were composed featuring one or more solo trumpets than in any other place.

The Golden Age of the Natural Trumpet (1600–1750)

The composer H.I.F. Biber (1644–1704) was active in Kremsier between 1666 and 1670. There he composed suites with trumpets and strings for the table music of the prince-bishop. The castle archives there contain his *Sonata Sancti Polycarpi*, one of the most magnificent compositions ever written for an ensemble of Baroque trumpets. It is scored for two choirs of four trumpets each, or eight in all, kettledrums, and basso continuo. Because of the harmonic limitations of the natural trumpets, the possibilities of modulation within this composition are reduced to C and G. However, Biber made necessity the mother of invention, creating masterful climaxes and a beautiful overall form by the use of ostinati and echo effects. This piece can be regarded as the quintessence of Baroque trumpet splendour. Thanks to the research of Eric Chafe (1975), we now know that this sonata received its first performance on the feast day of St Polycarp on 26 January 1673 in Salzburg, Biber's last place of residence. Biber seems to have been motivated to write the sonata by the election of Polykarp von Kuenberg, a nephew of the Salzburg archbishop, to the position of provost of the Salzburg cathedral. Biber sent a copy of the piece to Kremsier.

After Biber's departure from Kremsier, the music director there was a trumpeter, Pavel Josef Vejvanovský (1639/40–93). Among his surviving compositions there are many for trumpet(s) and strings, besides masses, motets and the like. In 1670, he composed a piece of table music with the title *Balletti pro Tabula*, a series of dance movements framed by two sonatinas. The instruments called for are two clarini, five viols, and basso continuo. In another work, *Sonata à 4 Be mollis* for trumpet, violin, two viols, and basso continuo, the trumpet sounds in G minor. This rare effect was made possible through the use of the seventh and fourteenth partials, seldom used because slightly too low in pitch, as the minor third of a minor chord on G.

The Golden Age of the Natural Trumpet (1600–1750)

Furthermore, Vejvanovský demanded and obviously played both *c*-sharp" and *e*-flat", that is, a semitone lower than the ninth and tenth partials respectively. Biber also composed a trumpet sonata and two duets in G minor, but with only a single lipped semitone, a *c*-sharp" in bar 101 of the *Sonata Xa5*.

During this period, two terms referring to trumpets, borrowed from Latin, emerged in Kremsier. The first is *tuba campestris*. In 1680, Vejvanovský composed a serenata for five *tubae campestris* kettledrums, four viols, and basso continuo. This Latin term is equivalent to 'field trumpet' and underlines the fact that an entire choir of trumpets is employed in this serenata. Moreover, Vejvanovský signed his name in scores as *tubicen campestris*; the title Field Trumpeter was, for him, a mark of honour. The other term is *tromba brevis*. Vejvanovský composed two works, among them a *Sonata Venatoria* or hunting sonata, for two *trombae breves*, strings, and basso continuo. This term, too, is easily understood; it means nothing other than 'short trumpet' and simply designates the D trumpet. The preferred tonality for trumpets in Kremsier, as well as in Vienna, was C. Both of the compositions by Vejvanovský employing two *trombae breves* are the only pieces in the entire solo repertoire of the trumpet in Kremsier written in the key of D. The D trumpet was called *tromba brevis* because it is shorter than the C trumpet. An inventory from Osseg in Northern Bohemia explicitly mentioning five trumpets in C and two in D proves that the C trumpet was an independent instrument, and not just a D trumpet lengthened by a whole-tone crook.

There were other composers who wrote for the Kremsier trumpeters. The two most important ones, Johann Heinrich Schmelzer (1623–80) and Antonio Bertali (1605–69), were active in Vienna, as were others such as Antonio Poglietti (d. 1683) and Ferdinand Tobias Richter (1649–1711), all of them

The Golden Age of the Natural Trumpet (1600–1750)

sending new compositions to the prince-bishop from time to time. In some works, such as Bertali's *Sonata Sublationis* from 1665, both *clarini* and *trombae* are called for. It was a custom in Austria and Moravia until about 1850 to divide the high and low trumpet parts from one another in this way, whereas in Germany, the terms utilized were *clarini* and *principale*. These terms, of course, did not designate different kinds of instruments, but rather the parts, high and low.

Vienna

It was at the Viennese imperial court that the art of clarino playing came into full bloom. All the arts flourished in Vienna, particularly music. It is well known that all the Habsburg emperors, from Ferdinand III (1608–57) to Karl VI (1685–1711), were themselves composers. The number of trumpeters employed there varied considerably. Around 1550 there were six trumpeters and a kettledrummer; in 1566–76 there were 15 trumpeters and a kettledrummer, a number reached only one other time, in 1643, and surpassed only once when 16 trumpeters and two kettledrummers received payment there in 1721. Yet in 1766 there were only six trumpeters, and from 1793 only four trumpeters and a kettledrummer. The greatest peaks were under Leopold I (reigned 1658–1705) and Karl VI (reigned 1711–40). Riedel has shown that the origins of the liturgical trumpet sonata are to be found not in Bologna, but in Vienna, where from the mid-seventeenth century solemn church sonatas with two or four trumpets, timpani, strings and often winds (cornetts and trombones) began to be composed.

Of the entertainments in which trumpeters took part and to which those in Dresden and Kremsier corresponded, we will emphasize only two: the equestrian ballet and the opera. Equestrian games had changed decidedly since the Middle Ages.

The Golden Age of the Natural Trumpet (1600–1750)

In the place of tournaments, during which the cracking of lances and the din of trumpets could be heard simultaneously, came equestrian ballets with intricate figures. At the Viennese court, home of the still world-famous Spanish Riding School, many such equestrian games or horse ballets were performed in the 1730s, '60s, '70s and '90s. The most splendid and famous of them had taken place on 24 and 30 January 1667 in the course of the wedding celebrations for Leopold I and Margarita of Spain – celebrations that lasted for two years!

As was customary, the entertainment proceeded thematically; in this case the theme was *La contesa dell'aria e dell'acqua* (The Contest of Air and Water). At the end, 'air' and 'water' joined in praising Leopold and Margarita. The rehearsals had begun four months previously; the number of participants came to a thousand, and the cost amounted to 600,000 talers. To bring the grand entertainment to a conclusion, the actual equestrian ballet with music by Schmelzer (*Arie per il balletto a cavallo*) was performed. Although only a six-part trumpet setting and (in two movements) a five-part string setting are preserved, 'molte trombe', at least four choirs of trumpets, and 'piu di cento stromenti d'arco, e di fiato', more than one hundred other string and wind instruments, took part in the festivities, according to copper engravings of the celebration.

Italians were preferred as opera composers, from Pietro Cesti (1623–69; his *Il Pomo d'oro*, 1667, received one of the most splendid opera performances of any) to Bertali, Ziani, Draghi, Pollarolo, Steffani, and later, Caldara. In the performances of opera, the use of two *Clarini* and two *Trombe* was customary. Both Clarino parts developed an unparalleled technique and reached hitherto unimaginable heights. Trills on e''', the twentieth partial, occurred frequently, and the upper boundary was not c''' and d''' as with J.S. Bach, but f''' and g''', the twenty-second and

The Golden Age of the Natural Trumpet (1600–1750)

twenty-fourth partials respectively. The composers of these most virtuosic of all Baroque trumpet parts were Johann Fux (1660–1741), Antonio Caldara (1670–1736) and Georg von Reutter, the younger (1708–72). Their trumpeter, Johann Heinisch (fl. 1727–50) was probably the greatest player of the natural trumpet, and one of the greatest players of all times.

Fux, the 'Hofcompositeur' between 1698 and 1741, occasionally wrote assessments of the court musicians, and from these we can construct a fairly accurate picture of their capabilities. For example, on 27 September 1727 it is said of Heinisch that he came recently into the imperial service as a successor to the court trumpeter Andreas Pernember, and that he 'distinguished himself and rendered excellent musical service'. On 14 May 1732 he is already marked as 'an entirely special virtuoso'

> in such a manner that no one can surpass him. Heinisch, has also happily discovered certain tones on the trumpet, which the chapelmasters indeed hitherto wanted, but no trumpeter was able to produce.

Fux recommended that Heinisch should receive not a modest salary increase, but rather a doubling of his salary from 200 to 400 talers on the basis of 'his uncommon merit'. In the 'certain tones' that 'no trumpeter was able to produce', Fux alludes to the above-mentioned tones of the extreme high register, which now began to appear in Viennese trumpet music.

The unique spectacle of Baroque opera was enhanced by the rivalry between singers and instrumentalists. In 1746, four years before his death, Heinisch played in *Artaserse* by Andrea Bernasconi (1706–84). The following report characterized his high playing in a trumpet aria:

> After this singer appeared another, who only recently came

from Venice. This singer sang an adagio aria like an angel, if it is allowed to say so. Heinisch, the famous trumpeter, played a solo in this aria so artful and high that it was nearly impossible that it could have been played by a human because the trumpet behaved like a little flute. At the end of this aria, this woman sang a trill so long and lovely that I truly believed that she would run out of breath, and thus Herr Heinisch made in the same manner a long and even longer trill on the trumpet with her.

Italy

Monteverdi's *Orfeo*

Until now it has been a common belief that Claudio Monteverdi, in his opera *L'Orfeo* (Mantua, 1607), introduced the trumpet into the realm of art music. In reality he did not go so far. In *L'Orfeo*, Monteverdi used the traditional court ensemble of five trumpets for the toccata, a fanfare sounded three times before the curtain went up. This followed the example of improvised trumpet toccatas heralding, for instance, the opening of Palladio's Teatro Olimpico in Vicenza in 1584. Monteverdi was well known for his love of detail; that in the *Orfeo* toccata he composed a piece that hitherto had been improvised is consistent with this attitude. Nevertheless, the toccata was purely functional music and had little to do with art music.

Of course, Monteverdi's toccata brought some innovations to the earlier improvised trumpet fanfares. By composing, he succeeded in making the structure of his toccata more transparent and lively than it had been improvised trumpet music. (*For comparison, see the example by Cesare Bendinelli, p. 72.*) Moreover, Monteverdi was the first to use other instruments – strings, two recorders and a large continuo band – in the Toccata. But in order

The Golden Age of the Natural Trumpet (1600–1750)

that the trumpets did not drown out the other instruments, Monteverdi requested that the trumpeters use mutes. The contemporary mute was made of wood and had the form of a goblet. A cylindrical hole passed through the mute's entire length. The mute was placed in the bell of the trumpet, thus

Trumpet mute from Marin Mersenne, Harmonie universelle, *Paris 1636/37*

shortening it and requiring a transposition of around a half or a whole step, depending on the gradation of shortening. Although Monteverdi used trumpets together with the other instruments in his opera *L'Orfeo*, the trumpets were used only in the toccata, a piece that traditionally sounded *before* the beginning of a dramatic work. Therefore there can be no discussion of the use of trumpets *in* Monteverdi's opera – a step he did not take.

Girolamo Fantini

Girolamo Fantini (1600–*c* 1675) was employed as a trumpeter at the court of the Grand Duke of Tuscany, Ferdinando II, from April 1631. The eight sonatas for trumpet and organ as well as numerous dance settings for trumpet and basso continuo which appear in his trumpet method *Modo per imparare a sonare di*

The Golden Age of the Natural Trumpet (1600–1750)

Girolamo Fantini
(Photo: Universitätsbibliothek, Basel)

Tromba (1638) are the first known examples of Italian art music with trumpet.

His tutor is similar in structure to Bendinelli's from 1614. After introductory exercises in the low register, both Bendinelli and Fantini present the customary military calls. At this point in the Fantini tutor, the dance settings and sonatas for trumpet and continuo follow.

Together with Girolamo Frescobaldi, the organist of St Peter's Basilica in Rome, Fantini took part in an historic performance for the Roman Cardinal Borghese around 1635. French trumpeters who heard this concert, probably the first in modern times for

trumpet and organ, reported that Fantini played not only the overtones but also the tones which lie between, which sounded

The Golden Age of the Natural Trumpet (1600–1750)

Four ship's trumpeters
from an engraving of Bengt Oxenstierna's palace, Lindholmen,
by Johannes van den Aveleen (1702).
Author's Collection
(Photo: Universitätsbibliothek, Basel)

'spurious' and 'inordinate'. One should not take their criticism too seriously, because, as we shall see, the trumpet in France remained limited to its traditional heroic role for a long time. The fact of the matter is that Fantini was a master of the technique of lipping. Many of his sonatas contain pitches outside the overtone series.

Moreover the tone a' (lipped downward from b-flat') occurs frequently.

The Trumpet in the Venetian Opera

In the Venetian opera it was popular for other instruments to imitate the trumpet in battle scenes and similar circumstances. The hunting call in G in Francesco Cavalli's opera *Le Nozze di Teti* (1639), hitherto regarded as trumpet music, is the earliest example of such imitation. In other operas by Cavalli (1602–76) such as *La Rosinda* (1651) and *L'Elena* (1660), he again recalled the sound of the trumpet without using the instrument itself. Apparently, only around 1670 were one or two trumpeters employed in the opera houses. The first opera in which two trumpets were explicitly required was *L'Adelaide* (1672) by Antonio Sartorio (1630–80). Here they played in the Sinfonia at the beginning of the opera. The function of this piece was probably identical with the toccata, namely to bring order to a noisy theatre. The repeated D-major chords (two whole notes) at the beginning of Sartorio's Sinfonia to *L'Adelaide* filled this function admirably.

The Golden Age of the Natural Trumpet (1600–1750)

Before long the trumpet aria also became popular. The majority stem from Sartorio, but other composers of the day, such as Pallavicino and Legrenzi, wrote trumpet arias in which the trumpet and voice alternated competitively one with the other. It often happened that the goddess Fama (Fame), whose attribute, not by chance, was the trumpet, sang a trumpet aria on stage. Even in the early Classical era Baldassare Galuppi (1706–85) wrote such a trumpet aria, 'Alla Tromba della Fama'.

The Trumpet in the Dramatic Music of Rome and Naples
The grand age of the trumpet aria in the Venetian opera occurred from *c* 1670 to *c* 1685. Around that time, the trumpet entered the opera and other dramatic productions throughout Italy. The last work of Alessandro Stradella (*c* 1644–82), *Il Barcheggio* (1681), contains two of the most beautiful sinfonias for trumpet, strings and basso continuo; the instrumental accompaniment of this serenata was performed by a cornetto (or trumpet, perhaps alternately), violin(s), and 'many trombones' (according to a note in the score). *Il Barcheggio* was performed in Genoa, although Stradella originally came from Rome. There the trumpet was played in the entertainments of Cardinal Pietro Ottoboni. Arcangelo Corelli (1653–1713) composed a trumpet sonata; Alessandro Melani (*c* 1630–1703) some solo cantatas with trumpet; Alessandro Scarlatti (1660–1725) a famous cantata, *Su le sponde del Tebro*, whose first aria, *Contentatevi*, demands a very good trumpeter, especially if – as notated in the original – two stanzas are performed. In Rome we read of episcopal trumpeters, and also of trumpeters associated with different embassies. The Pope himself also had a trumpet corps. Finally, in Naples, where he composed the majority of his operas, A. Scarlatti wrote many operas with highly virtuosic trumpet arias.

The Golden Age of the Natural Trumpet (1600–1750)

In addition to the goddess Fame, the trumpet symbolized war in Italian opera. The two strongest themes of contemporary librettos were 'Guerra' and 'Amore'. Therefore most arias in which the trumpet participates have texts like 'All'armi', etc. The normal range of the trumpet in such arias and sinfonias was c' to a'', i.e. from the fourth to the thirteenth partial. But occasionally composers like M.A. Ziani (1635–1715, *La Flora*), Corelli (trumpet sonata) and A. Scarlatti (*Su le sponde del Tebro*) require the sixteenth partial or high c'''. Actually this sounded a d''', because the instrument pitched in D was by far the most common.

The Trumpet in Bologna
The construction of the grand Basilica of San Petronio was begun in 1390, and the church was intended to become the largest in all Christendom. In the 1660s the proud residents of the city finally acknowledged that the original project could never be realized. The church as it now stands is nevertheless enormous. The nave, which was to have become the transept, is 132m long and 44m high; with the aisles the basilica is 60m wide. In this church under three chapelmasters – Maurizio Cazzati, 1657–71, Giovanni Paolo Colonna, 1674–95 and Giacomo Antonio Perti, 1696–1756 – more sonatas, sinfonias and concertos for trumpets were performed than at any other place except perhaps Kremsier. They were performed chiefly on 4 October, the Feast of St Petronius.

The number of performers at these festive services swelled after Cazzati's arrival in 1657 through the engagement of extra musicians, among them one to four trumpeters, so the number of performers corresponded to the vastness of the basilica. Our own practical experience gained in concerts on historical instruments in S. Petronio in 1984 and 1986 leads us to believe that composers introduced the trumpet for acoustical reasons beside the obvious symbolic ones: in the vast church it is the only instrument whose sound carries clearly. In 1663 under Cazzati, 28 regular and 58 extra musicians (altogether 86 singers and instrumentalists) are documented; under Colonna in 1687 there were 106 and in 1694, 105. On these three grand occasions the orchestra, without the singers, had a strength of 18, 31 and 40 members. The chief musical event was a concert mass in which trumpets frequently played, yet a prelude in the form of a trumpet sonata often preceded it.

In 1665 Cazzati published the first three sonatas for trumpets, strings and basso continuo. They are for C trumpet, although the first sonata, *La Caprara*, sounds in D because of the use of the mute, described above. The mottoes of this and one other sonata, *La Bianchina*, with their strong fanfare motifs, recall the opera toccata and show that the trumpet sonata in church music had the same function as the toccata in the opera. At the end of the trumpet parts to a later work by G. A. Vincenzo Aldrovandini (c 1673–1707), the *Sonata a sei – due Trombe* (I Bsp No. D. 11. 14), the theme of a Kyrie appears, from which it follows that this trumpet sonata introduced a mass (now unknown).

Trumpeters are documented here only since 1676. From 1679 until 1699 the trumpeter who was especially engaged for these festive occasions was Giovanni Pellegrino Brandi. Between 1704 and 1707 an anonymous trumpeter of the archbishop played together with a certain Angellino (the first time in 1703, the second 1704/05) and one Sellaro or Selloro (1706/07).

Cazzati's three sonatas required only a moderate high register, to the thirteenth partial, which was already known through Bendinelli and Monteverdi. But the next works, Petronio Franceschini's *Suonata a 7 con due Trombe* (1680) and four published sonatas by the 15-year-old Giovanni Bononcini, who

The Golden Age of the Natural Trumpet (1600–1750)

was to become a rival of Handel's in London, ascend to the sixteenth partial for the clear-sounding D trumpet. From this point on, D was the principal pitch of the trumpet not only in Bologna but throughout Italy.

The most important composer for trumpet at San Petronio was Giuseppe Torelli (1658–1709). In the past he was best known for his *concerti grossi* and other string music, but he was also the most productive Italian composer for the trumpet. He wrote at least 36 works for one, two, and four trumpets in two creative periods: 1686–95 when he was employed as a violist, and then later (after a pause when the church orchestra was temporarily dissolved) from 1701 until his death when he was employed as a violinist and concertmaster. Between 1695 and 1701 he stayed in Vienna and Ansbach where he became acquainted with the oboe as a solo instrument. From 1702 this instrument was also found frequently in the San Petronio ensemble.

In his early period Torelli wrote two especially virtuosic trumpet sonatas, Numbers 7 and 1 in the thematic catalogue compiled by Franz Giegling. Both of these works as well as some trumpet sonatas by the cellist Domenico Gabrielli (1659–90, not related to the Gabrieli family in Venice) ascend to the sixteenth partial and require the soloist – certainly Brandi – to be flexible and agile. The other trumpet works by Torelli and the remaining composers at San Petronio employ the trumpet less for its virtuosity than for its sound. In these pieces, the trumpet as a rule reached only the thirteenth partial and placed its clear sound at the service of the whole. Thus the trumpet is often not 'soloistic' in our modern sense of the word. Nevertheless the trumpet sonata remained a musical symbol of Bologna far into the eighteenth century. The famous music theorist and fatherly friend of Mozart, Padre G.B. Martini (1706–84), composed the last Bolognese trumpet sonatas and sinfonias, which were still played in the 1780s.

The Golden Age of the Natural Trumpet (1600–1750)

Interior of a French workshop for brass instruments
From Denis Diderot and Jean Le Rond d'Alembert, Encyclopédie ou Dictionnaire raisonné des Sciences, des Arts et des Métiers, *Paris 1751–80*
Fig. 1: A piece of sheet metal is placed on a long, round mandrel attached to the wall. The worker gives the hunting horn its first shape with the hammer.
a, b: The mandrel partly covered with the sheet metal.
Fig. 2: This worker fuses the separate parts together, from which according to need, a hunting horn, a trumpet, or another similar brass instrument will develop.
a, b, c, d: The forge e: the bellows
Fig. 3: Now the worker pours molten lead in the horn, allowing it to be bent; without it the bore loses its roundness.
f, g: The melting oven for the lead. h: the crucible
Fig. 4: The worker bends the lead-filled horn. When it has taken the final shape, the horn is heated one more time in order to remove the lead

France

French Instrument Makers

In 1599 the instrument makers in Paris came together to form an association. However, until the time of the French Revolution, all we know of many French brass instrument makers is their names, not their work, with the exception of a trombone by Colbert in Reims (1593) and hunting horns by Joseph Raoux (from *c* 1759) and Carlin (d. 1780), both in Paris.

The Golden Age of the Natural Trumpet (1600–1750)

The French Court Trumpeters
Under Louis XIV there were 12 military trumpeters divided into four *trompettes ordinaires ou de la chambre* and eight *trompettes non servants*. They performed their duty in groups of three or six members. In addition, there were 24 trumpeters of the royal bodyguard (*de la garde du corps*) from which four elite trumpeters, *des plaisirs du Roi*, were recruited. Because all of these trumpeters were subordinate to the King personally, they received their orders from him and not from superior officers. They themselves had a kind of independent officer's rank and were styled *chevalier*. In France during the Age of Absolutism the trumpeters symbolized only the 'Sun King'. The queen had only one trumpeter, if any at all. Even the brother of the king needed to ask for special permission to employ on occasion two or three trumpeters for his personal needs.

French Music for Trumpet Ensemble
In view of the strict hierarchical organization of the court trumpeters at Versailles, it is not surprising that it was in French trumpet music that the heroic *Affekt* was perhaps most perfectly preserved. The trumpeters from Lully to Rameau were less individual soloists than symbols of unbounded kingly might.

Surviving French trumpet music is generally in three or four parts, apparently depending on whether it was for the military trumpeters or the four *trompettes des plaisirs*. One of the Philidor manuscripts (F Pc Rés. 921) – André Danican-Philidor was the king's librarian – contains short movements for the three-part military ensemble. Much of the known music, however, seems to be four-part, real or implied.

The title of French trumpet pieces often tells much about their use. For example, there is a suite by Jean-Baptiste Lully (1632–87) entitled *Les Airs de Trompettes, timballes et hautbois faits par*

The Golden Age of the Natural Trumpet (1600–1750)

M. de Lully par l'ordre du Roy pour le Carousel de Monseigneur l'an 1686. Thus it is an equestrian ballet for four-part trumpet ensemble, kettledrums and four-part oboe ensemble. The music theorist Claude-François Menestrier (1631–1705), in his *Des ballets anciens et modernes* (1682), accounted for the use of trumpeters in equestrian ballet as follows:

> Trumpets are the most suitable instruments to make the horses dance, because [the horses] have time to take breath whenever the trumpeters breathe. No other instrument is so pleasing to them, because it is war-like, and because the horse, born grand, loves this sound, which urges it on.

Lully's carousel music is the only complete French music of this kind preserved. Normally the composers were content with writing, besides the oboe and string parts, only the first trumpet and the kettledrum parts. But on the basis of Lully's suite it is easy to complete the instrumentation of such compositions. One of the most festive works with this instrumentation is the *Concert de trompettes pour les festes sur le Canal de Versailles* by Michel Richard de Lalande (1657–1726). And today the Prelude to the *Te Deum* by Marc-Antoine Charpentier (1634–1704) is a very popular fanfare throughout Europe. It is however played on television for 'Eurovision' broadcasts with the incorrect instrumentation of a trumpet, a trombone in place of the fourth trumpet, kettledrums, and strings – the second and third trumpet parts are missing. On American television a theme from a suite by Jean-Joseph Mouret (1682–1738) serves a similar purpose: it heralds the broadcast of 'Masterpiece Theatre' and in its instrumentation is just as incomplete as Charpentier's 'Eurovision' theme.

A *Piece à double trompette et de different ton* in the above-mentioned Philidor manuscript presents us with a continuing

The Golden Age of the Natural Trumpet (1600–1750)

mystery. The trumpet melody proceeds in two seven-measure phrases; the first half is for a trumpet in C, the second half for a trumpet a fourth lower in G. A 'double trumpet'? Such an instrument is mentioned nowhere else; we cite it here only to point out one of the many open questions awaiting an answer.

In another group of works, that is, in his opera choruses, Lully also wrote for a trumpet solo, or even a pair of unison trumpets, a practice which Jean-Philippe Rameau (1633–1764) was to take up later.

Great Britain

The British Trumpet Makers

The most famous English trumpet maker, William Bull, a trumpeter in the 'King's Musick', was active between 1676 and 1707. His card advertised that he manufactured not only trumpets, but also horns, 'speaking trumpets' [megaphones], and various bottles of silver and brass. Three D trumpets by him survive, one of brass with silver decoration, and two of silver, one of which still has a C crook. Simon Beale (fl. 1660–80) was another trumpeter in the 'King's Musick'; a trumpet by him of brass with silver decoration dated 1667 survives. Another trumpet maker, John Ashbury (fl. 1675–1700) was a piper in the 'King's Musick'. The earliest preserved English trumpet, from 1651, and another from 1666, were made by Augustine Dudley; both are of brass with silver decoration. A pair of instruments each by Bull's successor, John Harris (fl. 1700–20), as well as an anonymous Glasgow trumpet maker (1669) are also preserved. William Shaw was a famous manufacturer of the late eighteenth and early nineteenth centuries.

Like the trumpet and trombone makers of Nuremberg, the British trumpet makers manufactured their instruments out of

The Golden Age of the Natural Trumpet (1600–1750)

'bastard brass', i.e. of brass with added ingredients, especially lead. The bell form of the surviving British trumpets from the seventeenth century corresponds approximately to the middle-Baroque bell from Nuremberg. However, one essential difference between the Nuremberg and the British trumpets is that the first yard and the bell of the British trumpet were not joined with a wood block as on those from Nuremberg. The stupendous ball took care of the necessary fastening; it is sometimes so large that the first yard was led through it, thus stabilizing the trumpet.

A special instrument, the 'flatt trumpet', came into use around 1685. It was a slide trumpet, called 'flat' because it could be played not only in major but also in minor or flat keys. Godfrey Finger (c 1660–1730), a composer who came to England from Olomouc, is supposed to have taught the court trumpeters to play on these slide trumpets. They did not move the entire instrument in and out, as on the German *Zugtrompete*, but rather moved only the second bow. Henry Purcell (1659–95) composed a movement for four 'flatt' trumpets in the fifth act of a dramatic work, *The Libertine* (1692), and revised it as funeral music for Queen Mary II (d. 28 December 1694); shortly thereafter, this music was played at his own funeral.

The English Court Trumpeters
Before Charles II returned to London at the restoration of the monarchy (1660), he lived in exile in Versailles. After his return, he introduced several French institutions to his court. For example, he organized his musical establishment in ways similar to those he knew in France. In England, following the French model, there were the '24 Violins' and the 'Wind Musick'. The 'Wind Musick' consisted of seven fifers and drummers under a 'Drum major' and of 16 trumpeters and a kettledrummer under a 'Sergeant-trumpeter'. For festive performances the members of

The Golden Age of the Natural Trumpet (1600–1750)

the '24 Violins', the 'Wind Musick', and the 'Chapel Royal' (the singers) joined together.

In contrast to France, where the trumpeters accompanied only the King, the English trumpeters were divided into four different regiments of the Life Guards. The first was assigned to the King, the second to the Queen, the third to the King's brother, the Duke of York, and the fourth to the children of the royal family or royal guests. As a rule a member of the trumpet corps was first admitted for a probationary period without remuneration, becoming later a trumpeter 'in ordinary'. The mounted trumpeters accompanied the Life Guards in the city, on trips, and in battle; they accompanied diplomats to peace negotiations and played at coronations, customarily receiving new silver instruments for the occasion. Moreover, there was a lively public concert life in London from the end of the seventeenth century onwards, and trumpeters were also heard in this context. For example, in 1713 a certain Twiselton, a trumpeter of the Duke d'Aumont, appeared in a benefit concert in London. He played a trumpet sonata by Arcangelo Corelli, a work that Corelli must have composed for this trumpeter on a Roman sojourn of Twiselton's. But the court trumpeters on such occasions were not allowed to appear without permission of the Sergeant-trumpeter. At the time of the Shores (*see below*), the Sergeant-trumpeter received annually £160, a trumpeter in ordinary £90, a singer £63, and a common instrumentalist £40. Trips, coronations, etc. were remunerated over and above this fee.

The Sergeant-trumpeter at the time of the Restoration was Gervase Price. He was held in high esteem and received a gilded trumpet and a silver hunting horn from the King. When James II became king in 1685, Price was confirmed in his position; he died in 1687. His successor was Matthias Shore, who had been admitted into the trumpet corps in 1682. William Shore, who

The Golden Age of the Natural Trumpet (1600–1750)

was either his son or brother and had joined the corps in 1679, followed him as Sergeant-trumpeter from 1700–07. Matthias' son John (*c* 1662–1752), the most famous of all English trumpeters, entered the 'King's Musick' in 1687 as an instrument maker and in 1688 as a trumpeter, and became the next Sergeant-trumpeter between 1707 and 1752. He is also credited with the invention of the tuning fork. His successor was Valentine Snow (d. 1770), who had already played the leading trumpet parts in Handel's oratorios for many years.

The Trumpet in English Art Music

Undoubtedly we are indebted to the three Shores for the trumpet finding a place in English art music. Matthias was a close friend of Henry Purcell, who introduced the trumpet in English art music in 1687 in a birthday ode for James II, 'Sound the Trumpet, Beat the Drum'. Purcell is one of the most original and ingenious composers in music history – qualities he certainly brought to his writing for the trumpet. He employed his trumpets, pitched in C or D, often in pairs, integrating them completely in the structure of the music and treating both trumpets independently of one another. Before Purcell, trumpeters appeared in dramatic productions only in the trumpet corps to announce the comings and goings of important persons with a 'tucket' or toccata. With Purcell however, the trumpet embraced the same function as in the Italian opera and was similarly treated. Some of the sinfonias and arias with trumpet from Purcell's 'The Yorkshire Feast Song' (1689), *Dioclesian* (1690), *The Fairy Queen* (1692), *The Indian Queen* (1695), the 'Ode for St Cecilia's Day' from 1692 or from the 'Te Deum and Jubilate' (1694) are among the most majestic works in the entire trumpet literature.

John Shore, who retired in 1695 because of a lip paralysis but was able to play again in 1697, earned the highest praise from his

The Golden Age of the Natural Trumpet (1600–1750)

contemporaries. He was granted the distinction of having led the English trumpet from the military world to the sphere of art music. Hawkins reported that Shore

> by his great ingenuity and application had extended the power of that noble instrument, too little esteemed at this day, beyond the reach of imagination, for he produced from it a tone as sweet as that of a hautboy.

A German composer, Gottfried Keller (d. 1704), who was active at the English court under the name of Godfrey Keller, published three trumpet sonatas in 1699. In his dedication to an 'English Princess' (Princess Anne of Denmark, later Queen Anne, in whose service John Shore was registered in that year) he wrote that the

> Trumpet [is] an Instrument formerly practis'd in ye rough Consorts of ye Field but now instructed in gentler Notes, it has learnt to accompany ye softest Flutes and can join with the most charming Voices.

Further, Keller wrote that the trumpet 'first reached this perfection at your court', and that

> one of [your trumpeters] is allowed to be ye best Master in ye world.

Many composers wrote trumpet sonatas for the Shores, especially for John Shore. We might mention here a suite by Jeremiah Clarke (1673/74–1707), two sonatas by Henry Purcell, works which stem from larger compositions now lost, a sonata by James Paisible (c 1650–1721), four by Godfrey Finger (c 1660– after 1723), three by Daniel Purcell (c 1663–1717), the brother of Henry, one by John Eccles (1668–1735), one by John Barrett (c 1674–1735), and finally four sonatas in D, two sonatas

The Golden Age of the Natural Trumpet (1600–1750)

in the unusual pitch of E, and a Suite in D by William Corbett (c 1680–1748) from the year 1713. The range of all these works extends from the fourth or even the third to the thirteenth partial; Purcell, in his dramatic works and church music, occasionally writes the sixteenth partial. Also, the Shores could lip the partials downwards, as an occasional *b*-natural' or an opportune *e*-flat" in an important final cadence in Purcell's 'Ode for St Cecilia's Day' shows. As in the works of the Bolognese school, the trumpet in these compositions generally alternated with the accompanying strings; only in the final cadences did they sound together.

George Frideric Handel (1685–1759), like Bach on his arrival in Leipzig, met with an existing trumpet tradition on his arrival in London (1710). He had already composed for the trumpet in his early operas *Almira* (Hamburg, 1704) and *Agrippina* (Venice, 1708); altogether 22 of his 40 operas (1704–41) contain trumpet parts. And he further developed the trumpet aria, known to him from Venetian opera and the operas of Alessandro Scarlatti. One of the most virtuosic and extensive is Melissa's aria *Desterò dall'empia dite* from the second act of *Amadigi* (1715) for soprano, trumpet, oboe, strings and basso continuo. Also, in the choruses, one to four trumpets are richly employed. Handel continued this practice in 18 of his oratorios from 1720 until 1751, of which *Messiah* (1742) is the most famous and beloved. When the trumpeter Sarjant played the bass aria from *Messiah*, 'The Trumpet Shall Sound', in the context of the Handel Jubilee Concert of 1784, he was vehemently censured by Burney because of too high an eleventh partial, which he was unable to lip down low enough. Nevertheless, Handel's own trumpeters, the ageing John Shore and his successor Snow, must have possessed considerable ability and, above all, great stamina.

In general, Handel's trumpet parts do not lie as high as Bach's, although they can also ascend to the sixteenth partial. But it often

The Golden Age of the Natural Trumpet (1600–1750)

happens in Handel's parts that one must play very long stretches in the full tutti. Besides the bass aria from *Messiah*, the Overture to *Atalanta* (1736, written expressly for Snow), the *Dettingen Te Deum* (1743) and the 'Music for the Royal Fireworks' (1749) are among the most strenuous parts by Handel. The two last works are written in the traditional manner for two 'clarini' and a 'principale'. The Fireworks Music was originally composed for a military band of trumpets, kettledrums and oboes, to which were added the then fashionable horns. It is thus in the tradition of the great French 'open air' music of Lully and Lalande. The original performance turned out splendidly (although the fireworks themselves were a failure); each of the three trumpet and horn parts was given to three players – nine trumpeters and nine hornists altogether. Perhaps two played while one rested.

Some English composers in the Handel tradition composed trumpet concertos. The sonatas of Purcell's day were couched in the Italian style; the concertos of Handel's day had the form of a French overture with an appended minuet. The most important concertos were published by John Humphries (*c* 1707–before 1740) in 1740 (op. 2), a cleric, the Revd Richard Mudge (1718–63) in 1749 and by Capel Bond (1730–90) in 1760.

The time of both Purcell and Handel, roughly 1690 until around 1800, is characterized by a specific English musical piece: the trumpet voluntary. This was an organ piece in which the natural trumpet was imitated. The most splendid trumpet melodies are to be found in the trumpet voluntaries of Jeremiah Clarke, Purcell, Maurice Greene (1695–1775), William Boyce (1710–79), John Stanley (1713–86) and others. Probably many of these melodies were well-known military marches, such as Clarke's 'Prince of Denmark's March', which he also set in his Suite for trumpet, oboes, strings and continuo.

SEVEN

The Trumpet in an Era of Decline (1750–1815)

The period between 1750 and 1815 was a time of crisis for the trumpet. On the one hand the art of clarino playing was brought to its zenith, and the court trumpet corps offered its most magnificent music. On the other hand, however, the compositional style had changed owing to a new bourgeois idea of society. The trumpet represented the old courtly culture and expressed one-sidedly an old-fashioned heroic *Affekt*. In an article in F.W. Marpurg's *Historisch-kritische Beyträge zur Aufnahme der Musik* (Berlin, 1754), the famous flautist J.J. Quantz (1697–1773) admitted that he had been offered the opportunity to become a trumpeter, an offer which he nevertheless refused, because 'good taste' was 'not to be cultivated' on the trumpet.

Culmination of the Court Trumpet Ensemble
The *Charamela real* of Lisbon
The following commentary appears in J.E. Altenburg's *Versuch*:

> [The German trumpeters] are sought [after] and promoted even at the most remote ends of Europe.
> Thus in 1722, the then King of Portugal, Christian II, had twenty German trumpeters and two kettledrummers simultaneously accepted into his service ... paying their travelling fees and giving them gorgeous liveries and considerable pay. (pp. 39 & 42)

There was no King of Portugal with the name Christian II; at this time João V ruled. However, many trumpeters with German names are found among the Lisbon court trumpeters, so we are tempted to apply Altenburg's commentary to that monarch.

In Lisbon the court trumpet corps, the successor to the alta ensemble of the sixteenth century, bore the name *Charamela real*. The trumpet was called *Clarim* without regard to register; even a

The Trumpet in an Era of Decline (1750–1815)

'principale' was called Clarim.

The national coach museum in Lisbon (Museu Nacional dos Coches) houses a splendid collection, the finest in Europe. The musical part of the collection consists of music books and trumpets. The music books of the Charamela real, through a stroke of good fortune, survive in nearly their entirety, and demonstrate that this trumpet ensemble was an imitation of the 24 *trompettes de la garde du corps* with four kettledrummers at Versailles. Nowhere else, as in Lisbon, is the music for a 28-part trumpet and kettledrum ensemble preserved.

The musicians were divided into four choirs, each with six trumpeters and a kettledrummer. Each trumpet choir consisted of two pairs of trumpets in the clarino register, a principale (called 'Clarim 5') and a 'filling' part called *Ripianno*. Occasionally, the first trumpet had to perform very virtuosic phrases; the second trumpet pair was subordinate to the first. The Ripianno part likewise played in the clarino register and doubled the melody at important places in a simpler form. The contents of the 26 music books (two which are missing are easy to reconstruct) make up 54 untitled processional sonatas. The last sonata is for four choirs, ten are for two choirs, and the remainder is for one choir of trumpets and kettledrums. However, all the pieces are contained in all of the part books, so that each part of the one-choir pieces was performed by four musicians. The moderate clarino register of the highest part extends from the sixth to the thirteenth partial. Although they do not promote the high register, the 54 processional sonatas require of the first player some degree of virtuosity and – because of the scarcity of rests – good endurance.

We are again indebted to good fortune that nearly all the trumpets of the Charamelos survive. There are 22 richly ornamented instruments of silver, whose ornamental parts – garland, ball and ferrules – are gilded. Twenty are from 1761,

The Trumpet in an Era of Decline (1750–1815)

two date from 1785 and fall consequently during the reign of Joseph I and Maria I, respectively, whose names are imprinted on the garland. They were probably made in a local workshop. These trumpets are pitched in modern D, the contemporary E-flat. The silk banners belonging to some of the instruments also survive, showing two angel trumpeters holding between them the royal crest. Until only recently this collection of music and instruments had escaped the attention of trumpet researchers.

The unparallelled splendour of this royal music can hardly be expressed in words (but the four-choir sonata, No. 54, can be heard on a Swedish recording made in 1980 for the BIS label).

Other Court Trumpet Ensembles
Various processional pieces of the Munich, Viennese, and other court trumpet ensembles from the period around 1760 until around 1810 are preserved. Six anonymous *Aufzüge* from Munich for four *Tropanno* (really two clarini, principale, and timpani) fit exactly Altenburg's writing about such pieces. Among other things, 'a lively theme' is required at the beginning, 'which can also start possibly with the kettledrums or with the principale'; 'either the two clarini or the principale, or even the kettledrums, are accustomed to giving variety with a short solo'; and 'the kettledrum and principale [parts] must be so structured that these [instruments] do not always blare and thus drown out both clarino [parts]'. (p. 105)

Two *Aufzüge* by Johann Dessary disclose the wish for greater possibilities of modulation, because in addition to the clarino I/II in C, principale in C, and kettledrums in C and G, two other trumpet parts in G and D are present. Also, a Divertimento by Josef Starzer (1726–87) for the unusual combination of two *Schallemay* (*chalumeaux*, an early type of clarinet), five trumpets and two pairs of kettledrums presents the possibility of touching

The Trumpet in an Era of Decline (1750–1815)

more keys than just C and G by using on the one hand the keys available to the chalumeaux, and on the other the keys of the trumpets and kettledrums. Here three trumpets are pitched in C, two in D, and the kettledrums in C, G, D and A. This piece must have been an instrumentation exercise for the young Wolfgang Amadeus Mozart (1756–91), because he copied the Starzer work, exchanging the chalumeaux for two flutes, and added some movements which he had selected from Christoph Willibald Gluck's (1714–87) opera *Paris und Helena* (1769), and reorchestrated them for these instruments. The piece bears the number KV 187 in the Köchel Catalogue of Mozart's works; another Divertimento (KV 188) with similar instrumentation appears to have originated entirely with Mozart. Starzer often took the first C-trumpet part and once the first D-trumpet part to the sixteenth partial. Mozart, who was not particularly fond of the trumpet, did not go this high in KV 188 as often as did Starzer.

Various *Aufzüge* of the Vienna trumpet corps show a similar solution to the problem of modulation through the inclusion of either two clarinets or other trumpets in strange keys. From these beginnings on the one hand and from the field music of military woodwinds on the other, developed the military music of the nineteenth century.

The High Point of Clarino Playing

Clarino playing reached its high point between 1740 and 1770, especially in Germany and Austria. One can divide the trumpet concertos of this time into three groups according to the treatment of the high register. In the first group the trumpet ascends, as in the works of J.S. Bach, to the sixteenth or eighteenth partial. The most important concertos of this group are by the following composers: Johann Friedrich Fasch (1688–

The Trumpet in an Era of Decline (1750–1815)

1758) and Georg Philipp Telemann (1681–1767) (for the Darmstadt court trumpeter and composer Adolf Friedrich Schneider), Johann Melchior Molter (c 1695–1765, three concertos for the Karlsruhe court trumpeter Carl Pfeiffer), Leopold Mozart (1719–87, a concerto from 1762, probably for the Salzburg Court trumpeter Johann Andreas Schachtner), Johann Wilhelm Hertel (1727–89, five concertos for the Schwerin Court trumpeter Johann Georg Hoese from Leipzig), and Johann Matthias Sperger (1750–1812, two concertos, dated Vienna 1778 and 1779). All are in D with the exception of three of the concertos by Hertel, which are in E-flat.

The trumpet part of Carl Friedrich Christian Fasch's (1736–1800) triple concerto for the unusual ensemble of trumpet, oboe d'amore, and violin (with strings and continuo) is in E. This Fasch, the son of Johann Friedrich and a pupil of Hertel, was a co-founder of the Berlin *Singakademie*. Two works by the Darmstadt chapel master Johann Samuel Endler (d. 1762), one a Suite for *Clarino piccolo*, two horns, strings and continuo, deserve attention because they require a high F trumpet. With the exception of the second Brandenburg Concerto by J.S. Bach and a work by Telemann (1721), the use of a natural trumpet in F was hitherto unknown.

A second group of concertos in which the trumpet ascends even higher was probably composed especially for the court in Fulda. In these works by Franz Xaver Richter (1709–89), Joseph Riepel (1709–82), and Gros, the line is not drawn at high c''' or d''', but frequently requires even e''' or f''', the twenty-second partial on the D trumpet. (A recently discovered work of this type by the famous composer of the Mannheim school, Johann Stamitz (1717–57), belongs to this group.)

However, the highest notes are found in the music of Austrian composers. The second trumpet concerto in C major by Johann

The Trumpet in an Era of Decline (1750–1815)

Michael Haydn (1737–1806), the brother of Franz Joseph Haydn, is the most virtuosic work that we know. Frequently the trumpet ascends to the twentieth and once to the twenty-second partial through daring leaps. The first trumpet concerto by Georg von Reutter, the younger (1708–72) requires the twenty-fourth partial, a concert g''', many times. The 'world record height', a concert a''', the twenty-fourth partial on the D trumpet, was reached once in the first movement of Michael Haydn's first trumpet concerto in D major.

The trumpeters who played these extremely strenuous pieces came after the famous Johann Heinisch, who was discussed above. His successor in Vienna was Ernst Bayer. Caspar Köstler, a court trumpeter in Salzburg, was a student 'of the very famous late Hrn. Heinisch' – 'he gave the trumpet a refined, very pleasing, singing tone; had a good kind of delivery, and one listens to his concertos and solos with much delight'.

Another Salzburg court trumpeter, writer, and friend of the Mozart family was the already mentioned J.A. Schachtner, a student of Köstler; he 'was quite an elegant player and one with good taste'. However, we must rank above these performers another Salzburg court trumpeter, J.B. Resenberger, famous for his mastery of the extreme high register. Leopold Mozart, from whom the commentary on the other Salzburg trumpeters originates, wrote in 1757 about Resenberger (whose name the publisher mistakenly gave as Gesenberger):

> [He] is an excellent trumpeter who has made himself very famous, especially in the high [register], through the extraordinary purity [of his sound], through his quickness in runs, and through his good trills.

In the works mentioned above and in others, the gentle side of the Baroque trumpet reached its highest state of development.

The Trumpet in an Era of Decline (1750–1815)

However, the ultra-high notes above the high c''' led nowhere. The further development of the trumpet took place not in the fourth, let alone the fifth, octave of the overtone series, but rather in the third and lower half of the fourth.

The Classical Style

At the same time as these works requiring a highly developed clarino technique, the composers of the so-called Classical style, Joseph Haydn (1732–1809), W.A. Mozart and Ludwig van Beethoven (1770–1827), wrote a new kind of music in which the trumpet had a completely different function. The new style made a tutti instrument of the once heroic trumpet, which formerly had led the melody. Sometimes a short fanfare which closed an allegro movement or a symphony called attention to the trumpeters' surviving court function. But heroic expression was not enough. The adaptable strings could better render the new range of expression, because in a musical work not one but several forms of emotion were now required.

The trumpet continued to play its heroic role, but only in climaxes. In order to adapt itself to the new multiplicity of keys, trumpeters employed instruments in F or sometimes G down to B-flat and A. The clarino register was reduced in Classical works to the twelfth partial (g''). The thirteenth partial, the a'' – except for some youthful symphonies by Franz Schubert (1797–1828) – was required only once: in Haydn's Symphony No. 101 (III, m. 76). With the exception of Schubert's first symphony, which occupies a special place, the high c''' occurred only twice in the symphonies of the Classical era, once in Haydn and once in Mozart. The eleventh partial, which the trumpeters of the Baroque era until Sarjant (1784) had had under control, was now problematic; it occurred with some frequency only in Haydn

Trumpete I–II in D

and Schubert. Beethoven preferred to write a rest in its place.

It would be false to claim that the loss of the clarino technique came about overnight or that the trumpeters of the Classical era were no longer able to play in the highest register. We saw above that Sperger composed concertos as late as 1778 and 1779 for the high trumpet. This fact confirms that trumpeters could still play in the high register. A trumpet method by Joseph Fröhlich from the late year of 1829 made this still clearer: he wrote of trumpeters of his day who without much difficulty played up to the twentieth and even to the twenty-fourth partial.

The loss of the high clarino register can be traced back to two other causes: one was the decline of the courtly order by which the too explicit heroic affect was perceived as old fashioned, and the other was the corresponding change in musical style.

One *Servizio di tavola* of Reutter, perhaps originally composed for Heinisch and performed in the years 1757, 1758 and 1759, shows the musical isolation of the high trumpeter. In all movements except one, both trumpeters play in the tutti-reinforcing style characteristic of the Classical period. But in the slow movement, which forms the exception, the first trumpeter performs an expressive *cantilena* ascending up to the twenty-second partial, a concert *f′′′′*.

The wide leaps in the second part were characteristic of the tutti-reinforcing trumpet parts of the Classical era, expecially in Beethoven. At places like the one illustrated (Beethoven's Seventh Symphony, Mvt 1), the overtone series admits no other possibilities.

Richard Wagner (1813–83), who wanted these and similar passages improved through the valve technique available in his day, proposed that the second trumpeter should play the *d′′* an octave lower. Hans von Bülow in this way 'corrected' a similar place in Beethoven's Eroica (Mvt. 1, mm. 655–663). But Felix

The Trumpet in an Era of Decline (1750–1815)

Weingartner showed more sensitivity. Indeed he admitted that Beethoven's works 'were written at a time prior to the reform of brass instruments through the introduction of valves, which has been in many respects beneficial'. And he felt in Beethoven's 'manner of writing an anticipatory longing for this reform'. Yet he did not always agree with 'corrections' of Beethoven's instrumentation through the new use of valves. For him, 'it is just these intervals which are often so characteristic; and just as a great master can often turn to advantage the very imperfection of the means at his disposal, so here this striking use of natural notes often corresponds exactly to the peculiarities of Beethoven's style'. The attempt at improvement, following Weingartner's view, 'would only have the opposite effect'.[2]

The Search for Chromaticism

Not only Beethoven, but composers and musicians in general felt the 'longing for reform' towards the end of the Baroque Era. Players and instrument makers in particular sought various ways to make the trumpet chromatic. This pertained not so much to the high notes of the clarino range, but rather to the third octave of the overtone series. Attempts were made to fill the gaps between the tones of this 'fanfare octave' by various means and chromatic mechanisms. These experiments with the stopped trumpet, the keyed trumpet, and the English slide trumpet led to the invention of the valve mechanism around 1815, and therewith to modern playing technique.

The fate of the city of Nuremberg, a centre of brass-instrument making, was closely bound to that of the baroque trumpet. While the Nuremberg masters continued making the old natural trumpet, in other cities new names sprang up. In Vienna there were the instrument building families Leichambschneider and

The Trumpet in an Era of Decline (1750–1815)

Kerner. Michael Saurle in Munich, Ignaz Lorenz in Linz, Haltenhof in Hanau, Köhler in London, and Halary in Paris all came forward with new kinds of instruments. Johann Leonhard Ehe III, from whom many splendid instruments are preserved, died in Nuremberg in 1771 in deepest poverty. No instruments made by the last Haas, Johann Adam, are known to have survived; he died of consumption in 1817 at the age of 47. In the nineteenth century only two instrument makers in Nuremberg acquired the title of Master.

The Stopped Trumpet (*c* 1775–*c* 1840)
Around 1750, a Dresden hornist, Anton Joseph Hampel, came upon the idea of 'stopping'. By the introduction of the hand into the bell, he could lower the pitch of the instrument a half or a whole tone. Michael Wöggel, court trumpeter in Karlsruhe, transferred this successful horn technique to the trumpet, *c* 1777, when he, in collaboration with the Augsburg instrument maker Johann Andreas Stein, bent the trumpet so that he could reach the bell with the hand. Stopped trumpets were commonly manufactured in the twice wound shape in either the old form or in a bent half-moon shape. The stopping was performed by the three fingers of the right hand.

The *Inventionstrompete* was a special kind of stopped trumpet. As with many of the then current novelties of the trumpet, the designation 'invention' originated first for the horn. J. Werner (Dresden) built the first *Inventionshorn* for Hampel in 1753. Although Weidinger's keyed trumpet was likewise called an Inventionstrompete (*see further below*), modern terminology holds that an Inventionstrompete is first equipped with several inserted tuning crooks, and second has a tuning slide. Commonly the tuning crooks of the Inventionstrompete are made in 'U'-form, and are inserted not at the mouthpiece end but in the

The Trumpet in an Era of Decline (1750–1815)

middle of the instrument where they serve as a tuning slide at the same time. Wöggel's stopped trumpet is said to have been an Inventionstrompete. Improved Inventionstrompeten were manufactured in the 1790s by A.F. Krause (Berlin).

The advocates of 'stopping' intended – though their hopes were unrealized – that the characteristic sound of the trumpet would be in no way lost through the stopping. In 1829 the Königlich Preussicher Kammermusikus, Karl Bagans, published an essay on the stopped trumpet. He wanted parts of the musical pieces, like those illustrated below, performed with ease.

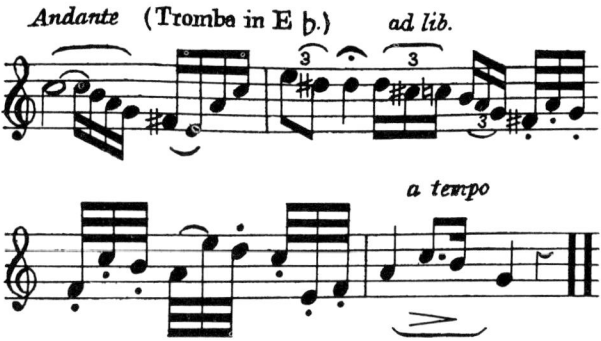

According to his remarks, the stopped halftones were easy to produce, yet he was forced to admit that the whole tones were 'purely and quickly tuned only with great difficulty'.

In France, David Buhl (1781– after 1829) was the leading trumpeter who played according to this method. His and many other French trumpet methods of that time mention two kinds of trumpets: the *trompette d'ordonnance* or cavalry trumpet in E-flat, on which the player did not use the stopping technique, and the *trompette d'harmonie* or orchestral trumpet in G, which was crooked down to lower keys and on which the player produced the lowered half steps through stopping.

The Trumpet in an Era of Decline (1750–1815)

In Beethoven and Schubert occasionally an *e*-flat" appears that was likely to have been produced with the help of this technique. According to the well-known instrumentation tutor by Berlioz, in the *Grand traité d'instrumentation et d'orchestration modernes* (1843), this tone could not enter freely and was used only with strong dynamics. In 1835 the music theorist Gottfried Weber was still more deprecatory. According to him, stopping 'on the trumpet . . . [was] absolutely not worth talking about'.

The Keyed Trumpet (*c* 1775–*c* 1840)
The earliest experiments to raise the fundamental of a brass instrument through the opening of one or more keys stretch back to the 1760s. Again experiments were made first with the horn. In November 1766, after several years of testing, Ferdinand Kölbel and his son-in-law demonstrated two keyed horns called *Amor-Schall* for Tsarina Katharina II in St Petersburg. C.F.D. Schubart wrote about the first trumpet with keys. This instrument, probably invented before 1777 by a Dresden trumpeter, was rejected because the characteristic trumpet sound 'disappeared nearly completely'; according to Schubart, the instrument had a sound that lay between the trumpet and the oboe. Wöggel, the previously-mentioned inventor of the stopped trumpet, was familiar with keyed trumpets and rejected them on similar grounds.

Other isolated attempts were undertaken by the Weimar Court trumpeter Schwanitz, whose one-hole trumpet with 'a small, leather slider' J.E. Altenburg had seen; around 1780–85 by a Thuringian named Ernst Kellner in Holland; and finally, around 1793 in Hamburg by an amateur trumpeter named Nessmann. Nessmann, in some way, concealed three keys under the coding of his trumpet, and in the same year produced all the half steps between c' and c'' 'pure and light, even in quick passages' for the

The Trumpet in an Era of Decline (1750–1815)

lexicographer Ernst Ludwig Gerber.

By far the most successful experimenter and at the same time the greatest virtuoso on the keyed trumpet was Anton Weidinger (1767–1852). He was also a friend of Joseph Haydn. In 1796 Haydn wrote his magnificent trumpet concerto in E-flat major for Weidinger and his keyed trumpet, a concerto which in our century stands at the heart of the solo trumpet repertory. For this concerto Weidinger's trumpet required at least three keys in order to raise the partials a half, whole, and a step and a half. Before 1800 Leopold Kozeluch and Joseph Weigl composed two other works for him.

In December 1802 Weidinger displayed his keyed trumpet with several works in Leipzig. A critic was carried away by the instrument:

> The instrument has yet its full, penetrating tone, but at the same time one so soft and tender, that one cannot render it softer on a clarinet.

At the same time Weidinger inspired through his musicality:

> The crescendo and decrescendo, the clear high register which cut to the quick, especially where Mr W[eidinger] kept more within the instrument's natural key are completely incomparable, and literally unprecedented.

A year later Johann Nepomuk Hummel (1778–1837), the new court composer at the Esterhazy palace, composed the other great concerto of the classical repertoire for Weidinger. This concerto in E major was originally performed there on New Year's Day 1804, as table music. Because of the key of this piece, we assume that Weidinger in the meantime had obtained a new, improved keyed trumpet, perhaps in a higher key, A-flat or G, with crooks, as indicated by most surviving examples in modern

The Trumpet in an Era of Decline (1750–1815)

museums. While the Haydn Concerto makes generous use of the clarino register ($c''-g''$), the low is cultivated in the Hummel Concerto; at least a fourth key is required.

Despite Weidinger's success and despite his enduring gains for the solo trumpet repertoire, his invention was not a total success. The keyed trumpet was used only for a while, until approximately 1840, in the military music of Austria and Italy. We hear of two Viennese keyed-trumpeters and especially of the Gambati brothers, who at the end of the 1820s played on keyed trumpets in Paris and London. (Alessandro Gambati later emigrated to New York.) But at that time valves (*see further below*) had already proved themselves the better system.

The English Slide Trumpet (*c* 1790–*c* 1885)
The origin of the nineteenth-century English slide trumpet is obscure. Actually it is none other than the English slide trumpet of Purcell's time with an additional return mechanism. According to a statement in John Hyde's *New and Compleat Preceptor for the Trumpet and Bugle Horn* (*c* 1799), the instrument was invented by Hyde and was built by an instrument maker named Woodham, deceased in 1795 or 1797. It is very likely that the unfortunate Sarjant, who at the 1784 Handel Jubilee Concert had experienced the famous difficulties with the eleventh partial and to whom Hyde alluded in his method, was responsible for this development. This is because in 1790/91 at Vauxhall Gardens, Sarjant played pieces by Handel which were unplayable on the natural trumpet, yet would lie well on a slide trumpet.

It is an unusual phenomenon that the slide trumpet persisted until nearly the end of the nineteenth century in England, while everywhere else valved trumpets had been in use for 40 years. The reason for its persistence is the strong personality of the greatest players of the slide trumpet in England, Thomas Harper,

The Trumpet in an Era of Decline (1750–1815)

Thomas Harper, junior (1816–98) with the slide trumpet
(Photo: R. Morley-Pegge)

father (1786–1853) and son (1816–98). The elder Harper was Hyde's successor in the most important London orchestras and English festivals, and was succeeded by his son, who only retired in 1885. The elder Harper firmly held on to his slide trumpet, improved it in 1833 with the London instrument maker Köhler, and wrote a famous trumpet method around 1835. His son kept up with the times more and wrote a cornet method. He appeared in concerts with both instruments, slide trumpet and cornet, playing difficult technical passages on the agile cornet. Towards the end of his career, however, the cornet seems to have gained the upper hand. Around 1875 in a new trumpet method, he stormed against the 'misappropriation of another instrument' (the cornet) 'for parts designated for the Trumpet'.

The Trumpet in an Era of Decline (1750–1815)

John Norton was another famous English slide trumpeter of the early nineteenth century. He played in 1823 next to the elder Harper and Hyde at the York Festival, and emigrated to Philadelphia in 1827. A few years later in New York, he pitted himself against the above-mentioned Alessandro Gambati in a 'trumpet battle', and won.

The slide trumpet was built in F. Crooks brought the pitch down to C or B-flat. The slide was used mostly for half and whole steps, and although the slide trumpet was not very agile, it was valued because of its noble, unadulterated sound. It was an orchestral rather than a solo instrument.

In France Adolphe Sax (1814–94) built a slide trumpet following the English principle, and in the thirties F.G.A. Dauverné (1800–74) – the teacher of Arban (*see below*) – devised an improvement of the Hyde model, by which the slide lay in front and underneath, and could be operated like a small trombone slide. But at this time in France the valved trumpet was also sufficiently known, and the slide trumpet had no justification for its existence.

Interestingly, in Germany in 1767 a mathematician named Hübsch, in a letter to J.E. Altenburg, proposed countering the imperfection of the natural trumpet through a slide. In his negative answer, Altenburg pointed out that the tower musicians had already used such an instrument for a long time, and that for the court trumpeters, who might welcome an improved instrument on which they could perform their difficult solo concertos, the slide trumpet is 'because of the burdensome pulling out and in certainly not practical'. Nevertheless Altenburg wished at the close of his letter 'that in respect to this heroic and musical instrument one could come to help Nature through artificial means if only a little'. The final help was the valve.

The Trumpet in an Era of Decline (1750–1815)

1   Natural trumpet in D (A=415) by Johann Leonhard Ehe II, Nuremberg (1663–1724)
Author's Collection

2   Fanfare trumpet in E-flat by Karl Hammerschmidt und Söhne, Watzkenroth (modern)
Basel, Historisches Museum, W. Bernoulli Collection

3   English slide trumpet in F by Köhler & Son, London (c 1850), 'T. Harper's Improved', 'R[oyal] I[talian] O[pera]'
Author's Collection

4   Keyed trumpet in G-flat by Alois Doke, Linz (c 1820)
Basel, Historisches Museum, W. Bernoulli Collection

5   Inventionstrompete in E-flat by I.G. Roth sen., Adorf (1826)
Basel, Historisches Museum, W. Bernoulli Collection

6   Valved trumpet in G by Antoine Courtois, Paris (c 1865), with piston valves
Trompetenmuseum Bad Säckingen

7   Valved trumpet in G by C.A. Müller, Mainz (c 1850), with Vienna valves and Mainz return mechanism
Trompetenmuseum Bad Säckingen

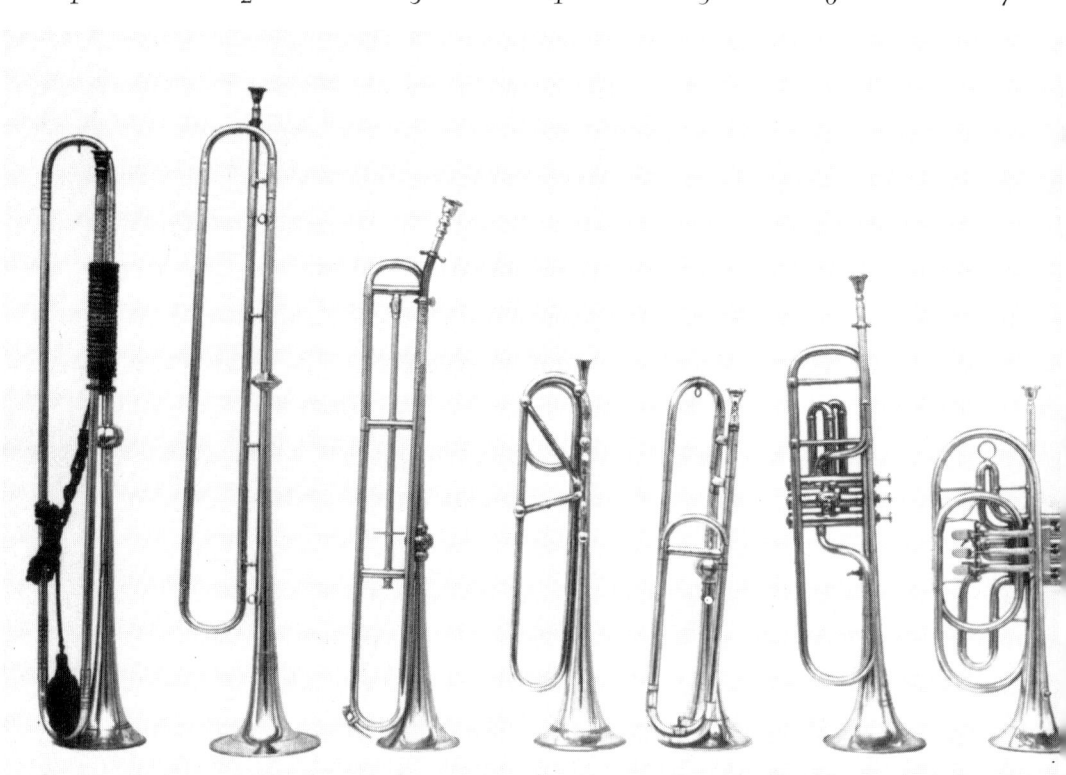

1   2   3   4   5   6   7

The Trumpet in an Era of Decline (1750–1815)

8   Cornet in B-flat by Laberte Humbert, Paris, an otherwise unknown instrument maker (c 1850), with tubular valves
Trompetenmuseum Bad Säckingen

9   Cornet in B-flat by Antoine Courtois, Paris serial number 1804 (c 1865), sold through S. Arthur Chappell, London, 'Koenig's Model', with piston valves
Author's Collection

10   Trumpet in B-flat with echo valve by C. Schäfer, Hannover (1903), with rotary valves and the inscription: 'Die Eltern ihrem lieben Gustav Bernhardt zur Weihnacht 1903'
Author's Collection

11   Trumpet in B-flat by Arno Windisch, Dresden (1974), with rotary valves
Author's Collection

12   Trumpet in B-flat by Vincent Bach Corporation, Elkhart, Indiana (USA), serial number 99770 (1976), with piston valves
Pforzheim, S. Schärr Collection

13   Trumpet in C with an ascending fourth valve for D tuning by Jerome Thibouville-Lamy, Paris, serial number 137896 (1921), with piston valves
Author's Collection

14   Piccolo B-flat trumpet by Henri Selmer, Paris, serial number 55323 (1970), with four piston valves
Trumpetenmuseum Bad Sackingen

8   9   10   11   12   13   14

EIGHT

The Modern Epoch of the Trumpet: From 1815 to Today

The Invention of the Valve
The Significance of this Invention

History can be written on two levels. On the one plane there are the almost daily events to record, which in a causative context are correlated with one another or else directed by chance. All in all these are small events, which nevertheless are conditioned by large, decisive, epochal factors which occur only rarely. On the second, higher plane of the history of the trumpet, there was a major landmark as early as c 1600: the entry of the trumpet into art music. This event had been prepared over a century through the cultivation of the clarino register.

The invention of the valve around 1815 had the same broad significance for the trumpet. This event also matured slowly, as it was an answer to an increasingly strong need for chromatics in the low register dating back to 1750. Through the valve, trumpet playing experienced a fundamental change.

The valve system incorporated the advantages of the previous systems of chromaticizing without the disadvantages. The disadvantages of the stopped trumpet was the unequal tone colour between the open and stopped notes. The keyed trumpet showed the same disadvantage, if to a lesser degree. In this context it must be said that the ideal sound of the Classical era still was not, as today, one of absolute homogeneity. The keyed trumpet in the concertos of Haydn and Hummel corresponded to this aesthetic of sound in precisely the same way as did the contemporary, still not fully mechanized, woodwind instruments. This sound ideal changed gradually, as may be deduced from Weidinger's career. At the beginning he was greatly celebrated, but later, somewhere from 1825 on, he played before half empty rooms; not until then did one note the inequality of the tone colour with open and closed keys. The slide trumpet did not show the supposed sound deficiency of the stopped and the keyed

The Modern Epoch of the Trumpet: From 1815 to Today

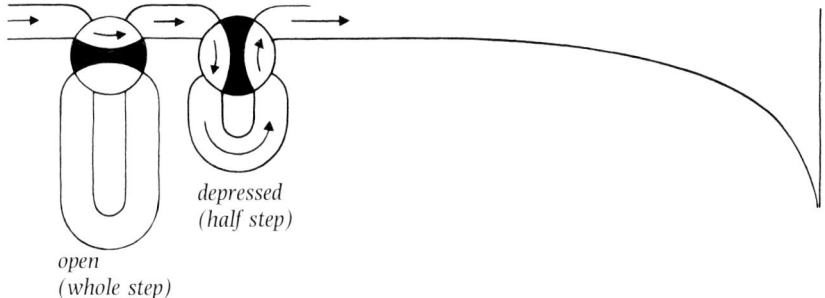

open
(whole step)

depressed
(half step)

trumpet, yet the slide mechanism was cumbersome.

With the valved trumpet the three disadvantages of the other systems were removed. First, the instrument was fully chromatic, without the gaps of the stopped trumpet. Second, its tone was homogeneous, except perhaps in the first valved trumpets. And third, the valved trumpet was agile.

The Principle of the Valve

While the tube length on the keyed trumpet was shortened, on the valved trumpet – as on the slide trumpet – it was lengthened. This was accomplished not through the physical process of pulling a slide, but rather through the mechanical process of positioning the valve. In this latter process there are in the main tubing one or more valves which either allow the air to flow unhindered through the main tubing, or divert it – like the points on a railway line – through short subsidiary tubing or valve slides, and then lead it back to the main tubing. According to the length of the valve slides the pitch is brought down a half, a whole, or a step and a half. All three valves can be operated singly or in various combinations. The accompanying drawing shows the principle of rotary valves with the valve mechanism open and closed.

The F or G Trumpet of the Nineteenth Century

Like the contemporary natural trumpet, the valved trumpet was first built in G, later in F. Crooks brought it down to E, E flat, D, C, B, and B flat, and sometimes to A. To the inherited trumpet technique – tonguing, slurs, and accuracy, especially in the high register – was added a new essential element: finger dexterity. While the Baroque trumpeter had needed to co-ordinate only lips and tongue, trumpeters with the new valved instrument had to reconcile three elements one with another: lips, tongue and fingers. One can easily imagine that because of the convenience and retention of tradition, and probably also because of the defects of the first valved instruments, there was much opposition to the new instrument, especially from the older players. One of them cursed about 'the emasculation of the trumpet and horn through the introduction of valves'. Even around the middle of the century, the leader of the Dresden opera orchestra himself thought the valved trumpet could not sound at all because it was not airtight. The valved trumpet found a quick entry in military music, yet it was also gradually accepted in symphonic music.

Some Kinds of Valves
Before we consider the introduction of the valved trumpet in the concert and opera orchestra as well as its treatment by some representative composers, a short chronological summary of various valve types and their inventors is given. At the outset it must be stated that hardly any area in brass research presents such a labyrinth of conflicting information as the valve. The fundamental difficulty is caused by the fact that no illustrations survive to accompany the first reports or patents. Thus it is that Baines, Dahlqvist, and Heyde, the three who have done the most recent original research, have come to differing conclusions. The following synopsis is an attempt to present the various forms of valve in chronological order. We do not doubt that future research will change some of the details.

The first invention of a kind of valve mechanism must be attributed to an Irishman, Charles Clagget. Sadly the wording of his patent application, tendered in 1788, is unclear, and instruments by Clagget do not survive. Thus he had no influence on the historical developments.

On the other hand, the time was ripe for development when the

The Modern Epoch of the Trumpet: From 1815 to Today

hornist Heinrich Stoelzel played on a valved horn in Berlin in July 1814. The firm of Griessling & Schlott had manufactured his instrument, of which no clear description survives; the form of the valve has variously been termed a double-piston valve leading to the Vienna valve (Dahlqvist) or a tubular valve (Heyde).

However, four years later Stoelzel, together with one Friedrich Blühmel, obtained a patent for the so-called 'square' or 'box valve' which had a four-cornered form outside. Trumpets were furnished for the first time with these valves in 1820. A little later Stoelzel and Blühmel separated, each disputing with the other about the authorship of the original invention. At this time Blühmel claimed to have developed the idea – not a working model – of a valve as early as 1811. It was called *Röhren-Schiebe-Ventil* (scarcely translatable) or *Schieberröhren* ('slider tubes'), the latter term being used later to designate the tubular valve, a famous and long-lived type also associated with Stoelzel's name, particularly in France. After the separation, the Karlsruhe instrument maker W. Schuster manufactured instruments for Blühmel whose square valves were then called 'Schuster valves'.

An F trumpet with three tubular valves was brought from Berlin to Paris in 1826. There F.G.A. Dauverné immediately recognized the enormous possibilities of the new instrument. He not only wrote three early valved trumpet methods, in which he gave a precise account of the course of events, but also had the first French valved trumpet made. J.-C. Labbaye first attempted it in 1826, but without success. Two years later Halary manufactured the first French valved trumpet; his instruments had only two valves instead of three.

In 1827 Blühmel attempted to apply for a patent in Berlin for a so-called *Drehbüchsenventil*, but it was refused. This valve might have been the first rotary valve altogether, but since neither

159

The Modern Epoch of the Trumpet: From 1815 to Today

Blühmel's description nor instruments survive, the question must remain open.

The invention of the double-tube 'Vienna valve' – still in use today on the 'Vienna horn' – is commonly attributed to the Viennese Leopold Uhlmann. In reality, however, his invention, for which he received a patent in 1830, must have applied only to certain improvements on the previously existing double-tube model such as the enclosure of the movable tubes to avoid contact with dust and an enclosed clock spring return mechanism. The surviving drawing to his patent also shows a water key, probably the first in history.

Previous types of double-tube valves are mentioned or illustrated in Andreas Nemetz's methods for valved horn (Vienna, 1829) and valved trumpet (1828). Still earlier developers of this type of valve included C.F. Sattler of Leipzig, who is stated to have improved Stoelzel's valve in 1819, adding a third valve and changing their placement; and Joseph Riedl (d. 1840) and Anton Khayl (1787–1834), who in 1823 introduced an improvement which probably had to do with the return mechanism.

The invention of the rotary valve by Riedl followed in the next decade. In the literature we generally read the date 1832, but Dahlqvist has located the original patent, which dates from 1835. Riedl called it a 'Rad-Maschine' (wheel valve). His invention is held to have been anticipated not through Blühmel's *Drehbüchsenventil* but through the work of an inventive American, Nathan Adams (1783–1864). Around 1824, Adams had built a trumpet with three valves which can be considered as rotary valves. Unfortunately, Adams stood, as had Clagget earlier, aside the historical development.

Another widely disseminated type of valve was the *Berliner Pumpventil* (Berlin pump valve), patented in 1835 by Wilhelm Wieprecht. Here the piston is short and very thick and permits the

The Modern Epoch of the Trumpet: From 1815 to Today

construction of the airway in one plane. Adolphe Sax built his instruments with these valves when he opened his workshop in Paris in 1842, calling them 'cylindres'.

A last, unsuccessful type of valve, the disc valve, was patented in 1838 by an Englishman, John Shaw, and was built by John Augustus Köhler (d. 1878). The idea may have come from Halary, who three years earlier had devised a disc valve, without having it patented however. But already in 1824 Shaw had obtained a patent for a still earlier form of this valve.

Finally the piston valve is to be mentioned, a mechanism which François Périnet developed in 1839 from the already existing tubular valve. The new valve removed the sharp angles and the valve slides leading down from the valve casing. All valve slides now stood at right angles to the valve casing, and the airways ran optimally not only with open but also with closed valves. Further inventions represented only improvements of existing systems and need not be mentioned here.

The Introduction of the F or G Valved Trumpet into the Orchestra

As already mentioned, the opposition to the new valved instrument at first was very great. Although developed in 1820, the valved instrument was only gradually taken up around 1840 in the concert and opera orchestra. But many composers at that time still wrote for the natural trumpet, and even the players who had decided in favour of the valved trumpet preferred to play these and older works on the natural instrument, not on the valved one. Even in the second half of the preceding century, trumpeters played both instruments, as a beautiful French double case in the author's possession shows. This case, built of plain wood and lined with red velvet, provides a place for an

The Modern Epoch of the Trumpet: From 1815 to Today

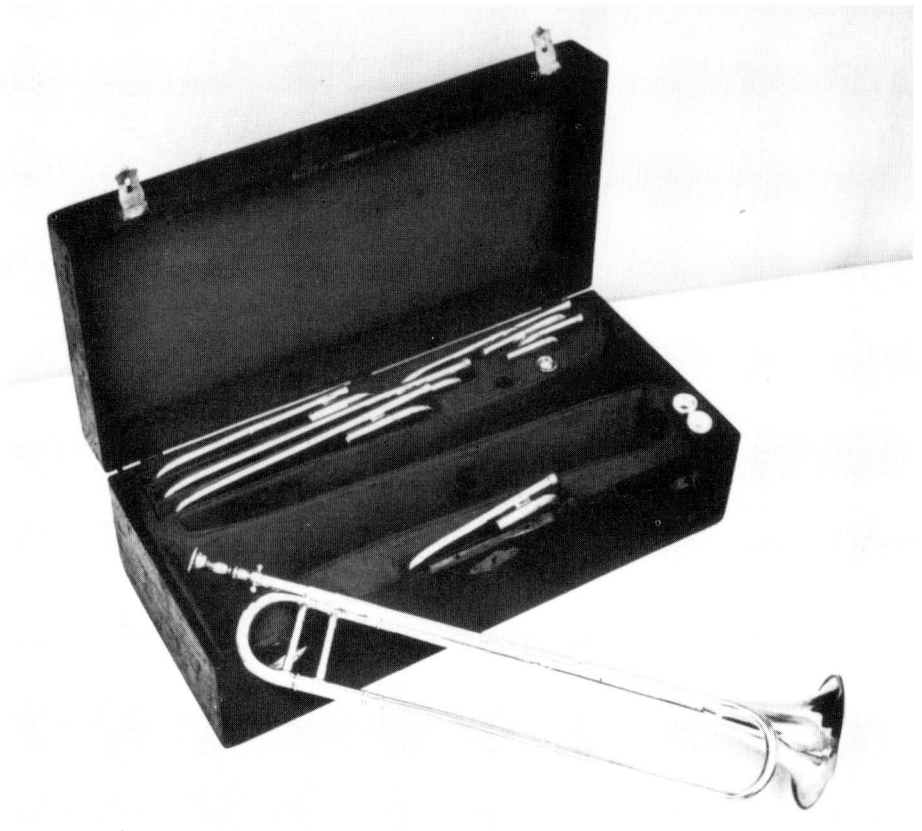

French double case with orchestral trumpet (stopped trumpet) in G with its crooks by Gautrot & Marquet of Paris around 1865. One can see the impressions of the three valve tips of a missing valved trumpet in G. The original owner was thus still in the position to play this instrument as well as the natural trumpet Author's Collection (Photo: F. Hoffmann, Basel)

orchestral natural trumpet in G with all crooks to B-flat, as well as a valved trumpet – unfortunately not preserved – which the same crooks probably fit. On the inside of the case lid one can still see the impressions of the three valve tips. In France the natural trumpet is believed to have existed side by side with the valved trumpet until 1891. In Leipzig in the year 1850 E. Sachse played his own *Concertino für einfache Trompete* (Concertino for simple trumpet), i.e. the natural trumpet.

Although the valve mechanism was an essential improvement and had lasting effects on the technique of trumpet playing, oddly

The Modern Epoch of the Trumpet: From 1815 to Today

enough it brought no enlargement of the trumpet repertoire. On the contrary, the nineteenth century was an epoch in which the trumpet was employed chiefly as an orchestral instrument. This is again analogous to the situation of woodwind instruments. They too were mechanized in the nineteenth century, however they had already passed their heyday as solo instruments. For the brass as for the woodwind, one bought the full chromatic range (with uniform timbre on all notes) at the price of greater richness of sound. The leading composers wrote their famous concertos for string instruments and for the piano; not for wind instruments.

There follow some brief notes on the use of the trumpet in famous works.

In France the valved trumpet found a ready reception in the opera orchestra thanks to Dauverné's foresight. According to his account, Chelard's *Macbeth* (1827) was the first work in which the valved trumpet was specified. The next works in France which contained valved trumpet parts were Berlioz's *grande ouverture Waverley* (op. 1, 1828) and the overture to *Les francs-juges* (op. 2, 1828), Rossini's *Guillaume Tell* (1829), Halévy's *La juive* (1835) and Meyerbeer's *Les Huguenots* (1836).

Richard Wagner lived in Paris between 1839 and 1842 and adopted this kind of instrumentation in his first opera *Rienzi*, which was premiered in Dresden in 1842. It contains parts for two valved and two natural trumpets in the orchestra pit, as well as for six valved and six natural trumpets on stage. By this time the valved trumpet appears to have been accepted in Germany, for Berlioz travelled there in 1843 and found it available everywhere.

Felix Mendelssohn-Bartholdy (1809–47) and Robert Schumann (1810–56), who in their early works had composed for the natural trumpet, as well as Johannes Brahms (1833–97), wrote

The Modern Epoch of the Trumpet: From 1815 to Today

for the valved trumpet in the old, classical way: they wrote in pairs and, especially with Mendelssohn and Brahms, mostly within the overtone series. Brahms, who in his youth had played the natural horn, contemptuously called valved horns – and with them probably also the valved trumpet – *Blechbratschen* (tin violas). Yet he seems to have written 12 *études* for a trumpet-playing friend in his younger days as a pub musician (according to their editor Max Zimolong (1972), who learned about the origin of these pieces from older Hamburg musicians who often used to play music with Brahms). Even so, their authenticity has been questioned by Michael Musgrave in his Brahms book written in 1985.

If Brahms was most conservative in the treatment of brass, the older Schumann proved more progressive. When Schumann began to write for the valved trumpet around 1848, he used it in the low register as earlier he had used the natural trumpet. Whether he liked the low register, or wrote in this manner because the high notes on the valved instrument 'spoke' with difficulty we cannot say.

The most important trumpet composers of the period 1850–90 were Wagner, Anton Bruckner (1824–96) and Giuseppe Verdi (1813–1901). Wagner (from *Tannhäuser*, 1844) and Bruckner (from his Third Symphony forward, 1873) broke with the tradition of trumpets set in pairs and increased their number to three; with Wagner up to 12 additional trumpets are found on stage (in the meadow scene of *Die Meistersinger* [III/v], 1868, as many as possible). Both of these composers slowly increased their demands on the players' stamina; Wagner also increased the demands put on the high register. The organist Bruckner appeared at many times – in his Fifth, Seventh and Eighth Symphonies for example – to forget that the brass section is not an organ stop, and wrote without regard to human fatigue. As to the

The Modern Epoch of the Trumpet: From 1815 to Today

high range, Bruckner wrote a concert *b*-flat″ in his *Te Deum* (1883–84) and in his Eighth Symphony (1885–90). A *b*-natural″ in the fourth movement of his Fifth symphony originated with Franz Schalk, who – of course with Bruckner's consent – had reinforced the score with brass. Wagner required the concert *c‴* in *Parsifal*. Wagner and Bruckner were also the first to give the trumpet gentle, sustained cantilena passages.

In the Romantic era the trumpet also led a double life. During the Baroque era there had been both field pieces and clarino works: the trumpet continued to be used for both during the Romantic era. Berlioz, in his instrumention tutor, called the sound of the trumpet 'noble and brilliant', 'suitable in expressing martial splendor . . . and vigorous, violent and lofty feelings'.[3] But a gentle cantilena played by the trumpet, besides producing in the high range joyful and yet manly affections, is lent a degree of majesty and festivity that can be attained with no other instrument. Bruckner employed two trumpets *sehr leise* in the first movement of his Eighth Symphony (1885), albeit not with a cantilena, but rather with a simple repeated signal, while the remainder of the orchestra played *forte*. He explicitly designated the trumpets as the presage of death.

The manner of writing for two cornets and two trumpets (in the case of Berlioz, natural trumpets), whereby the cantilenas and also the technically difficult places were given to the cornets, was established in France around 1833 by Hector Berlioz (1803–69).

It is hard to determine when the valved instruments were introduced in Italy because the expression *tromba con chiavi* can designate the keyed as well as the valved instrument. According to Berlioz, keyed trumpets were played in many Italian orchestras until the 1840s. Chromatic trumpet parts had existed in Italian opera since Donizetti's *L'elisir d'amore* (1832) and *Lucrezia Borgia*

The Modern Epoch of the Trumpet: From 1815 to Today

(1833) and Bellini's *Beatrice di Tenda* (1833). Perhaps the chromatic trumpet parts in Giuseppe Verdi's *Nabucco* (1842) and *I lombardi* (1843) were still played on keyed trumpets. Verdi required two trumpets in his early operas and added two cornets in the later ones; *Falstaff* (1893) had three trumpet parts. In contrast to Berlioz, whose trumpet parts were intended for natural trumpets, Verdi wrote similar parts for trumpets and cornets, and heroic melodies were often reinforced by trumpets.

Transposition was soon added to the technical demands on the high register and sound production which Wagner and Bruckner had placed before their trumpeters. According to Richard Strauss, the 'Wagnerian method' of notation for the trumpet consisted of 'writing in all keys so as to leave the trumpet part in C major as much as possible', whereby 'one can then leave the choice of the most suitable key to the individual trumpeter'. (Berlioz, *Treatise*, p. 282)

At the beginning of this book we noted that trumpeters are accustomed to thinking of the overtone series always in C; with a D or B-flat trumpet the series sounded a tone higher or lower respectively. Composers, with the exception of Italian or Italian-influenced composers of the Baroque era, kept to this way of thinking and writing. Wagner and R. Strauss still attempted to notate the trumpets in keys which, on paper, always gave C major. However, the procedure was simply untenable. Because these composers wrote highly chromatic music, the trumpet tunings had to change literally every few measures. The third act of *Lohengrin* offers an example of the excess to which this method can lead. The stage trumpets, in pairs, play fanfares in E-flat, D, F and E. Finally the 15 trumpeters (12 on the stage, three in the orchestra) join, in five different tunings, to play a fanfare which closes on a C-major chord.

In his early stage works Wagner always allowed his trumpet-

The Modern Epoch of the Trumpet: From 1815 to Today

ers time to change their tuning. But in the later works he often altered the tuning from one note to another. The strange arrangements of the wind parts in Bruckner's symphonies show frequent tuning changes – up to 62 times in the Fifth Symphony with nine different tunings – while Bruckner himself almost never alters the tuning. Obviously the trumpeters played such works on a single instrument, but on it they had to bring every other tuning immediately into the proper sounding pitch through transposition. With diatonic music, transposition is not so difficult, but with many accidentals and remote keys, it indeed becomes more complicated. Therefore transposition is central in the modern training of a trumpeter so that the trumpeter masters the principle of transposition to all keys, and learns the most important orchestra parts as if by memory.

The brothers F. and E. Sachse were perhaps two of the best German trumpeters of the middle of the nineteenth century. The first brother was 'first staff trumpeter and member of the court orchestra of the royal Hanovers'; the other worked in Weimar. Around 1850 he brought out *études* for the E-flat trumpet which still serve as transposition exercises today.

Another prominent German trumpeter of this time was Adolf Scholtz (1823–84) from Breslau. By around 1850 he was performing solos on the B-flat trumpet. During the following 20 years he played Bach's trumpet parts with the greatest confidence, firstly on the B-flat trumpet, then on the little Flügelhorn in high F. However, because he possessed little initiative, he never appeared outside Breslau.

On his trip to Germany (1843), Berlioz missed no opportunity to refer to the superiority of the German orchestral trumpeters, an observation that Wagner also made. Berlioz did not know to which of the two trumpeters named Sachse he should award the palm, and observed in his instrumentation treatise (1844) that 'a

Trumpet in E-flat

passage [such as that above] most German and English players would attack without hesitation [on the natural trumpet]' while in France it 'would be considered very risky'. (Berlioz, p. 281)

We attribute the inferiority of the French at that time, at least in the high register, to their pronounced predilection for the cornet.

The Cornet's Threat to the Trumpet

According to Dauverné (*Méthode Théorique & Pratique de Cornet à Pistons ou à Cylindres*, Paris 1840, p. 9), the cornet sprang from the posthorn in 1831 when Halary (Jean-Louis Antoine, 1788–1861) constructed a posthorn with valves. The normal tuning of the cornet was B-flat (sometimes C); its lowest tuning, G, was the highest tuning of the French trumpet. (Later the valved trumpet in France was also built in F instead of G.) Because the tubing of the cornet was shorter and more conical than that of the trumpet, the cornet was considerably more agile. The danger of blunders in the high range was less and, although the cornet tone was described as less noble, less incisive, less carrying – for Richard Strauss it was 'an abomination' – it was beautiful, tender and pleasing. Soon the new instrument was at home in military music, and especially as a virtuosic instrument in salon music. Dauverné called it 'the soul of the Quadrille'.

The first cornetist with a comprehensive technique was Joseph Jean-Baptiste Laurent Arban (1825–89), a student of the above-mentioned Dauverné. His *Grande Méthode*, which he wrote in 1864, when he was a teacher at the Academy of Military Music, still forms today the foundation of cornet as well as trumpet technique. Between 1869–74 and 1880–89 Arban was Professor of Cornet at the Paris Conservatory; since his time, there has been a double class, one for trumpet, one for cornet. (The trumpet

The Modern Epoch of the Trumpet: From 1815 to Today

class began with Dauverné in 1833: from 1869 the trumpet and cornet classes were conducted in parallel and from 1948 onwards each of the two professors instructs 12 students, among them four cornetists.)

Nearly everywhere – in France, Belgium, England and the USA – the cornet endangered the existence of the trumpet. Indeed, its tone was less noble, but it was easier to play. We have already seen that around 1875 the younger Harper in England was warning against the cornet gaining the upper hand. The music theorist Gevaert wrote in his instrumentation treatise of 1885 that the cornet had supplanted the trumpet in the orchestra in countries of the Latin tongue, under the false name *trompette à pistons*. Edwin Franko Goldman reported a similar situation about a generation later from the USA.

But the use of the cornet had two positive aspects. Firstly, the solo status was regained, for since the beginning of the nineteenth century the trumpet had been an orchestral instrument, not a solo one. The few trumpet concertos from the nineteenth century are merely exceptions to the rule. (We will briefly consider the cornet soloists of the nineteenth and twentieth centuries and their amazing technique at the end of this book.) Secondly, the cornet pushed the trumpet into a new age as B-flat tuning was also introduced for the trumpet.

The Introduction of the B-flat Trumpet into the Orchestra

B-flat trumpets, short instruments in the cornet range, were already made in Germany before 1830 and were soon played in military bands, many times under the French-derived name *piston* (mostly an abbreviation for *cornet à pistons*, but also short for *trompette à pistons*). By around the middle of the century the increasing difficulties of orchestral literature caused trumpeters, who resisted the cornet because of its sound, to take up this instrument. The B-flat trumpet or its close relative, the C trumpet, has remained the standard trumpet instrument up to the present day.

The B-flat trumpet has more projection and better accuracy in the high register than the old F trumpet, but at the same time it has a less full tone in the middle and low registers. Thus, with the transition to the B-flat trumpet, one above all gained the necessary certainty in the high register at the price of greater fullness of tone in the low register. As an important conductor of the day, Mahler, who thought that the multiplication of stringed instruments in the orchestra since Beethoven logically required an increase of the winds, had the trumpet parts in many classical works doubled, as for example in the final movement of Beethoven's Ninth Symphony. This doubling proved necessary, because the impoverished-sounding B-flat trumpet had already taken over in Mahler's time. In order at least to hint at the full tone of the old natural trumpet, which people at that time still remembered, a doubling of the parts was required.

The transition from the long G or F to the short B-flat trumpet took place first in Germany. The Dresden trumpeter Albert Kühnert (d. 1889) appears to have been one of the first who recognized the possibilities of the B-flat trumpet. Between 1850 and 1860 he began to alternate between the F and B-flat trumpets. By 1870 the B-flat trumpet had apparently been taken over by the first trumpeters of the major orchestras of Germany, although some older trumpeters continued to play second and third parts on the F trumpet. Around 1900 a Dresden trumpeter (P.E. Richter) complained that many trumpeters learned only the B-flat trumpet.

In Austria, especially in the Vienna Philharmonic, the change

The Modern Epoch of the Trumpet: From 1815 to Today

appears to have taken place somewhat later, around 1880–85. Interestingly, at the beginning of the twentieth century, the trumpeters of the Vienna Philharmonic did not play on the B-flat or C trumpet with rotary valves customary today, but rather on the C trumpet with piston valves by F. Besson (Paris). The beginnings of the much lauded traditional sound of the Viennese trumpeters are thus to be found later, probably in the thirties. In Russia the change to the B-flat/A trumpet apparently also occurred around 1880–85. Peter Tchaikovsky's (1840–93) B-flat trumpet parts from before this time – e.g. as in *Francesca da Rimini* (1877), where two cornets and two B-flat trumpets are required – appear to have been composed for the old trumpet of double length. His Fourth Symphony (1878) is still for the F trumpet, yet the majority of his works after 1885 are for the B-flat/A instrument (e.g. the Fifth Symphony, 1888).

Teste, the first trumpeter at the Paris Opera, introduced not the B-flat trumpet but rather the C trumpet in France (1874). (His instrument was actually a D trumpet with C slides.) The opposition to the B-flat trumpet was greatest in England. Here it was called the 'trumpetina', and introduced after the death of the younger Harper who had played the slide trumpet and the F trumpet until the end of his career (1885). Harper's successor, Walter Morrow (1850–1937) was an impassioned advocate of the long trumpet, and thought that the cornet seductively affected the young people because they did not wish to do so many strenuous, tone-forming exercises. Morrow's student, the great Ernest Hall (1890–1984), first definitively introduced the B-flat trumpet in England around 1912. In the USA the cornet was often played instead of the trumpet; as late as the 1920s one could find both instruments in the orchestra.

The most important composers of the period from 1890 to 1915 were: in Austria and Germany: Gustav Mahler (1860–

1911) and Richard Strauss (1864–1949), in France Claude Debussy (1862–1918) and in Russia Peter Tchaikovsky and Nicolai Rimsky-Korsakov (1844–1908). Strauss increased the demands on the trumpeters in all ways to the utmost. In his operas and symphonic poems he expanded the high range to *d-flat'''* and *d'''*, not only in the forte, but also – which is appreciably more difficult – in the piano. Furthermore such high tones were also required in slurred passages. These works reached the same height as those of the Baroque clarinists. Moreover, since the middle of the nineteenth century all areas of playing had been expanded: dynamics, expressive content, mechanics, finger technique and transposition.

Because of their technical difficulties, the works of Richard Strauss require the B-flat trumpet and sometimes also the C. In *Ein Heldenleben* (1898) he wrote for three B-flat and two low E-flat trumpets. *Also Sprach Zarathustra* (1896), with its feared, octave-leaping signal from *c''* to *c'''*, demanded the C instead of the old F trumpet.

One place in the *Sinfonia Domestica* (1903) surpassed even the Zarathustra call in difficulty.

Hermann Pietzsch, a famous Düsseldorf trumpeter and editor of orchestra studies and often-played *études*, stated in 1906 that the C trumpet was used with increasing frequency.

In his First Symphony (1888), Mahler raised the number of trumpets to four. In the last movements of the Second, Sixth and Eighth Symphonies he even required as many as ten, six and eight trumpets respectively. From the Third Symphony (1895) onwards he wrote apparently unsystematically, sometimes for the F and sometimes for the B-flat trumpet. At a large climax in his Eighth Symphony (1907) he once wrote a high concert *e-flat'''*, but permitted the lower octave as an alternate possibility. Richard Strauss and Mahler both wrote the high concert *c'''* as a note sustained over four measures, as for example in Mahler's Eighth Symphony (*see example 1 above*).

No doubt under the influence of the French cornetists with their nimble technique, Claude Debussy required considerable finger dexterity in addition to expressive playing.

In 1874 J.B. Arban wrote about the German and French influence in Russia: 'hitherto the German artists and their music were praised in St Petersburg, [now] our virtuosos . . . have surpassed them'. Russian composers from this time wrote for full-toned and strong brass, as did the Germans, yet also required flexibility and virtuosity, as did the French. Rimsky-Korsakov, in his *Osnovï orkestrovki* (1913), characterized the sound of the B-flat/A trumpet in the low range as 'troubled, as though threatening danger'.[4] At the same time he wrote some of the most virtuosic passages in the entire orchestral literature, as example 2 (*see above*) from *Scheherazade* (1888) shows. Here a very fast double tongue is required.

Furthermore, the ingenious orchestrator Rimsky-Korsakov 'invented' two kinds of trumpet in *Mlada* (1892), which in reality were modifications of existing instruments. The one called *Tromba alta in Fa* was an F trumpet with wider bore, and was used only in the low range. The other was the high E-flat/D trumpet. (*See the chapter* 'The Use of Small Trumpets'.)

The Modern Epoch of the Trumpet: From 1815 to Today

Factories

In the second half of the nineteenth century and as a result of the Industrial Revolution, the first musical instrument factories developed in France, England and the USA. It is difficult to determine when the older French firms changed over to factory production. Here are some important dates:

- In 1842 Adolphe Sax founded a firm in Paris.
- In 1850 John Henry Distin & Sons began to manufacture brass instruments in England.
- In 1856 Gustave Auguste Besson (1820–75) invented the *système prototype*, after which, for the first time, each component of a musical instrument was standardized.
- In 1859 the John F. Stratton Co. was founded in New York. Stratton appears to have been the first to seek cheap labour in Europe.
- In 1860 the firm Hawkes & Co. was founded in London. From that developed the well-known firm Boosey & Hawkes in 1930. (In 1868 Boosey & Co. bought the firm of Distin & Sons.)
- Before 1867 machine production was introduced by Thibouville-Lamy. This firm led in the construction of French trumpets between 1880 and 1925.
- Around 1870 the Boston Musical Instrument Manufactory was founded.
- In 1875 C.G. Conn (1844–1931) founded his firm in Elkhart, Indiana. Since that time most American brass instruments have been built in Elkhart by this and other firms located there.

The absence of German names is striking. German and Austrian firms have traditionally remained small and specialized. Bells and valve sections are for example manufactured by different specialized firms, and sold to the assembler, who joins his own tubing with these pre-fabricated parts and sets his own name on the finished product.

The Orchestral Trumpet in the Twentieth Century

As already noted, Richard Strauss made the highest demands on the orchestral trumpeter. So did Mahler, although he demanded less than Strauss in terms of transposition because he limited himself to the B-flat and F tunings. Since that time composers and orchestral players alike have standardized B-flat and C tunings. The A tuning, popular at the beginning of the twentieth century, especially in Russia, has disappeared from use.

The composers after Mahler and Richard Strauss maintained or even increased the high technical expectations. In this connection, three composers of the so-called 'new Viennese School' might be named: Arnold Schönberg (1874–1951), Anton von Webern (1883–1945) and Alban Berg (1885–1935). Igor Stravinsky (1882–1971), the student of Rimsky-Korsakov, took over the small D trumpet from his master in *Le sacre du printemps* (1913) and in the *Symphony of Psalms* (1930). Vincent d'Indy (1851–1931) had already done this in his Second Symphony (1903, E-flat trumpet) and in *Jour d'été à la montagne* (1905, D or E-flat) as had Maurice Ravel (1875–1937) in *Boléro* (1927). One often plays these parts today on a piccolo trumpet in high B-flat or A.

Among the composers of the present day who have written significant trumpet parts, Benjamin Britten (1913–76), Bernd-Aloys Zimmermann (1918–70), Luciano Berio (b. 1925) and his student Vinko Globokar (b. 1934) as well as Hans Werner Henze (b. 1926), Karlheinz Stockhausen (b. 1928), Richard Henderson

The Modern Epoch of the Trumpet: From 1815 to Today

(b. 1950), and Stanley Friedman, may be mentioned here. To the already existing technical difficulties (apart from the by-now-forgotten transposition) are added problems like the hearing of difficult intervals, accuracy in extreme leaps and often with dynamics adverse to the instrument, the playing of extreme high notes up to f''' and g''' (to some extent on the piccolo B-flat trumpet) and the solution of complicated rhythms, not to mention the avant-garde techniques, like playing and singing at the same time.

Among the most important works of the recent past demonstrating today's technical level are the trumpet concerto (1948) by Henri Tomasi (1901–71), the concertino for piano, string orchestra and trumpet (1948) and the second concerto for trumpet (1954) by André Jolivet (1905–75) and *Ottetto di ottoni* (1968) by Goffredo Petrassi (b. 1904). In the author's opinion, the most significant trumpet concerto of our time – and also the most difficult – is that written in 1955 by B.-A. Zimmermann. It is an attempt at a synthesis of three elements: spiritual ('Nobody Knows the Trouble I've Seen') chorale variation, and dodecaphonic technique. Avant-garde techniques are displayed in *Atem* (1969–70) and *Morceau de concours* (1968–71) for trumpet and sound track by Mauricio Kagel (b. 1931), two works in whose development the author participated, Globokar's *Fluide* (1967) for brass and percussion ensemble, his *Echanges* (1973), as well as his *Res/As/Ex/Ins-pirer* (1973) for any wind instrument. Many playing techniques in these works were borrowed from jazz. Globokar was the first to require blowing, not only by exhaling but by inhaling as well.

Karlheinz Stockhausen occupies an ambivalent position. One of his earlier works for ensemble, *Aus den sieben Tagen* (1968), consists of text pieces: the performers make up their own music through the inspiration of the moment, the group, and

Stockhausen's poetic texts which guide them. Another solo piece of his for any instrument, *Spiral* (1969), consists exclusively of plus and minus signs; the performer applies them to certain parameters such as volume, pitch, etc., improvising on random sounds received on the spot on a short-wave radio. However, Stockhausen's present writing for his gifted trumpeter son Markus (b. 1957), employs conventional notation, presenting problems only of range and endurance.

The National Schools of Trumpet Playing

France
The teachers at the Paris Conservatory and the instruments played by them are the best indicators of French taste. A brief summary of the most important French trumpeters since Teste might look something like this:

- Merri Franquin (1848–1934; professor between 1894 and 1925), who with Thibouville-Lamy in 1912 introduced a four- and in 1916 a five-valve C/D trumpet.
- Eugène Foveau, his student (1886–1957; professor between 1943 and 1957), who played on an instrument by Couesnon and is commonly regarded as the greatest French orchestral trumpeter of his time.
- Raymond Sabarich (1909–1966; professor between 1948 and 1966), the teacher of Maurice André, who preferred the Selmer trumpet.
- Ludovic Vaillant (1912–1974), a Foveau student and professor since 1957, who was faithful to Couesnon, and in 1951 was one of the first to make a long playing record of Bach's Second Brandenburg Concerto.
- Maurice André (b. 1933), who in 1967 was named successor to Sabarich and plays a Bach C and Schilke E-flat as well as

The Modern Epoch of the Trumpet: From 1815 to Today

*Maurice André with a piccolo B-flat trumpet
(Photo: Gerard Loucel, Paris/EMI/Electrola)*

The Modern Epoch of the Trumpet: From 1815 to Today

piccolo B-flat/A trumpets (formerly Selmer). He is the most celebrated trumpeter of our day. His endurance is especially noteworthy, a quality he may have inherited from his father (also named Maurice, 1901–67), a tenacious amateur trumpeter. Also noteworthy and consistent with the style of the day is his totally equal articulation in all registers.
- Pierre Thibaud (b. 1929), a Foveau student who was active in jazz for a long time before he turned to classical music and became, in 1975, the successor of Vaillant at the conservatory.
- Marcel Antoine Lagorce (b. 1932), André's successor as professor, a highly respected orchestral trumpeter and teacher.

Other important French trumpeters are Roger Delmotte (b. 1925), first trumpet at the Paris Opera from 1950 to 1985 and from 1951 teacher at the Versailles conservatory, and several brilliant soloists of the younger generation: Thierry Caëns (b. 1958), a student of André and professor at the Dijon conservatory; Bernard Soustrot, a student of André; Guy Touvron (b. 1950), André's most famous pupil who is professor in Lyons; and Marc Ullrich (b. 1954), a pupil of Delmotte, André, and the author who is first trumpet in the radio symphony orchestra in Basel.

Perhaps through the strong influence of the cornet, the French trumpet school was and remained more soloistic than orchestral. French orchestral trumpeters became famous more for temperament and brilliant technique than for a large sound.

Germany/Austria
The German and the Austrian trumpet school on the other hand has been famous since the middle of the nineteenth century for its orchestral playing. Because this area was not as centralized as in France, a similar summary would be much too complicated. Consequently the list is restricted to smaller data.

The Modern Epoch of the Trumpet: From 1815 to Today

- Julius Kosleck (1825–1905) was the originator of the misnamed 'Bach trumpet' in the year 1884 (*see further below*). Actually he was a cornetist, and the instrument on which he played the works of Bach was in the A tuning of a cornet in B-flat/A. His trumpet method of 1872 (for the F trumpet and the cornet) contains the good advice that one should not press the mouthpiece too hard against the lips when blowing, especially in the high register.
- Heinrich Täubig was the first trumpeter in the Leipzig Gewandhaus Orchestra and a leading interpreter (on the short valve trumpet in D) of Bach parts.
- Hellmut Schneidewind (b. 1928), his student, played at first in Leipzig and went to West Germany in 1956 where since that time he has been active in the Cologne Radio Symphony Orchestra (first trumpet, 1956–84).
- Rolf Quinque (b. 1927), another student of Täubig and also a member of the Gewandhaus Orchestra, was first trumpet of the Munich Philharmonic from 1957 until 1971. His speciality was the extreme high register, as found in the trumpet concerto by F.X. Richter, which he performed for the first time in the present day and has since played publicly over 30 times.
- Franz Dengler, the eminent first trumpeter of the Vienna Philharmonic, was famous for his round, soft tone and his melodic style. He was the teacher of two important soloists: Helmut Wobisch and Adolf Scherbaum.
- Helmut Wobisch (1912–80), a member of the Vienna Philharmonic, made the first long playing record of the Haydn concerto in 1952, a milestone on the road to the revival of the trumpet's solo status in the second half of the twentieth century.
- Adolf Scherbaum (b. 1909) was, until the appearance of Maurice André, the leader in the rediscovery of the trumpet as

The Modern Epoch of the Trumpet: From 1815 to Today

Adolf Scherbaum with a C trumpet
(Photo: Werner Neumeister, Munich)

a solo instrument. Before the war he played virtuoso pieces on the B-flat; after the war he played Baroque music on the piccolo B-flat trumpet, a tuning which he was the first to use in order to render D trumpet parts. His speciality was the Second Brandenburg Concerto, which he performed publically throughout the world over 400 times and recorded a dozen times.
- The family tree of trumpeters of the Dresden *Staatskapelle* includes Eduard Seiffert (who in passages by Richard Strauss and others discussed above sometimes played the small F trumpet), Wilhelm Simon (1897–1968, an excellent teacher who played everything on the B-flat trumpet and whose specialities were the difficult parts by Wagner, Bruckner and Strauss), and today Kurt Sandau (b. 1936, who, like Seiffert,

The Modern Epoch of the Trumpet: From 1815 to Today

acts rather freely in the selection of instruments with rotary valves).

A discussion of the trumpet in Germany would be incomplete without mention of the Berlin Philharmonic Orchestra, the leading orchestra of the country and one generating great pride. Some of the better-known first trumpeters are Richard Stegmann (1898–1985), with the orchestra 1913–25, then professor at the Bavarian State conservatory in Würzburg, 1938–1954, author of a well-known trumpet method and of transposition studies; Paul Spörri (b. 1909), 1927–43 (*see also below*); and the above-mentioned Scherbaum, 1943–45. The two first trumpeters at present are Konradin Groth (b. 1947) and Martin Kretzer; their predecessors were Horst Eichler (b. 1920) and Fritz Wesenigk (b. 1923).

Two East German trumpeters who have become well known are Willy Krug (b. 1925), first trumpeter in the East Berlin radio orchestra and a very gifted soloist, who developed the Scherzer piccolo B-flat/A trumpet which has become quite popular; and Ludwig Güttler (b. 1943), a former member of the Dresden Philharmonic who has achieved great popular success in the West with his renditions of Baroque music.

Three young West German trumpeters to watch in the future are Günter Beetz (b. 1953), a free-lance soloist, Hannes Läubin (b. 1958), first trumpeter in the Hamburg radio orchestra and the oldest of three trumpet-playing brothers who are all professional musicians, and Reinhold Friedrich (b. 1958), a student of Thibaud and the author who is first trumpeter in the Frankfurt radio orchestra. Finally we should mention Friedemann Immer (b. 1948), who has specialized on historical instruments, working frequently with Nikolaus Harnoncourt and also performing Bach's Second Brandenburg Concerto on the natural trumpet all over the world.

The Modern Epoch of the Trumpet: From 1815 to Today

In Germany the B-flat tuning is generally preferred; in Austria the C. In German and Austrian orchestras in which trumpets with rotary valves are still used, two makes were traditionally favoured: J. Monke and Heckel. The Monke trumpets from Cologne have a bore of 11.2mm and a large bell, and are used by the Berlin Philharmonic. The somewhat narrower Dresden Heckel trumpet (10.9mm) is played in Dresden and Vienna. Heckel's successor is Windisch; other trumpets with similar bores are built today by Scherzer (Augsburg), Scherzer (Markneukirchen), Lechner (Bischofshofen nr Salzburg), and Ganter (Munich). The pedigree of Cologne trumpet-makers goes back from Josef Monke (1882–1965) to Leopold August Schmidt (d. 1921) and his father F.A. Schmidt (active from 1848). Josef Monke is said to have developed the screw-rim mouthpiece in the year 1908. Today his firm is led by his daughter Liselotte (b. 1923); another Cologne firm is led by his son Wilhelm (b. 1913).

United Kingdom
The modern English trumpeters are nearly all students of either the above mentioned Ernest Hall, an exponent of the traditional trumpet school with straight, even tone, or of George Eskdale (1897–1960), an early cornetist and dance musician, who caused a sensation with a recording of Bach's Second Brandenburg Concerto under Adolf Busch in the year 1936 (on a small F trumpet). The leading English trumpeters today are Philip Jones (b. 1928), director of the wind department at the Guildhall School of Music and the leader of an internationally famous brass ensemble from 1951 to 1986, and John Wilbraham (b. 1944), former first trumpet of the BBC Symphony Orchestra and a well known soloist on the piccolo B-flat trumpet, together with John Wallace (b. 1949), first trumpeter of the Philharmonia Orches-

The Modern Epoch of the Trumpet: From 1815 to Today

tra, Michael Laird (b. 1942) and Crispian Steele-Perkins, two versatile free-lance musicians who have also performed frequently on modern reproductions of historical instruments.

Russia
The Russian school was originally influenced by Germany. At the founding of the conservatory in St Petersburg in 1860, a German, Wilhelm Wurm (1826–1904), who had lived there since 1848, became the first trumpet teacher. Four years later, Nikolai Rubinstein founded the Moscow conservatory, engaging Wurm and another German, Karl Zimmermann, to teach the trumpet. Tsarist Russia was open to touring cornet virtuosos from many countries. Among the visitors the names of Jules Levy (1871–72), Jean-Baptiste Arban (1873–77) and Vincent Bach (1914) stand out. Levy recollected long conversations with the Tsarevitch, who himself played the cornet. Others settled for good: Oskar Böhme, who had been born in Dresden (1870–1938); Wilhelm (Vassily) Brandt (1869–1923), who from 1869 to 1923 was soloist at the Bolshoi theatre, from 1889 to 1911 teacher at the Moscow conservatory, and from 1912 to his death, teacher at the Saratov conservatory; and the Belgian Emile Joseph Trognée (1868–1942), who settled in St Petersburg. In 1899 Böhme published his Concerto in E Minor for a full-blown Romantic work strongly reminiscent of violin concertos by Mendelssohn and Bruch. The original version was recently discovered and recorded by the Norwegian trumpeter, Lars Næss.

The founder of the modern Russian trumpet school was Mihail Tabakov (1877–1956) who played in the orchestra of the Bolshoi Theatre from 1897 until 1938. As a teacher he underscored the importance of a good tone and called it 'the valuable capital of an artist'. His student, Timofei Dokschitser

The Modern Epoch of the Trumpet: From 1815 to Today

(b. 1921) has been soloist in the Bolshoi Theatre since 1945 and the successor of Tabakov at the Gnesin Music Academy. He was originally a cornetist, but changed to a B-flat trumpet by Selmer in 1958. He is well known for his impassioned expression.

USA
The modern American trumpet school is a mixture of the French and the German schools, but stands closer to the German, because in America orchestral work is central in a trumpeter's training.

When the American orchestras were founded in the second half of the nineteenth century, many musicians came from abroad, especially from Germany, in order to find employment in the 'New World'. One such musician was Karl Rodenkirchen, first trumpeter at the founding of the Chicago Symphony Orchestra in the year 1891; he played cornet until 1898 and then, until 1902, the trumpet. His successor, Paul Handke (fl. 1903–12) came from Vienna; there he had prepared a handwritten copy of the solo part of the trumpet concerto by Haydn, which he brought along to Chicago. At this time, the concerto was still relatively unknown.

The other large American orchestras, such as the Boston Symphony Orchestra and the New York Philharmonic, oriented themselves to the German school, though in the wave of anti-German sentiment following the First World War, many German musicians in Boston, among them the orchestra's director Dr Karl Muck, were dismissed and Frenchmen engaged in their places. Thus for example the nine-year-old Roger Voisin (b. 1918) came to America with his father René (1893–1952). René played the second part in the section. At 16, Roger became the youngest member of the orchestra and moulded the sound of the wind section as first trumpet between 1949 and 1967. He

The Modern Epoch of the Trumpet: From 1815 to Today

played on a four-valve Thibouville-Lamy C trumpet (*see above*). Around the turn of the century Max Schlossberg (1870/76–1936) emigrated from Russia to New York; he was an extremely influential teacher and wrote an important trumpet method.

Finally to be mentioned is the Viennese Vincent Bach (1890–1976). He travelled originally as a cornet virtuoso to America, where he was invited to play first trumpet in a symphony orchestra. In this way he spent a season (1914/15) in Boston and the following year and a half with the Diaghilev Ballet in New York. After the First World War, he went over to the manufacture of instruments and mouthpieces, because he had been trained in Vienna as a mechanical engineer. His trumpets and mouthpieces became more and more desired and are played today throughout the world.

The immigrant European musicians gave impetus to American musical life and taught the next generation well. Among the native American trumpeters of the next generations might be named: William Vacchiano (b. 1912), the student and successor of Schlossberg, who, in the course of his long career as first trumpet of the New York Philharmonic (1935–73) also trained numerous professional students; Adolph Herseth (b. 1921) who since 1948 has held the first position in the Chicago Symphony Orchestra, the orchestra with the most forceful, but also the most balanced and virtuosic brass; and Armando Ghitalla (b. 1925), the successor of Voisin in Boston and now professor at the University of Michigan, who is famous above all for his distinctive solo playing.

Some other highly respected younger orchestral players are Thomas Stevens (b. 1937), first trumpeter of the Los Angeles Philharmonic, who has become noted especially for his interpretations of contemporary music; Charles Schlueter (b. 1940), who came to his first-chair position in the Boston Symphony by way of

The Modern Epoch of the Trumpet: From 1815 to Today

Cleveland and Minneapolis; Philip A. Smith (b. 1952) of the New York Philharmonic; and Richard Giangiulio of Dallas, who received part of his training in Paris. Gerard Schwarz (b. 1947), Vacchiano's favourite student and successor, has renounced the trumpet after a number of highly successful recordings and is making a second career as a conductor.

Modern life-style has made it possible for some younger trumpeters to seek their living as soloists and teachers, without making orchestral playing their main musical activity. Anthony Plog (b. 1947) of Los Angeles, composer and soloist, and David Hickman (b. 1950), professor at Arizona State University and a fine soloist, are two of the most prominent trumpeters of this type who come to mind.

A unique phenomenon is Carl ('Doc') Severinsen (b. 1927), whose amazing technique – a fusion of 'classical' and jazz elements – has been heard five nights weekly for over 20 years on the North American TV 'Tonight Show'.

After the Second World War a change took place in the musical relations between Europe and America. While around the turn of the century European directors and musicians had fertilized American musical life, after the Second World War many Americans emigrated to Europe. Often they were opera singers who found no employment in their homeland. But equally often they were brass players whom Europe suited better for various reasons. Today American trumpeters are members of orchestras in Rome, Zürich, Munich, Stuttgart, Frankfurt, Düsseldorf, Cologne, Kassel, Rotterdam, The Hague, and Bergen.

In Europe, it is highly unusual for women to play the trumpet, but it is less exceptional in America. Two highly talented American female trumpeters have even made careers for themselves in Europe: Janis Marshelle Coffmann (b. 1949; a former pupil of Louis Davidson at Indiana University), who also played

The Modern Epoch of the Trumpet: From 1815 to Today

for a time in the Munich Philharmonic and the Stockholm radio orchestra; and Carole Reinhart (a former pupil of Edward Treutel at the Juilliard school), who is now professor at the Vienna conservatory.

Another native American phenomenon is the young Wynton Marsalis (b. 1961), of unusual technical ability, whose career is developing – with equally unusual marketing support – in both classical and jazz idioms.

American-made trumpets are commonly the leaders today. Some of the well-known makes are Bach (*see above*), Benge (like the Bach instrument, derived from the F. Besson, Paris), Schilke (especially famous for high trumpets, but also well-known as advisor to the Japanese firm Yamaha, who has also advanced to a world-class position) and Getzen. Morever, trumpets by Calicchio, Conn, Martin, and Holton are played in jazz and entertainment orchestras.

Scandinavia

Two players from the generation born around 1920 have been of more than local importance: Harry Kvebæck (b. 1925) of Oslo and Knud Hovaldt (b. 1926) of Copenhagen. In particular, Hovaldt felt that Scandinavian players could move out of their geographical isolation only if they were to study in other countries. Two of his Swedish pupils, Bengt Eklund (b. 1944) of Gothenburg and Bo Nilsson (b. 1940 – no relation to the composer of the same name) of Malmö, did just that, Eklund studying in Chicago and Basel, and Nilsson in those two places and in Paris. The first results of this expansion are beginning to be felt. Not only has Nilsson's experience already made him one of the world's most sought-after teachers, but also one of his pupils, Håkan Hardenberger (b. 1961), went on to study with Thibaud in Paris, won prizes in international competitions, and has embarked on a soloist's career.

The Modern Epoch of the Trumpet: From 1815 to Today

The Transition from the Small to the Large Bore around 1950

After the Second World War, the differences in the national schools described above began to diminish. This drawback was in part produced by the ever-increasing size both of the symphony orchestras and concert halls, and the resulting search for brass instruments with larger bores and, consequently, greater volumes of sound. This process appeared to have begun first with the horns (with the transition from French-made instruments to German horns, as seen in the career of Dennis Brain), then with the trombones, and lastly with the trumpets. Throughout the world, locally manufactured instruments were generally abandoned in favour of American made trumpets. Before the war, locally made instruments with a bore of 10.9 to 11.2mm were preferred in Germany and France; the bore of a modern orchestral instrument however measures between 11.66 and 11.74mm. These instruments require more air; therefore the study of breathing technique appears to be more important than ever. Obviously brass sections in orchestras from Minneapolis to Moscow have come to sound nearly the same. But fortunately a few orchestras – Berlin, Leipzig, Dresden and Vienna – hold fast to their older rotary-valved instruments and to their own distinctive sound; and other orchestras in which piston-valved trumpets are employed, starting with Chicago (around 1975) and now including even the Orchestre de Paris (1985), are starting to use rotary-valved trumpets as well for some of the repertory.

The Use of Small Trumpets

The modern orchestral trumpeter no longer finds the B-flat trumpet totally sufficient, as did many players before the Second

The Modern Epoch of the Trumpet: From 1815 to Today

World War. The ever increasing demands on the trumpet, the rediscovery of Baroque works for trumpet and the special effects of the *avant-garde* since Stravinsky have all led to the construction and use of trumpets in higher keys. Moving from the B-flat and C trumpets, the most common high trumpets are those found in the following keys: D (earlier used for Baroque works, today hardly at all), E-flat (used for solo works like the Haydn concerto as well as for certain orchestral passages), F (earlier often used for the first part in Bach works, especially for the Second Brandenburg Concerto, today seldom used), G (today popular for Bach works), and B-flat/A (the so-called 'piccolo B-flat trumpet' which is the most universally used high trumpet from Bach to Stravinsky). There are even piccolo C trumpets.

The D trumpet appears to have been used for the rendering of Bach works already around 1870 in Brussels, around 1890 in Germany, and after 1892 in England where it was at first constructed in a straight form. The D trumpet with valves is half as long as the natural trumpet in D from the Baroque era. The first high G trumpet was built in 1885 by F. Besson (Paris) for Teste, who played the Bach Magnificat on it. As a consequence, Besson manufactured other high trumpets in F/E-flat and E-flat/D.

The first trumpeter of our time to play Bach's Second Brandenburg Concerto with success was A. Goeyens of Brussels. He played it for the first time on 23 February 1902 on the high F trumpet and later, around 1906 or 1907, on the piccolo B-flat. Other early trumpeters who came to grips with this difficult work were Ludwig Wehrle (Cologne, in November 1905, on an F trumpet by Alexander of Mainz), Herbert Barr (at the Leeds Festival 1922, on an F trumpet by Besson), and Paul Spörri (Berlin and Basel, who in 1932 made the earliest recording with Edwin Fischer, likewise on the F trumpet). As mentioned above, Adolf Scherbaum was the first to use the piccolo B-flat trumpet for

The Modern Epoch of the Trumpet: From 1815 to Today

D trumpet parts as well.

In England, the most conservative country in Europe around the turn of the century, the B-flat trumpet was adopted last. Today some English orchestral trumpeters are among the most progressive, using the E-flat or even the piccolo B-flat trumpet in place of the B-flat or C. As around the turn of the century, a gain in accuracy and brilliance in the high register was realized at the cost of fullness of tone.

The Rediscovery of the Natural Trumpet

In our century various attempts have been made to play the natural trumpet again. Although the recorder and harpsichord are once again played everywhere, the Baroque trumpet defied resuscitation for some time. The likely explanation for this is that the wind technique of the Romantic Era and the early twentieth century had become remote from Baroque practice.

We might first briefly consider the so-called 'Bach trumpet' of the nineteenth century. Julius Kosleck, the Berlin trumpeter and cornetist, devoted several years of study to the high range of Bach parts. He also developed a straight, valved instrument in A, a fifth higher than the Baroque natural trumpet, on which he played publicly for the first time in November 1881 in the garrison church in Berlin. He also used this two-valved trumpet, which he had had made ostensibly after an old busine, at the Eisenach Bach Festival in 1884. His success was so great that he was invited to England, where on 21 March 1885 the B Minor Mass was performed for the first time in its entirety in this country with the trumpet parts in the correct register. In England, and probably earlier at Eisenach, the special instrument received the unfounded name 'Bach trumpet'. The instrument was copied by Kosleck's English colleagues Morrow and John Solomon (1856–

The Modern Epoch of the Trumpet: From 1815 to Today

1953) and was produced in 1886. Its use however was abandoned as early as 1892, when trumpets in the short D tuning, a fourth higher, were built.

In Germany the notion of the 'Bach trumpet' has obstinately persisted up to the present day, although the instrument has nothing to do whatsoever with the trumpet of Bach's day, and is not used anymore in this form. Music lovers and critics should make use of the terminology of the modern professional musician for the present day high trumpet, speaking simply of 'high' or 'piccolo' trumpet, or naming it after its key, e.g. 'piccolo B-flat trumpet'.

An unsuccessful attempt to introduce the Baroque trumpet was undertaken in 1931 by the collector Hans Eberhard Hoesch of Hagen, who had three D trumpets from 1767 reconstructed by the noted makers, Alexander of Mainz. A similar attempt was made by Werner Menke in 1934, by whose commission the same firm constructed a two-valved trumpet with the tubing length of the Baroque trumpet.

The first to enjoy success was Walter Holy (b. 1921) in 1960 with a new construction by Otto Steinkopf and Helmut Finke. This coiled trumpet was a reproduction of the instrument of Gottfried Reiche. Unfortunately the new construction was given the false name 'clarino', a concept that, as we have seen, was used in the Baroque era to designate the high *register* of the trumpet but not to designate a form of the instrument. Whatever the case may be, Holy's success was guaranteed through Steinkopf's brilliant invention of a three-hole system that on the one hand did away with the defective intonation of the eleventh and thirteenth partials, and on the other hand improved the problematic accuracy in the high range through the alternate elimination of even and uneven partials. Holy introduced this 'Jägertrompete' throughout the world as first trumpeter of the

The Modern Epoch of the Trumpet: From 1815 to Today

Cologne Baroque Orchestra, the *Cappella Coloniensis*.

After an initial period of collaboration with Steinkopf and Finke from 1962, our own attempts, dating from 1967, have among other things the purpose of restoring the inimitable sound of original instruments in the full trumpet ensemble. We had noticed that playing the Steinkopf-Finke instrument with its small bell and modern mouthpiece receiver did not prepare us adequately for working with original instruments from the seventeenth and eighteenth centuries. The German bell firm Meinl & Lauber (now Ewald Meinl) built for us a trumpet after Haas. In the interim, trumpets by Hans Hainlein (1632) and J.L. Ehe III (1746) have also been reconstructed. Since about 1980 we have been collaborating with Rainer Egger (Basel) on reproductions of an original trumpet by J.L. Ehe II (1663–1724) and of original mouthpieces, which are considerably larger than modern ones and require special practice to develop the necessary lip musculature.

The natural trumpet has been taught at the Schola Cantorum Basiliensis since 1973, and in 1985 collaboration with the Trumpet Museum in nearby Bad Säckingen was instituted for the purpose of working not only with copies, but also with original instruments.

In the meantime other makers have begun to make historical reproductions of earlier instruments, notably the brothers Heinrich and Max Thein of Bremen, who have succeeded in creating a Baroque alloy; good instruments have also been produced by Rudolf Tutz of Innsbruck, Geerd van der Heide of Putten, Netherlands and, for a time, by the Historical Brass Workshop of Boston. Robert Barclay of Ottawa, who has also written about the workmanship involved in making old brass instruments (*see Bibliography*), and John Webb of London, should also be mentioned. At the moment there is intense activity in

The Modern Epoch of the Trumpet: From 1815 to Today

England, generated by a veritable boom in early music recordings. With all due respect, however, we are obliged to state that the trumpets generally used there seem to represent a step backwards, due to the use of modern components (production-line bell, thick-walled tubing, tapered mouthpiece receiver, modern mouthpiece). Modern playing techniques and especially mouthpieces are hard to give up! But on the other hand, modern mouthpieces on old trumpets give a nasal sound. Recently John Webb (London) has started to make replicas of old English trumpets, and it is to be hoped that their quality will entice English players to forsake the inferior instruments they now use.

At the time of writing (1988), some makers have made historical reproductions of later instruments: Egger, Webb and Meinl of keyed trumpets, Webb of English slide trumpets, and Robb Stewart (Hollywood) of nineteenth-century American band instruments. No one has yet made a 'classical' trumpet suitable for the works of Haydn, Mozart, Beethoven and Schubert.

An Introduction to the Style and Technique of the Modern Trumpet

The modern orchestral school was decidedly influenced by the most important works of the nineteenth and early twentieth centuries. Two peculiarities of playing technique may be mentioned here. Wagner invented the 'inaudible entry', an orchestral crescendo in which the single instruments entered one after the other. At the beginning of our century this method engendered a style of playing long tones with an imprecise beginning, through which an immediate swelling of the sound was accomplished. Another striking peculiarity is seen in passages with short, fast, tongued notes. Because of the enlarged size of the orchestra, it could happen that fast semiquavers were not clear enough to be heard in the common tumult of sound. Thus at the end of the nineteenth or at the beginning of the twentieth century one tongued these notes very short and pointed, not *ta, ta, ta,* but *tat, tat, tat* to achieve that clarity. With time, this and the above-mentioned articulation were regarded as bad habits and were removed from the modern school of playing.

While the many teaching methods of the nineteenth century – certainly borrowing from the soft tonguing strokes of the Baroque – always named three or four possible articulations, today the ideal articulation demands that every note, high and low, receives exactly the same attack. Only the hard stroke *ta* and the soft stroke *da* are used. The illustrious teacher James Stamp (1905–86) recently added the breath or 'poo' attack.

The playing technique of the orchestral trumpeter has also been influenced by jazz. Various manners of playing and muting have been taken over. More important still, the trumpeter has learned to persevere for a long time in the register above high c''' (in jazz up to c'''' and even higher). This is accomplished not by pulling back the corners of the mouth in a smile, as had earlier been practised, but rather by pushing the stiffened corners forward a bit, although allowing the lip muscles themselves to relax as far as possible.

Nevertheless the trumpet remains overall the most strenuous instrument of all. The high notes are produced not only with increased lip tension, but especially with increased air pressure, controlled from the diaphragm and formed in the oral cavity by the tongue. This pressure is strongest in the chest. In 1961 three doctors in Basel, Dr H. Nidecker, Prof. Dr H. Herzog, and Dr H.R. Richter, of whom Nidecker and Richter are active brass players, executed a series of filmed x-ray experiments with wind players in order to study exertion in playing. They pointed out afterwards that the requisite air pressure for blowing the trumpet is far higher than for other instruments, as for example the trombone, tuba or oboe. While this so-called intra-thoracic pressure for high trumpet tones can rise to 1.5 atmospheres above normal – a value which corresponds to the air pressure in a VW tyre – with the low brass instruments with large mouthpiece cup it reaches scarcely a third of this value. The highest pressure with the tuba, for example, comes to only 0.5 atmospheres above normal. (With woodwind instruments the pressure is still far less, with the oboe merely 0.25 atmospheres above normal.) Moreover, the three doctors concluded that such an activity, which furthered the lungs in this manner, was healthy.

Nowadays the listener is often overly impressed by the physical strength of a trumpeter and neglects the musical side of the performance. Obviously the trumpet still possesses its old double nature: at once both strong and elegant.

Soloists

We might conclude this consideration of the twentieth century with a short retrospective view of the already forgotten soloists from the turn of the century and their art.

After the Second World War the trumpet began to be accepted again as a solo instrument in so-called 'classical' music. And we must state from our own experience that it is not at all easy to resume an interrupted soloistic tradition. The last real soloists of the past were the Baroque trumpeters and Anton Weidinger. When we play their repertoire after 150 years, we must not only relearn their flexible style, but also acquire again their artistic freedom. With an orchestral player who lives permanently under the dictates of a baton, this quality wears away all too easily.

However, there have always been soloists in the twentieth

The Modern Epoch of the Trumpet: From 1815 to Today

century. They worked not in symphonic music, but in the realms of entertainment, e.g. in military music and in jazz. Thanks to the soloistic tradition in these musical sectors, such soloists expressed a personal freedom and sense of communication which we 'classical' trumpeters, trained in the orchestral school of playing, must learn again.

The Cornetists
The first and greatest cornetist of salon and military music was the already mentioned J.B. Arban (1825–89). To his generation belonged also L.A. St Jacome (1830–98), Jules Levy (1838–1903) and Alessandro Liberati (1847–1927). The most outstanding member of the second generation was Herbert L. Clarke (1867–1945), who between 1893 and 1917 played with the famous miliatry band of John Philip Sousa and around 1906 discovered and taught diaphragmatic breathing. Another cornetist of that time was Bohumir Kryl (1875–1961) who was famous for his low notes of the so-called pedal register. (We designate as 'pedal tones' the first partial in each of the seven possible fingerings from little c down to great F-sharp.) To the third generation belonged the Englishmen Jack Mackintosh (1891–1979) and George Swift (1911–86), and likewise the Americans Del Staigers (1899–1950) and Rafael Mendez (1911–81). In Germany we might name Kosleck and Hugo Türpe (1860–1900), later the trumpeters Willi Liebe (1905–77) and Franz Willy Neugebauer (1904–75). The repertoire of these soloists consisted of countless pieces in the same form: theme and variations.

With the exception of the first two, Kosleck and Türpe, recordings by these soloists survive. Although the recording technique at that time was not as highly developed as today, it is still possible to hear clearly how these people played. Although it is difficult to generalize, the soloists of the very early twentieth century used little or no vibrato, and many used a certain kind of rubato – a then very popular rhythmic freedom which cannot be rendered in musical notation. The rubato of c 1900–25 consisted of anticipating the final note or notes of a phrase. (If it is impossible today for us to imitate the style of the turn of the century without documents in sound, how illusory it is then to pretend to have a true 'feel' for the Baroque style only from the music and on the basis of some little written instruction!)

The Soloists in Jazz
Louis Armstrong (1900–71) was undoubtedly the most influential soloist of jazz. Not only was he the first to extend the trumpet's high range up to f''' (concert e-flat$'''$), but he also set the standard in jazz phrasing. Armstrong had already developed his style, which influenced the progress of jazz as a whole, before his legendary recordings made between 1925 and 1928 with his group 'The Hot Five' and 'The Hot Seven'. He played until 1928 on the cornet and after that on the trumpet. Armstrong's important white contemporary Bix Beiderbecke (1903–31) played jazz in the so-called Chicago style, again at first on the cornet and later on the trumpet. His self-willed, lyrical improvisations are still a model for many jazz trumpeters today.

Other important trumpeters in the following jazz epochs are Dizzy Gillespie (b. 1917) in 'Bebop' and Miles Davis (b. 1926) in 'Cool Jazz'. Gillespie and Davis are opposites. Gillespie, who in blowing puffs out his cheeks, is an extroverted showman, disposing of countless notes per second in all registers. Davis is so introverted that he sometimes turns his back to the audience. The few notes that he plays are vibratoless and yet highly expressive, especially through the variety of tone colours which he gives them. One technique frequently used by jazz musicians, including Davis, to alter the tone colour is the 'half valve': one or more valves

The Modern Epoch of the Trumpet: From 1815 to Today

Maynard Ferguson in action. Whoever believes he plays with the so-called 'non-pressure system' should note the little finger of his right hand and how he presses the instrument against his mouth
(Photo: Willard Alexander, Inc., New York)

are depressed only part way; giving a distant and strange tone.

Other highly influential jazz artists include Harry James (1916–83), who possessed a formidable classical-style technique, and Clifford Brown (1930–56), whose long and brilliantly conceived solos still influence modern instrumentalists.

In jazz there are high register specialists who play even higher than the two Baroque experts Heinisch and Resenberger. In addition to Cat Anderson (1916–81) (the high trumpeter with Duke Ellington (1899–1974) for many years), is Maynard Ferguson (b. 1928), a native Canadian who first (1950–53) became famous with the orchestra of Stan Kenton (b. 1912) and since 1970 has led his own orchestra. Both play in the highest register from concert b-flat″ upwards to around concert e-flat″″.

Afterword

At the beginning of this book it was established that no instrument had changed so much in the course of time as the trumpet. Yet the tone quality of the trumpet stretches through its history like a continuous thread. The many sides of the trumpet can always be reduced to a double nature: that of 'sounding an alarm' and 'blowing' in ancient Israel; that of field pieces and clarino compositions in the Baroque era; and that of fanfares and *cantilena* during the Romantic period. The cornetists and jazz musicians add further dimensions, but here also the old opposition of the two natures is present.

The format of this book required conciseness. Much remains to be written; for example, considerations of the Belgian and Italian schools of trumpet playing, brass chamber music of the twentieth century, military music since the early nineteenth century, the German and Swiss *Posaunenchor* tradition, the new playing techniques of the avant-garde, and much else besides, especially in the field of jazz. However, these must be reserved for another book, or even another author.

At this point I would like to express my thanks to those without whose help this book could not have been written. Above all I name here the instrument collector Ernst W. Buser (Binningen near Basel), who was the true initiator of this book and who repeatedly offered helpful suggestions. To him and to the late Revd Dr Wilhelm Bernoulli (Greifensee) I am especially grateful for the loan of important instruments from their collections. In this way it was possible for me to provide illustrations of instruments chiefly from Swiss collections, although in 1985 the Buser collection was transferred to the Trumpet Museum in Bad Säckingen, West Germany.

I am deeply indebted to Reine Dahlqvist, whose dissertation on the history of the trumpet took over ten years to write and who generously shared many aspects of his research with me in an

Afterword

extensive correspondence. Many new points of view in this book can be traced back to his suggestions, for example the references to Goeyens, Heinisch, Hoese, Resenberger, Türpe, and to Fröhlich's trumpet method. These three individuals read and improved the finished manuscript.

Prof. Wulf Arlt, then Director of the Schola Cantorum Basiliensis, is to be heartily thanked for a research grant in the autumn of 1975 which enabled me to study the unique music and instruments of the 'Charamela real' *in situ*. Dr Detlef Altenburg, who has published the most significant book on the baroque trumpet to date, is likewise to be thanked for his contributions, both in his book and in correspondence. My thanks go at the same time to Rainer Egger for his help with the question of brass instrument construction, to the late Joseph Wheeler for his observations on the nineteenth century, to Daniel Morgenthaler for his drawings, to Stephen Glover for the production of many musical examples, to Alfredo Bernardini for his tip on Ubaldo Montini, and to my students at the Conservatory and at the Schola Cantorum Basiliensis for their indispensable help. I am also indebted to the many institutions which have loaned me pictorial material and who, in the course of the book, are credited in the corresponding places.

* * * *

This book was originally written in 1976, appeared in 1977 and again with certain corrections in 1978. The author translated the first half of the text in 1979 for a series of lectures delivered at the Victorian College of the Arts in Melbourne, Australia. The remainder was translated in 1986 by an old friend and former student, Steven E. Plank of Oberlin College, with great expertise and sensitivity, by the way, and our special thanks go to him for this and other contributions to the field of musicology.

Afterword

Looking at the book again after a decade, one can see that much has happened during this period. Some new research has been done, particularly on the Middle Ages and on the valve. Happily, many new artists have come up, and sadly, many old ones have gone from us. Since we have taken a keen interest in many of these developments and know personally most of the new and old colleagues in question, we felt it necessary while checking the translation to bring the book up to date by the addition of at least a minimal amount of new information. It was not possible, however, to expand the book, for reasons of both time and economy; and so the statement made above still stands: much remains to be written.

Perhaps this work could serve as a point of departure for future scholarly or practical work. The nineteenth century, for example, could furnish the terrain for many a doctoral dissertation: on the use of keyed trumpets in Italian orchestras, on trumpet and cornet methods, on the virtuoso literature for the cornet versus that for trumpet, on the development of valve return mechanisms, and so on. Also, we need good historical reproductions of natural and valved trumpets in F or G for concert performances.

One project which we intend to undertake personally has to do with performance practice. Since trumpeters do not seem comfortable reading books on subjects not related directly to their instruments and a wealth of information can be gleaned from old tutors – for cornett as well as for cornet – it seems a good idea to collate some of it in the hope that future performers' stylistic proficiency will catch up with their already formidable technical proficiency. We have made a start here, in the chapter entitled 'The Playing Technique of the Baroque Trumpet'. Beyond those words . . . much remains to be written.

Translator's Afterword

The historical study of musical instruments brings together the interests of both music historian and performer. For the historian, the instruments of the past are aural bridges across chasms of time – artefacts with a living voice from a now silent past. For the performer, the instruments are simultaneously teacher and medium, because, in many cases, the contextually appropriate instrument for a piece of music, both in its actual sound and in the techniques it encourages, does much to define the 'sonic world' of the piece. The modern performer might choose to accept or reject historical instruments and their period techniques – although the case for historically informed performance is strongly put today – but the knowledge of a piece gained by the consideration of the instrument for which it was written is germane, if not critical, to either approach.

Modern musicology has nurtured the historical study of musical instruments. Indeed, Guido Adler's landmark essay 'Umfang, Methode und Ziel der Musikwissenschaft' (*Vierteljahresschrift für Musikwissenschaft*, 1885) – an essay in which the groundwork for the modern, scientific study of music was laid – made it a fourth supplemental branch of a four-part historical scheme that also included the study of notation, musical forms, and musical laws. Adler's 'sanction' of organology was timely, both from the standpoint of instrument collections which developed in the nineteenth century (e.g. collections at Berlin, Brussels, The Hague, Nuremberg, and New York, *inter alia*), and in the light of the awakening interest in historical performing practice. Among the earliest modern studies of instruments was Curt Sachs' *Real-Lexikon der Musikinstrumente* (1913), 'the first effort to systematize knowledge of musical instruments on a worldwide basis' (*The New Grove*). Many works, including the present one, owe a debt to Sachs' pioneering work.

The history of the trumpet has been essayed by several authors

Translator's Afterword

during the past century, and the instrument was examined in the more distant past as well. Sebastian Virdung's *Musica getutscht* (1511), the earliest printed book on musical instruments, and its slightly younger, versified sibling, *Musica instrumentalis deudsch* (1528; 1545) by Martin Agricola, both depict several varieties of trumpet. In both works, little about the trumpet is offered beyond the illustrations. Michael Praetorius, the seventeenth-century music encyclopaedist, wrote of the Virdung treatise that 'this work is not actually very old, and nothing particular is to be gleaned from it about the use and character of the diagrammed instruments'. A frustrating situation that Praetorius' landmark *Syntagma musicum* (1614–20) in part redressed. The second volume of the *Syntagma musicum*, 'De Organographia', is devoted to musical instruments. The organization of the volume suggests its scope. Praetorius begins with a section on nomenclature, in which he presents a system of classification. This is followed by his record of the range and properties of various instruments. This section is extensive, presenting material on nearly 50 types of instruments, including trumpets. (Of them he mentions various pitches and shapes, and even includes some evaluation, e.g. that coiled instruments are not as good in tone as are straight ones.) Two sections on the history of the organ follow, and the volume is concluded with a 'Theatre of Instruments' in which the instruments discussed are depicted in now familiar woodcuts.

In France shortly after Praetorius, the cleric Marin Mersenne published his *Harmonie universelle* (1636–37), a significant part of which is devoted to the study of instruments. The work is often 'scientific' in its tone and interests. Thus, the section on the trumpet, for example, includes a discussion of why the harmonic series is so ordered, though his discussion of practical matters is minimal.

Johann Ernst Altenburg's *Versuch einer Anleitung zur heroisch-*

musikalischen Trompeter- und Pauker-Kunst (1795) is the most extensive of the 'pre-modern' works on the trumpet. Altenburg, motivated by the decline of the trumpeters' status and art, wrote a treatise that was both historical and practical. His historical discussion is an attempt to improve the status quo by establishing the glories of the instrument's past. Similarly, his practical discussion also proceeds out of the state of decline. The waning of the trumpeters' guilds saw the passing of an enclosed system of training, i.e. from master to pupil, all within the confines of the guild. Thus, Altenburg's practical advice would seem an attempt to perpetuate the 'secrets' of the art, since the system no longer did so.

Early modern studies of the trumpet include several works written in the closing decades of the nineteenth century by Hermann Ludwig Eichborn, a musicology pupil of E. Bohn and a trumpet student of Adolf Scholtz of Breslau. Eichborn's *Das alte Clarinblasen auf Trompeten* (1894) expressed the view that the revival of the clarino art was futile—a waste of time. Furthermore, this 'futility' did not seem to be a critical matter. He writes accordingly:

> Now it would be sad for a Handelian oratorio or a work by Bach, if its impression were dependent on the historically faithful reproduction of a trumpet part, and is it not anyhow a laughable matter to require in all details a completely historical performance of older music?
>
> (Nun, es wäre wohl traurig um ein Handel'sches Oratorium oder ein Werk von Bach bestellt, wenn sein Eindruck von der originalgetreuen Wiedergabe einer Trompetenstimme abhängig wäre, und ist es nicht überhaupt eine Lächerlichkeit, eine historisch genaue Aufführung älterer Musik bis in alle Einzelkeiten zu veriangen!) [p. 44]

Translator's Afterword

These views of Eichborn provided in part the impetus for a later study by Werner Menke: *Geschichte der Bach- und Handeltrompete* (1934). Menke was very much motivated by practical concerns, and was distressed that the difficulty of the trumpet part would discourage performances of music by Bach and Handel. His approach was at times empirical: 'Performance has demonstrated the correctness of my theories to a very high degree' (p. 117), and his goal was performance: 'I trust that science and practical experiment will ratify my line of thought and that the result will be the more frequent performance of neglected masterpieces' (p. 7). His book discusses the early history of the instrument, surveys various works by Bach and Handel, and considers players and instruments (including a lengthy section on mouthpieces). The work concludes with a 'solution' to the problems posed by the modern performance of clarino parts, viz. an instrument whose length, bell, and metal thickness would correspond to those of historical natural trumpets, but which was outfitted with two valves, because the trumpeter will 'produce the natural tones only imperfectly and because our ear will reject as ugly the production of notes not in the natural scale by forcing the natural tones' (p. 117). Menke had such instruments made by Alexander of Mainz.

The 1970s, spurred on by an ever-growing sensitivity to historical instruments, saw a flurry of trumpet research published, including Detlef Altenburg's extensive three-volume dissertation *Untersuchungen zur Geschichte der Trompete im Zeitalter der Clarinblaskunst (1500–1800)* (1973), Don Smithers' *The Music and History of the Baroque Trumpet before 1721* (1973), a second edition of Philip Bate's *The Trumpet and the Trombone* (1978), and Edward Tarr's *Die Trompete* (1977), the latter of which is presented here in English translation. *The Trumpet* surveys the history of the instrument as manifested in its

Translator's Afterword

construction, its literature, its role in contemporary life, its players, and its playing techniques. It is a rich contribution to the tradition of study outlined above, and the opportunity to further its audience with an English version is a welcome one indeed.

Edward Tarr's prominence as a trumpet soloist, prolific scholar, and teacher uniquely qualifies him to write a history of the trumpet from antiquity to the modern day. A trumpet student of Roger Voisin and Adolph Herseth, he has nurtured diverse performing interests, which range from virtuoso Baroque works on historical instruments to twentieth-century compositions on modern trumpets. He has had an enormous influence on the revival of the Baroque trumpet by his own example in recordings and concerts, by his tutelage, and by his work with instrument builders Rainer Egger (Basel) and the firm of Meinl & Lauber (Geretsried) in the reconstruction of historical instruments. Musicological studies with Prof. Leo Schrade (Basel) in 1959–64 have also led to an active scholarly life, characterized by numerous editions (including the complete solo trumpet works of Giuseppe Torelli and Monteverdi's *L'Orfeo*) and historical studies (including 69 articles in *The New Grove Dictionary of Music and Musicians* [1980]). He presently teaches at the Schola Cantorum Basiliensis (Baroque trumpet and cornett), the Basel Conservatory (trumpet), and the Karlsruhe *Hochschule* (trumpet). Since 1985, he has been the curator-director of the Trumpet Museum in Bad Säckingen.

At this point, it is a pleasure to express my gratitude to those who have helped to bring this project to completion. As this is a 'collaborative translation', my heartiest thanks must go to Edward Tarr, for his willingness to collaborate, for the characteristic skill and spirit with which he did so, and for all that he continues to teach and inspire. I am grateful, too, to my colleague, Prof. Richard Hoffmann of Oberlin, for his invariably good-natured consultations concerning the translation. And finally, I am grateful for a sabbatical leave from Oberlin College which has enabled this project to be finished in a timely fashion.

S.E.P.
Oberlin, 1988

Bibliography

General

BAHNERT, Heinz, HERZBERG, Th., and SCHRAMM, Herbert, *Metallblasinstrumente*, Leipzig 1958

BAINES, Anthony, *Brass Instruments*, London 1976

BATE, Philip, *The Trumpet and the Trombone*, London 1966

BERNER, Alfred, 'Geschichte der Trompeteninstrumente', *Die Musik in Geschichte und Gegenwart* 13, Kassel et al. 1966, 771

BERNOULLI, Wilhelm, 'Meine Sammlung historischer Blechblasinstrumente und Trommeln', *Brass Bulletin* 5/6, 1973, 85

FITZPATRICK, Horace, *The Horn and Horn-Playing . . .*, London 1970

LANGWILL, Lyndesay G., *An Index of Musical Wind-Instrument Makers*, Edinburgh 1980

MORLEY-PEGGE, Reginald, *The French Horn*, London 1960

SACHS, Curt, *Reallexikon der Musikinstrumente*, Berlin 1913

TARR, Edward H., 69 articles in *The New Grove Dictionary of Music and Musicians*, London 1980. See also *The New Grove Dictionary of Musical Instruments*, London 1984

The Early History of the Trumpet until the Late Middle Ages

ERNST, Fritz, 'Die Spielleute im Dienste der Stadt Basel im ausgehenden Mittelalter', *Basler Zeitschrift für Geschichte und Altertumskunde* 44, 1945

FLEISCHHAUER, Günter, 'Buccina und Cornu', *Wissenschaftliche Zeitschrift der Martin-Luther-Universität Halle-Wittenberg* IX/4, 1960

HAMMERSTEIN, Reinhold, *Die Musik der Engel*, Bern 1962

HEYDE, Herbert, *Trompete und Trompeteblasen im europäischen Mittelalter*, Dissertation Leipzig 1965

HICKMANN, Hans, *La trompette dans l'Egypte ancienne*, 1946, facs. rpt.: Nashville 1976 (*Brass Research Series*, No. 4)

MEUCCI, Renato, 'Riflessioni di archeologia musicale: gli strumenti militari romani e il lituus', *Nuova Rivista Musicale Italiana* XIX, 1985, 383–94

POLK, Keith, 'Wind Bands of Medieval Flemish Cities', *Brass and Woodwind Quarterly* I, 1968, 93–113

— 'Municipal Wind Music in Flanders in the Late Middle Ages', *Brass and Woodwind Quarterly* II, 1969, 1–15

SACHS, Curt, *Geist und Werden der Musikinstrumente*, Berlin 1929

— *The History of Musical Instruments*, London 1942

— *The Rise of Music in the Ancient World*, London 1944

SEEBASS, Tilman, *Musikdarstellung und Psalterillustration im frühen Mittelalter*, 2 vols, Bern 1973

WILLE, Gunther, *Musica Romana*, Amsterdam 1967

ŽAK, Sabine, *Musik als 'Ehr und Zier'*, Neuss 1979

ZEBINGER, Franz, 'Ikonographie zum Instrumentarium der Etrusker mit besonder Berücksichtigung der Blasinstrumente', *Alta Musica* VII, 1984, 6–23.

Bibliography

The Trumpet in the Renaissance

ANGLES, Higini, *La musica en la corte de Carlos V*, Barcelona, 2nd ed., 1965

DOWNEY, Peter, 'A Renaissance Correspondence concerning Trumpet Music', *Early Music* IX, 1981, 325–329

— 'The Renaissance Slide Trumpet – Fact or Fiction?' *Early Music* XII, 1984, 26–33

— *The Trumpet and Its Role in Music of the Renaissance and Early Baroque*, Dissertation Belfast 1983

EGGAR, Rainer, and WALKER, Lorenz, 'Die Zugtrompete der Renaissance', *Das Musikinstrument* 7 (July 1985), 22–3

HÖFLER, Janez, 'Der trompette des menéstrels und sein Instrument', *TVer* 29, 1979, 93–133

JAHN, Fritz, 'Die Nürnberger Trompeten- und Posaunenmacher im 16. Jahrhundert', *Archiv für Musikwissenschaft* VII, 1925, 23

LEECH-WILKINSON, Daniel, 'Il libro di appunti di un suonatore di tromba del quindicesimo secolo', *Rivista italiana di musicologia* 16, 1981, 16–39

MARIX, Jeanne, *Histoire de la musique et des musiciens de la cour de Bourgogne sous la règne de Philippe le Bon (1420–1467)*, Strassburg 1939

RAVIZZA, Victor, *Das instrumentale Ensemble ... in Italien*, Bern 1970 (*Publikationen der Schweizerischen Musikforschenden Gesellschaft*)

SAFOWITZ, Vivian, 'Trumpet Music and Trumpet Style in the Early Renaissance', Master's thesis University of Illinois 1965

THEIN, Heinrich, 'Zur Geschichte der Renaissance–Posaune von Jörg Neuschel (1557) und zu ihrer Nachschöpfung', *Das Zink Buch. Basler Jahrbuch für historiche Musikpraxis*, V, 1981, 377–404

WELKER, Lorenz, ' "Alta Capella" – Zur Ensemblepraxis der Blasinstrumente im 15. Jahrhundert', *Basler Jahrbuch für historische Musikpraxis* VII, 1983, 119–165

The Golden Age of the Natural Trumpet

ALTENBURG, Detlef, *Untersuchungen zur Geschichte der Trompete im Zeitalter der Clarinblaskunst (1500–1800)*, 3 vols., Regensburg 1973 (*Kölner Beiträge zur Musikforschung*, vol. 75)

— 'Zum Repertoire der Hoftrompeter im 17. und 18. Jahrhundert', *Alta Musica* I, 1976, 47

— 'Zum Repertoire der Türmer, Stadtpfeifer und Ratsmusiker im 17. und 18. Jahrhundert', *Alta Musica* VI, 1980, 9–32

ALTENBURG, Johann Ernst, *Versuch einer Anleitung zur heroisch-musikalischen Trompeter- und Pauker-Kunst*, Halle 1795, facs. rpt.: Leipzig 1972; Eng. trans. by Edward H. Tarr, Nashville 1974

BARCLAY, Robert, 'Preliminary studies on trumpet making techniques in 17th and 18th century Nürnberg', *Studia Organologica. Festschrift für John Henry van der Meer für seinen fünfundsechzigsten Geburtstag*, ed. by Friedemann Hellwig, Tutzing 1987, 11–31.

BENDINELLI, Cesare, *Tutta l'arte della Trombetta*, 1614, facs. rpt. by Edward H. Tarr: Kassel et al. 1975, *Documenta musicologica* II, 5 (Eng. trans. by Edward H. Tarr, Nashville 1975)

Bibliography

CRINON, Michel, *La trompette et son répertoire en Angleterre à l'époque de Henry Purcell*, Master of Music Education thesis, Paris 1974

DAHLQVIST, Reine, *Bidrag till trompeten och trumpetspelets historia fran 1500-talet till mitten av 1800-talet*, Dissertation Gothenburg 1984

EICHBORN, Hermann, *Das alte Clarinblasen auf Trompeten*, Leipzig 1894, facs. rpt.: Nashville 1975

FANTINI, Girolamo, *Modo per imparare a sonare di tromba*, Frankfurt 1638, facs. rpt. by Edward H. Tarr, Nashville 1972 (Eng. trans. by Edward H. Tarr, Nashville 1976)

HALFPENNY, Eric, 'Musicians at James II's Coronation', *Music & Letters* XVIII, 1951, 103

MENKE, Werner, *Geschichte der Bach- und Händeltrompete*, London 1934 (Eng. trans. by Gerald Abraham, rpt. Nashville 1972)

MACCRACKEN, Thomas J., 'Die Verwendung der Blechblasinstrumente bei J.S. Bach unter besonderer Berücksichtigung der Tromba da tirarsi', *Bach-Jahrbuch* 1984, 59–89

MERSENNE, Marin, *Harmonie universelle* (Paris 1636–37), (Facs. rpt. by François Lesure, Paris 1965 (Eng. trans: *The Books on Instruments* by Roger Chapman, The Hague 1957)

PECHSTEIN, Klaus, 'Die Merkzeichentafel der Nürnberger Trompeten- und Posaunenmacher von 1640', *Mitteilungen des Vereins für Geschichte der Stadt Nürnberg* 59, 1972, 198

PRAETORIUS, Michael, *Syntagma musicum*, 3 vols., Wolfenbüttel 1614–20, facs. rpt. by Wilibald Gurlitt, Kassel 1958–59, *Documenta musicologica*, First Series (Eng. trans. Vol. II by Harold Blumenfeld, rpt. New York 1980)

PRINZ, Ulrich, *Studien zum Instrumentarium Johann Sebastian Bachs mit besonderer Berücksichtigung der Kantaten* (Dissertation, Tübingen 1979)

RIEDEL, Friedrich W., *Kirchenmusik am Hofe Karls VI. (1711–1740)*, Munich–Salzburg 1977

SMITHERS, Don, *The Music and History of the Baroque Trumpet before 1721*, London 1973

— 'Gottfried Reiches Ansehen und sein Einfluss an die Musik Johann Sebastian Baches', *Bach-Jahrbuch* 1987, 113–150

TARR, Edward H., and WALKER, Thomas, '"Bellici carmi, festivo fragor": Die Verwendung der Trompete in der italienischen Oper des 17. Jahrhunderts', *Hamburger Jahrbuch für Musikwissenschaft* III, 1978, 143–203

TARR, Edward H., 'The Coiled Hunting Instrument by J.W. Haas in the Bad Säckingen Trumpet Museum', *Brass Bulletin* 54, 1986, 8–22

— 'Die Musik und die Instrumente der Charamela real in Lissabon', *Forum musicologicum* II, 1980, 181–228

— 'Der singende Stil in der Trompetenmusik des 17. Jahrhunderts', *Studien zur Aufführungspraxis und Interpretation von Instrumentalmusik des 18. Jahrhunderts* 19, 1982, 40–47

WEIGEL, Christoph, *Abbildung der gemeinnützlichen Hauptstände*, Regensburg 1698

WÖRTHMÜLLER, Willi, 'Die Nürnberger Trompeten- und Posaunenmacher des 17. und 18. Jahrhunderts', *Mitteilungen des Vereins für Geschichte der Stadt Nürnberg* 45, 1954, 208 and 46, 1955, 372

The Era of Decline and the Modern Epoch of the Trumpet

AVGERINOS, Gerassimos, *Künstler-Biographen: Die Mitglieder im Berliner Philharmonischen Orchester von 1882 bis 1972*, Berlin 1972

BAGANS Karl, 'Über die Trompete in ihrer heutigen Anwendbarkeit im Orchester', *Berliner Allgemeine musikalische Zeitung* VI, 1829, 337

BRIDGES, Glenn, *Pioneers in Brass*, Detroit, 2nd ed. 1968

BRIXEL, Eugen, 'Die Trompetenschulen von Andreas Nemetz als Spiegel der Bläserausbildung und Bläserpraxis im frühen 19. Jahrhundert', *Alta Musica* VII, 1984, 157–70

CARSE, Adam, *The Orchestra in the XVIIIth Century*, Cambridge 1940

DAHLQVIST, Reine, 'Some Notes on the Early Valve', *Galpin Society Journal* XXXII, 1980, 111–24

— *The Keyed Trumpet and Its Greatest Virtuoso, Anton Weidinger*, Nashville 1975, Brass Research Series, No. 1

ELIASON, Robert, 'Brass Instrument Key and Valve Mechanisms Made in America before 1875 . . .', Dissertation University of Missouri 1968

FLADMOE, Gary G., *The Contributions to Brass Instrument Manufacturing of Vincent Bach, Carl Geyer, and Renold Schilke*, Dissertation Urbana 1975

GLOBOKAR, Vinko, 'Entwicklungsmöglichkeiten der Blechblasinstrumente', *Brass Bulletin* 5/6, 1973, 15

HAINE, Malou, *Adolphe Sax*, Brussels 1980

HEYDE, Herbert, 'On the Early History of Valves and Valve Instruments in Germany (1814–1833)', *Brass Bulletin* 24, 1978, 9–33; 25, 1979, 41–50; 26, 1979, 69–82; 27, 1979, 51–61

— *Das Ventilblasinstrument. Seine Entwicklung im deutschsprachigen Raum von den Anfängen bis zur Gegenwart*, Leipzig 1987

KORNER, Friedrich, *Studien zur Trompete des 20. Jahrhunderts*, Dissertation Graz 1963

KRIVIN, Martin, 'A Century of Wind Instrument Manufacturing in the United States, 1860–1960', Dissertation State University of Iowa 1961

MATHEZ, Jean-Pierre, *Joseph Jean-Baptiste Laurent Arban (1825–1889)*, Moudon 1977, English trans. in preparation

NÆSS, Lars, *Oskar Böhme: Konsert for trompet; ess-moll, opus 18. Den angivelig eneste trompetkonsert fra tidsrommet 1803–1980*, 2 vols., Thesis University of Oslo 1983

PIERRE, Constant, *La facture instrumentale à l'Exposition Universelle de 1889*, Paris 1890

— *Les facteurs d'instruments de musique . . .*, Paris 1893

PIETZSCH, Hermann, *Die Trompete als Orchester-Instrument und ihre Behandlung in den verschiedenen Epochen der Musik*, Heilbronn, 2nd ed., 1903 (new printing: Ann Arbor, Michigan, n.d.)

ZORN, Hans, *Die Trompete in der deutschen Orchestermusik von ca. 1750 bis ins 20. Jahrhundert*, Dissertation Innsbruck 1972

Notes

1 This and subsequent quotations from the Altenburg treatise follow the author's published translation, *Essay on an Introduction to the Heroic and Musical Trumpeters' and Kettledrummers' Art*, Nashville 1974, here p. 17.
2 Translation follows that of Jessie Crosland in *On the Performance of Beethoven's Symphonies*, London 1907, pp. V, VI, & VIII.
3 This and subsequent quotations from the Berlioz treatise follow the translation of Theodore Front in *Treatise on Instrumentation*, enlarged and revised by Richard Strauss, New York 1948, here p. 285.
4 Translation follows that of Edward Agate in *Principles of Orchestration*, ed. Maximillian Steinberg, New York 1964, p. 23.

Index

Adams, Nathan   160
Adler, Guido   203
Aeschylus   24, 25
Africa   19
Agricola, Martin   92, 204
Aldrovandini, G.A. Vincenzo   126
Alexander (Mainz)   192, 206
Alta ensembles   35, 47, 48–49, 55, 56–58, 84
Altenburg, Detlef   66, 111, 201, 206
Alter Bass   103
Alto e basso   70
Ammann, Jost   77
Amor-Schall   149
añafil   37
anafir   36
Angelico, Fra   79
Animal horns   32, 33, 60
Apocalypse   33, 34
Arabia, see Saracen
Arlt, Wulf   201
Articulation   91–92, 194–195
Ashbury, John   131
Assyria   21, 30
Aufzüge (processional sonatas)   139, 140, 141
Augsburg   68, 147, 183

Bach, J.S.   14–15, 89, 93, 104, 105–110, 112, 118, 136, 141, 142, 167, 177, 180, 181, 182, 183, 190, 191, 205, 206
Bach, Vincent   177, 184, 186, 188
'Bach trumpet'   7, 110, 180, 191–192
Baines, Anthony   32, 39, 81, 158
Ballestra, Reimundo   102
Banderole   11
Barclay, Robert   193
Barrett, John   135
Basel (see also Schola Cantorum Basiliensis)   46, 50, 60–62, 67–68, 80, 84, 188, 190, 195, 207
Basso   70
Burgkmaier, Hans   81
Bate, Philip   206
Beale, Simon   131
Bebop   198
Beethoven, Ludwig van   144, 145, 146, 149, 170, 194
Bellini, Vincenzo   166
Benedict XI, Pope   104

Benge, Eldon   188
Bent tubing   53, 54, 84
Berg, Alban   175
Berio, Luciano   175
Berlin   81, 97–98, 111, 142, 148, 159, 182, 183, 189, 190, 191, 203
Berlioz, Hector   149, 163, 165, 166, 167
Bernardini, Alfredo   201
Bernasconi, Andrea   119
Bernouli, Wilhelm   8, 200
Bertali, Antonio   116–117, 118
Besson, F.   188, 190
Besson, Gustave Auguste   174
Biber, H.I.F.   89, 115, 116
Blühmel, Friedrich   159
Bohn, E.   205
Bologna   45, 54, 64–65, 114, 117, 125–127, 136
Bond, Capel   137
Bononcini, Giovanni   126–127
Boosey & Hawkes   174
Borcht, Peter van der   69
Boston   185, 186, 193
Boston Musical Instrument Manufactory   174
Boyce, William   137
Brahms, Johannes   163–164
Brain, Dennis   189
Britten, Benjamin   175
Brotherhoods (see also Guilds)   35, 46, 63
Bruch, Max   184
Bruckner, Anton   9, 16, 164–165, 166, 181
Buc(c)ina   25, 26, 37, 38
Buisine   38
Bull, William   131
Bülow, Hans von   145
Buq   37
Buq-al-nafir (nafir)   37
Būqāt   36
Burgundy   55–56, 57
Burney, Charles   136
Busch, Adolf   183
Buser, Ernst   200
Busine   32, 38, 40, 48, 54

Caldara, Antonio   118, 119
Calicchio   188
Capistrum   26–27
Carlin   128
Cassiodorus   33

215

Index

Cavalli, Francesco   123
Cazzati, Maurizio   125, 126
Cesti, Pietro   118
Chafe, Eric,   115
Charamela real   66, 138–140, 201
Charpentier, Marc-Antoine   130
Chatzotzrah   22–23, 24, 25, 29, 32
Chaucer, Geoffrey   41
Chelard, Hippolyte André   163
Chicago   185, 186, 188, 189
Chicago style (jazz)   198
Chief Court Trumpeter   112–113
China   30
Choir pitch   108
City trumpeters   45–46, 80
Concerto Palatino della Signoria   45, 64–65
Clagget, Charles   158, 160
Clairon   41
Clareta   62, 73, 74
Claretter   74
Claretto   73
Clarim   138–139
Clarin trumpeter   73
Clarino   73, 192
Clarino part   70, 73, 102, 103, 106, 117, 118, 137, 140
Clarino piccolo   142
Clarino player   73, 105, 172
Clarino playing   23, 73, 86, 95, 102, 117, 138, 141–144, 145, 165
Clarino register   72, 73, 84, 103, 139, 144, 145, 146, 156, 192
Clarion   41–42, 54–55
Clariounes   41–42
Clarke, Jeremiah   135, 137
Claro   41–42
Classical style   144–146
Classicum   40–41, 47
Clemencic, René   81
Colbert   128
Cologne   180, 183, 187, 190
Colonna, Giovanni Paolo   125, 126
Concert trumpeter   86
Confrérie de Saint-Julien   46
Conn, C.G.   174, 188
Cool jazz   198
Cor Sarrazinnois   37
Corbett, William   135–136
Corelli, Arcangelo   124, 125, 133
Cornett   64, 65, 75, 105, 117, 124
Cornet (à pistons)   16, 108–109, 152, 155, 165, 166, 168–169, 171, 180, 184, 186, 197–198
Cornu   25, 26, 27, 41, 53
Cöthen   107, 108–109, 110
Couesnon   177
Court trumpeter   43–44, 66–78
Courtly trumpet corps   47, 48, 63, 68–73, 85, 86, 103, 138, 138–141
Cousins   58
Cranach, Lucas   69
Crusades   31, 35–36

d'Indy, Vincent   175
Dante   54

Dahlqvist, Reine   158, 159, 160, 200–201
Debussy, Claude   172, 173
Dessary, Johann   140
Diderot, Denis   128
Didjeridu   19, 20
Distin, John Henry & Sons   174
Dokaku   30
Doll, Hans   99
Donizetti, G.D.M.   165–166
Double trumpet   130–131
Downey, Peter   73
Draghi, Antonio   118
Dran   78
Dresden   67, 81, 98, 104, 112–114, 117, 147, 149, 158, 163, 170, 181–182, 183, 184, 189
Drone   48, 50
Droschel, Conrad   99
Dudley, Augustine   131
Dufay, Guillaume   58
Dung   31

Eccles, John   135
Egger, A.   59
Egger, Rainer   193, 194, 201, 207
Egypt   20–21
Ehe, Friedrich   102
Ehe, Georg   99
Ehe, Isaac   99
Ehe, Johann Leonhard I, II, III   99–100, 147, 193
Eichborn, Hermann Ludwig   205–206
Elkhart, Indiana   174
Endler, Johann Samuel   142
Eschenbach, Wolfram von   48
Etruria   24, 25

Factories   128, 174–175
Fasch, Carl Friedrich Christian   142
Fasch, Johann Friedrich   141–142
Felttrumet   74
Ferrules   10, 11, 139
Fesselius   22
Festivals
    Eisenach Bach Festival   191
    Handel Jubilee (1784)   136
    Leeds Festival   190
    York Festival   153
Field piece playing   86, 165
Field trumpet   116
Field trumpeter   75–79, 95
Finger holes   87, 192
Finke, Helmut   192, 193
Fischer, Edwin   190
Fladdergrob,   70
Flatt trumpet   132
Flavius Josephus   22
Flavius Vegetius   26
Florence   45, 56
Flügelhorn   75, 167
Formis frescoes   38–39
Franceschini, Petronio   126
Franchois, Johannes   58
Frank, Johann David   102
Frank, Johann Jacob   102

Freiburg, Heinrich von   58
Frescobaldi, Girolamo   122
Friedman, Stanley   176
Fronsperger, Leonhardt   76, 77, 78
Fulda   142
Fux, Johann   119

Gabrieli, Andrea   65
Gabrieli, Giovanni   65
Gabrielli, Domenico   127
Galpin, F.W.   81
Groppo   93
Galuppi, Baldassare   124
Ganter (Munich)   183
Garland   10, 11, 36, 139
Gerber, Ernst Ludwig   150
Gervasoni, Carlo   80
Getzen   188
Gevaert, F.A.   169
Giegling, Franz   127
Glaretan Trometen   74
Globokar, Vinko   175, 176
Glover, Stephen   201
Gluck, Christoph Willibald   141
Greece   24
Greene, Maurice   137
Griessling & Schlott   159
Grob   103
Grocheo, Johannes de   42, 47, 49
Gros   142
Grossin, Estienne   58
Guilds   67–68, 94–98, 112, 114

Haas, Ernst Johann Conrad   100, 102
Haas, Johann Adam   147
Haas, Wolf Wilhelm   100, 102, 193
Hadrian's Arch   28
hai lo   30
Hainlein, Hans   99, 102, 193
Hainlein, Sebastian   79, 80, 99
Hainlein family   101
Halary   147, 159, 161, 168
Halévy, Elias   163
half valve   198–199
Hamburg   149, 164, 182
Hampel, Anton Joseph   147
Handel, G.F.   32, 134, 136–137, 151, 205, 206
hao t'ung   30
Harmonic series (overtone series)   11–16
Harnoncourt, Nikolaus   182
Harris, John   131
Harsthorn   75
Haussmann, E.G.   101, 105, 106
Hawkes & Co   174
Hawkins, John   135
Haydn, Franz Joseph   143, 144, 150–151, 156, 180, 185, 190, 194
Haydn, Johann Michael   14, 142–143
Heckel   183
Heerhorn   75
Heide, Geerd van der   193
Henderson, Richard   175–176
Henze, Hans Werner   175
Hertel, Johann Wilhelm   142

Herzog, H. (Dr)   195
Heyde, Herbert   8, 49, 158, 159
Hiller, Ferdinand   9
Historical Brass Workshop (Boston)   193
Hoesch, Hans Eberhard   192
Holton   188
hora   30
Hübsch   153
Hummel, Johann Nepomuk   150–151, 156
Humphries, John   137
Hyde, John   151, 153

India   30
Innsbruck   67, 74, 111, 193
Imperial Protection (*see also* Guild)   67–68
intra-thoracic pressure   195–196
Inventionshorn   147
Inventionstrompete   147–148
Israel   21–23, 29

Jäger Trommet   101
Jägertrompete   110, 192
Jannequin, Clement   75–76
Jazz   17, 176, 188, 195, 197, 198–199
John of Janua   40–41
John of Spain   36
Jolivet, André   176

Kagel, Mauricio   176
Karlsruhe   142, 147, 159, 207
Karnyx   26, 28
Keller, Gottfried (Godfrey)   135
Kellner, Ernst   149
Kenton, Stan   199
Kerner   147
Khayl, Anton   160
Klaritte   62
Klarytter   74
Knüpfer, Sebastian   105
Köhler, John Augustus   147, 152, 161
Kölbel, Ferdinand   149
Kozeluch, Leopold   150
Krause, A.F.   148
Kremsier   114–117, 125
Kuhnau, Johann   105
Kümmelmann, Hans   99

La pa   30–31
Labbaye, J.-C   159
Lalande, Michel Richard de   130, 137
Lantins, Arnold de   58
Lechner   183
Leges Palatinae   44, 84
Legrenzi, Giovanni   124
Leichambschneider   146
Leiden   46
Leipzig   101, 104–111, 136, 142, 150, 160, 162, 180, 189
Linssner, Elias   99
Lipping   14, 60, 87–90, 123, 136
Lisbon   66, 138–140
Lituus   25–26, 28, 39
London   81, 132, 133, 136, 147, 151, 152, 174, 193, 194

217

Index

Loqueville, Richard de 58
Lorenz, Ignaz 147
Lully, Jean-Baptiste 129–130, 131, 137
Lurs 27–28, 29, 31, 53
Luther, Martin 32, 33, 113

Mahler, Gustav 16, 170, 171–172, 173, 175
Mannheim 142
Marpurg, F.W. 138
Martini, G.B. 127
Martin 188
Meinl & Lauber 59, 193, 194, 207
Melani, Alessandro 124
Memling, Hans 54, 55
Mendelssohn-Bartholdy, Felix 163–164, 184
Menestrier, Claude-François 130
Menke, Werner 192, 206
Mersenne, Marin 76, 100, 121, 204
Messa di voce 93
Meucci, Renato 25
Meyerbeer, Giacomo 163
Molter, Johann Melchior 142
Monke, Josef 183
Monke, Liselotte 183
Monke, Wilhelm 183
Monteverdi, Claudio 120–121, 126, 207
Montini, Ubaldo 79, 80, 201
Morgenthaler, Daniel 201
Mouret, Jean-Joseph 130
Mouthpiece pressure 89–90, 180, 199
Mozart family 143
Mozart, Leopold 14, 92, 142, 143
Mozart, Wolfgang Amadeus 127, 141, 144, 194
Muck, Karl 185
Mudge, Richard 137
Müller, Hans 99
Munich 67, 70, 74, 81, 140, 147, 180, 183, 187, 188
Municipal Musicians 63–66
Musgrave, Michael 164
Mute 121, 126, 195

Nagel, Michael 102
Naples 124–125
National Schools of Playing (modern)
  France 177–179
  Germany/Austria 179–183
  Russia 184–185
  Scandinavia 188
  United Kingdom 183–184
  United States 185–188
Nemetz, Andreas 160
Nessmann 149–150
Neuschel family 80–81
New York 151, 153, 174, 185, 186, 187, 203
Nidecker, H. (Dr) 195
Nuremberg 52, 68, 74, 80, 81, 84, 99–102, 131–132, 146, 147, 203

Oceania 19

Paisible, James 135
Pallavicino, Carlo 124
Paris 52, 128, 147, 151, 159, 161, 163, 168, 171, 174, 187, 188, 189, 190
Pedal tones 197
Périnet, François 17, 161
Perti, Giacomo Antonio 125
Petrassi, Goffredo 176
Pfeiffer, Heinrich 101
Philadelphia 153
Philidor, Andre Danican 129
Piston 169
Plutarch 20
Poglietti, Antonio 116
Pollarolo, C.F. 118
Posaune 32–33, 38
Posaunenengel 32
Posthorn 168
Praetorius, Michael 14, 60, 70, 72, 101, 103, 204
Principale part 106, 117, 137
Prague 114
Principale playing 23
Prinzipal 70, 103
Purcell, Daniel 135
Purcell, Henry 132, 134, 135, 136, 137
Pusune 38

Quantz, J.J. 38
Quinta 70

Rameau, Jean-Philippe 129, 131
Raoux, Joseph 128
Rapa 30–31
Rapal 30–31
Ravel, Maurice 175
Reutter, Georg von (the younger) 14, 119, 143, 145
Richter, Franz Xaver 142, 180
Richter, H.R. (Dr) 195
Richter, Ferdinand Tobias 116
Riedel, Friedrich 117
Riedl, Joseph 17, 160
Riepel, Joseph 142
Rimsky-Korsakov, Nicolai 172, 173, 175
Ripianno 139
Robbia, Luca della 42–43, 50, 54
Rome (Ancient) 25–27
Rome (modern) 122, 124, 125, 133, 187
Rossini, G.A. 163
Rubato 198
Rubinstein, Nikolai 184

Sachs, Curt 19, 203
Salpinx 24, 25, 32, 33
Salzburg 115, 142, 143
Sānkha 30
Saracens 29, 32, 33, 35–38
Sartorio, Antonio 123–124
Sattler, C.F. 160
Saurle, Michael 147
Sax, Adolphe 153, 161, 174
Scarlatti, Alessandro 124, 125, 136
Schalk, Franz 165
Schallemay (chalumeaux) 140–141
Scheidt, Samuel 103
Schein, Johann Hermann 104

218

Index

Schelle, Johann   105
Scherzer   182, 183
Schilke, Renold   177, 188
Schmelzer, Johann Heinrich   116, 118
Schmidt, F.A.   183
Schmidt, Jacob   102
Schmidt, Leopold August   183
Schnitzer, Anton I   83, 102, 000 [illus]
Schnitzer, Anton the Younger   99
Schnitzer family   80, 81–82, 83, 101
Schola Cantorum Basiliensis   58, 90, 193, 201, 207
Schönberg, Arnold   175
Schrade, Leo   207
Schubart, C.F.D.   149
Schubert, Franz   144, 145, 149, 194
Schumann, Robert   163–164
Schuster, W.   159
Schütz, Heinrich   103, 113
Schwanitz   149
Selmer   177, 179, 185
Sergeant-trumpeter   132, 133, 134
Shawms   35, 36, 37, 47, 56, 58, 64, 66
Shaw, John   161
Shaw, William   131
Ship's trumpeters   123
Shofar   32
Siena   79, 80
Slide trumpet style   59, 60
Smithers, Don   206
Snb   20, 29
Sonata (part)   70
Sonata (trumpet ensemble piece)   72, 76
Soprano (register)   73
Sousa, John Philip   197
Sperger, Johann Matthias   142, 145
St. Petersburg   149, 173, 184, 185
Stadtpfeifereien (city pipers)   45, 63, 104, 105
Stamitz, Johann   142
Stanley, John   137
Starzer, Josef   140–141
Steffani, Agostino   118
Steiger, Jacob   50, 51, 80, 84
Steinkopf, Otto   192, 193
Stein, Johann Andreas   147
Stengel, Jorg (Neuschel)   66, 75
Stewart, Robb   194
Stockhausen, Karlheinz   175, 176–177
Stockholm   188
Stoelzel, Heinrich   159, 160
Stopping (hand)   82, 86, 147–149
Stradella, Alessandro   124
Stratton, John F.   174
Strauss, Richard   16, 166, 168, 172, 173, 175, 181
Stravinsky, Igor   175, 190

Tchaikovsky, Peter   171, 172
Telemann, Georg Philipp   142
Temperament   13, 86–87
Thein, Heinrich   193
Thein, Max   193
Thibouville-Lamy, Jerome   174, 177, 186

Thurner Horn   61
Tibet   31
Tirucinnam   30
Titus Arch   22, 23
Toccata   120, 121, 134
Tomasi, Henri   176
Torelli, Giuseppe   92, 127, 207
Tower playing (Abblasen)   60–61, 64, 105
Transposition   166–167, 175, 176
Trillo   93
Trills   93
Tromba   73, 117, 118
Tromba alta in Fa   171
Tromba brevis   116
Tromba con chiavi   165
Tromba da tirarsi   109, 110
Trombetta   54, 73
Trombetta antiqua   73
Trombetti della Signoria   45
Trombone (*see also* Posaune)   56, 58, 60, 64, 65, 74, 75, 80, 84, 105, 117, 124, 130, 196
Trompe   42
Trompete   39, 54, 55
Trompette   39, 54, 55, 58
Trompette d'harmonie   148
Trompette d'ordonnance   148
Trompette de guerre   55–56
Trompette des Ménestrels   55–56
Trompettes de la garde du corps   129, 139
Trompettes des plaisirs du Roi   129
Trompettes non servants   129
Trompettes ordinaires ou de la chambre   129
Tropanno   140
Trumpa   39
Trumpet
  African   19
  B-flat   7, 8, 16, 17, 155, 166, 167, 169–173
  Biblical   9, 21–23, 50
  C   16, 155, 170, 171, 172
  Celtic   28
  Chinese   30
  coiled (Jägertrompete)   110, 192
  didjeridu   19
  double   130–131
  Egyptian   20–21, 50
  English   100
  English slide   146, 151–153, 154, 156–157, 171, 194
  field   116
  folded   53–54, 55, 56, 80, 84, 110
  French   100
  German   100
  Greek   24
  high D   175, 190
  high E-flat   173, 190
  high F (natural)   142
  high F (valved)   181, 183, 190
  high G   190
  Indian   30
  invention   147–148, 154
  Italian   100, 101, 110–111
  jazz   17
  keyed   146, 147, 149–151, 154, 156, 157, 165, 166, 194

219

Index

low F (G) valved   15–16, 154, 157, 161 ff, 171
megaphone   19
natural   7, 8, 10–11, 15, 55, 56, 84, 85 ff, 110, 137, 146, 154, 161, 162, 163, 165, 166, 168, 191, 194
Oceanian   19
piccolo   7, 8, 155, 175, 181, 182, 190, 191–192
Roman   25–27
s-shaped   33, 53, 54, 56, 61
Saracen   36–38, 50
slide   54, 56, 58, 59–61, 80, 84, 132
small   189–191
stopped   146, 147–149, 156, 157, 162
Teutonic   27–28
Tibetan   31
Welsh   100, 101
valved   15–18, 153, 157, 158, 162, 165
Trumpet components
  ball (knob)   10–11, 30, 31, 36, 132, 139
  bell   10–11, 52, 101–102, 132
  bore   7, 189
  bow   10
  mouthpiece   8, 11, 42, 50, 51, 80, 183, 193, 194
  valve *see* valve
  water key   17–18, 160
  yard   10
Trumpet technique (Baroque)   85–93
Trumpet technique (modern)   194–195
Trumpet voluntary   137
Trumpeters (incl. cornetists)
  André, Maurice   7, 177–179, 180
  Achias   24
  Altenburg, Johann Caspar   111–112
  Altenburg, Johann Ernst   9, 22, 23, 26, 27, 73, 78, 86, 88, 89, 91, 92, 93, 98, 100, 101, 103, 111–112, 114, 138, 140, 149, 153, 204–205
  Anderson, Cat   108, 199
  Angellino   126
  Arban, Jean Baptiste   153, 168, 173, 184, 197
  Armstrong, Louis   198
  Bach, Vincent   184, 186
  Bagans, Karl   148
  Barr, Herbert   190
  Bayer, Ernst   143
  Beale, Simon   131
  Beetz, Gunter   182
  Beiderbecke, Bix   198
  Bendinelli, Cesare   70–72, 73, 74, 75, 76, 78, 82, 83, 86, 87, 93, 103, 120, 122, 126
  Böhme, Oskar   184
  Brandi, Giovanni Pellegrino   126, 127
  Brandt, Wilhelm (Vassily)   184
  Brown, Clifford   199
  Buhl, David   76, 148
  Bull, William   131
  Clarke, Herbert L.   197
  Coffmann, Janis Marshelle   187–188
  Dauverné F.G.A.   153, 159, 163, 168, 169
  Davidson, Louis   187
  Davis, Miles   198
  Dengler, Franz   180
  Dokschitser, Timofei   184–185
  Eichler, Horst   182
  Eklund, Bengt   188
  Eskdale, George   183
  Fantini, Girolamo   73, 76, 87, 91, 121–123
  Ferguson, Maynard   199
  Foveau, Eugene   177, 179
  Franquin, Merri   177
  Friedrich, Reinhold   182
  Fröhlich, Joseph   145, 201
  Gambati brothers   151, 153
  Ghitalla, Armando   186
  Giangiulio, Richard   187
  Gillespie, Dizzy   198
  Goeyens, A.   190, 201
  Goldman, Edwin Franko   169
  Göseke, Hans   73
  Groth, Konradin   182
  Güttler, Ludwig   182
  Hall, Ernest   171, 183
  Handke, Paul   185
  Hardenberger, Håkan   188
  Harper, Thomas (Jr.)   152, 169, 171
  Harper, Thomas (Sr.)   151–152, 153
  Heinisch, Johann   87, 108, 119–120, 143, 145, 199, 201
  Hentzschel, Caspar   94–95
  Herseth, Adolph   186, 207
  Hickman, David   187
  Hoese, Johann Georg   142, 201
  Hovaldt, Knud   188
  Hyde, John   151, 153
  Holy, Walter   192
  Immer, Friedemann   182
  James, Harry   199
  Jones, Philip   183
  Kosleck, Julius   180, 191, 197
  Kostler, Caspar   143
  Kretzer, Martin   182
  Krug, Willy   182
  Kryl, Bohumir   197
  Kühnert, Albert   170
  Kvebæck, Harry   188
  Lagorce, Marcel Antoine   179
  Laird, Michael   184
  Läubin, Hannes   182
  Levy, Jules   184, 197
  Liberati, Alessandro   197
  Liebe, Willi   197
  Mackintosh, Jack   197
  Marsalis, Wynton   188
  Mendez, Rafael   197
  Morrow, Walter   171, 191
  Næss, Lars   184
  Nessmann   149–150
  Neugebauer, Franz Willy   197
  Nilsson, Bo   188
  Norton, John   153
  Orologio, Alessandro   75, 114
  Pernember, Andreas   119
  Pezel, Johann   105, 107
  Pfeiffer, Carl   142
  Pietzsch, Hermann   172
  Plog, Anthony   187

220

Index

Price, Gervase 133
Quinque, Rolf 180
Reiche, Gottfried 87, 101, 105–106, 110–111, 192
Reinhart, Carole 188
Resenberger, J.B. 14, 143, 199, 201
Richter, P.E. 170
Rodenkirchen, Karl 185
Ruhe, Ulrich Heinrich 110, 111
Sabarich, Raymond 177
Sachse, E. 162, 167
Sachse, F. 167
Saint Jacome, L.A. 197
Sandau, Kurt 181–182
Sarjant 136, 144, 151
Schachtner, Johann Andreas 142, 143
Scherbaum, Adolf 7, 180–181, 182, 190–191
Schlossberg, Max 186
Schlueter, Charles 186
Schneider, Adolf Friedrich 142
Schneidewind, Hellmut 180
Scholtz, Adolf 167, 205
Schwanitz 149
Schwarz, Gerard 187
Seidemann, Jacob 67
Seiffert, Eduard 181
Sellaro 126
Severinsen, Carl 'Doc' 187
Shore family 135, 136
Shore, Matthias 133, 134
Shore, William 133–134
Shore, John 134, 135, 136
Simon, Wilhelm 181
Snow, Valentine 134, 136, 137
Solomon, John 191–192
Spörri, Paul 182, 190
Staigers, Del 197
Stamp, James 195
Steele, Perkins, Crispian 184
Stegmann, Richard 182
Steiger, Jacob 50, 51, 80, 84
Stevens, Thomas 186
Stockhausen, Markus 176
Swift, George 197
Tabakov, Mihail 184
Täubig, Heinrich 180
Teste 171, 190
Thibaud, Pierre 179, 182, 188
Thomsen, Magnus 76, 78, 103
Treutel, Edward 188
Trognée, Joseph 184
Türpe, Hugo 197, 201
Twiselton 133
Vacchiano, William 186, 187
Vaillant, Ludovic 177, 179
Vejvanovský, Pavel Josef 115–116
Voisin, René 185
Voisin, Roger 185–186, 207
Wallace, John 183–184
Wehrle, Ludwig 190
Weidinger, Anton 147, 150–151, 156, 196
Wesenigk, Fritz 182
Wilbraham, John 183
Wobisch, Helmut 180

Wöggel, Michael 147, 148, 149
Wülcken, Johann Caspar 111
Wurm, Wilhelm 184
Zimmermann, Karl 184
Trumpetina 171
Tuba 7, 8, 25, 26, 27, 29, 32, 33, 37, 39, 41
Tuba campestris 116
Tubatores 45
Tubilustrium 27
Tucket 134
Tutankhamun 20
Tutz, Rudolf 193
Tyrrhenica tuba 25

Uhlmann, Leopold 160

Valve 15, 146, 151, 153, 156–161
  Berlin pump 160–161
  box 159
  disc 161
  double tube 160
  Drehbüchsenventil 159–160
  piston 17, 161
  return mechanism 17–18, 160
  rotary 17–18, 159–160, 182, 183, 189
  Schuster 159
  square 159
  tubular 159, 161
  Vienna 159, 160
  wheel 160
Vejvanovský, Pavel Josef 115–116
Venice 123–124, 136
Verdi, Giuseppe 164, 166
Versailles 129, 132, 139
Vienna 46, 70, 74, 75, 98, 108, 116, 117–120, 127, 140, 141, 142, 143, 146–147, 151, 160, 170–171, 180, 183, 185, 186, 188, 189
Virdung, Sebastian 61, 204
Virgil 25
Volgan 103
Vulgano 70

Wagner, Richard 9, 16, 145, 163, 164, 166, 167, 181, 194
Webb, John 193, 194
Weber, Gottfried 149
Weber, Anton von 175
Weigel, Christoph 100
Weigl, Joseph 150
Weimar 107–108, 110, 149, 167
Weingartner, Felix 146
Weissenfels 111–112
Welker, Lorenz 58, 60
Wheeler, Joseph 201
Wiepracht, Wilhelm 160
Windisch 183
Woodham 151
Wörthmüller, Willi 101

Yamaha 188

Žak, Sabine 32–33, 39, 47
Ziani, M.A. 118, 125
Zimmermann, Bernd-Aloys 175, 176
Zimolong, Max 164

221

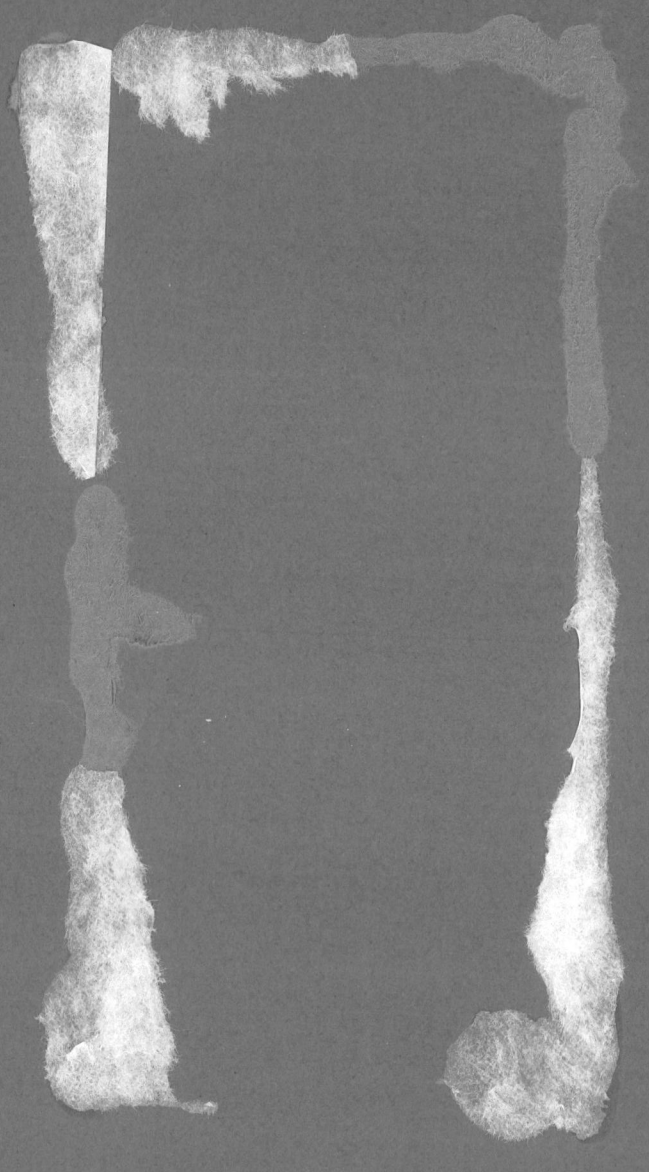